FREE VIDEO

Essential Test Tips Video from Trivium Test Prep!

Thank you for purchasing from Trivium Test Prep!
We're honored to help you prepare for your exam.
To show our appreciation, we're offering a

FREE *Essential Test Tips* Video

Our video includes 35 test preparation strategies that will make you successful on your big exam. All we ask is that you email us your feedback and describe your experience with our product. Amazing, awful, or just so-so: we want to hear what you have to say!

> To receive your **FREE** *Essential Test Tips* **Video,** please email us at
> **5star@triviumtestprep.com.**

Include "Free 5 Star" in the subject line and the following information in your email:

1. The title of the product you purchased.
2. Your rating from 1 – 5 (with 5 being the best).
3. Your feedback about the product, including how our materials helped you meet your goals and ways in which we can improve our products.
4. Your full name and shipping address so we can send your **FREE** *Essential Test Tips* **Video**.

If you have any questions or concerns please feel free to contact us directly at:
5star@triviumtestprep.com.

Thank you!
– Trivium Test Prep Team

Addiction Counselor Exam Study Guide:

2 Full-Length Practice Tests and Prep Book for IC&RC ADC, NCAC I, and CASAC

Elissa Simon

Copyright ©2023 by Trivium Test Prep

ISBN-13: 9781637983591

ALL RIGHTS RESERVED. By purchase of this book, you have been licensed one copy for personal use only. No part of this work may be reproduced, redistributed, or used in any form or by any means without prior written permission of the publisher and copyright owner. Trivium Test Prep; Accepted, Inc.; Cirrus Test Prep; and Ascencia Test Prep are all imprints of Trivium Test Prep, LLC.

DISCLAIMER: IC&RC was not involved in the creation or production of this product, is not in any way affiliated with Trivium Test Prep, and does not sponsor or endorse this product.

Image(s) used under license from Shutterstock.com.

Table of Contents

Online Resources vii

Introduction ix

1 Psychoactive Substances and Their Effects — 1

What Is Substance Use Disorder? 1
Effects of Substance Use 11
Long-Term Consequences of
Substance Abuse 17
Answer Key 23

2 Screening and Interviewing the Client — 25

Clinical Screening 25
Intake and Screening Tools 30
Interviewing the Client 33
Answer Key 40

3 Assessments — 43

Conducting Assessments 43
Assessment Instruments 47
Answer Key 57

4 Treatment Planning — 59

Developing a Treatment Plan 59
Collaborating with the Client and Other
Entities 64
Answer Key 67

5 Referrals and Service Coordination — 69

Scope of Practice and Referrals 69
Community-Based Prevention 75
Service Coordination 79
Answer Key 82

6 Recovery Beyond Primary Treatment — 83

Discharge Planning for Ongoing Recovery ... 83
Multiple Pathways and Continuum of Care . 89
Answer Key 96

7 Counseling — 99

The Therapeutic Relationship 99
Monitoring and Evaluation 106
Engaging Families and Concerned Others 111
Developing Life Skills 116
Answer Key 120

8 Group Counseling — 123

Working with a Group 123
Attributes in a Group Counseling
Context 131
Answer Key 134

9 Professional Practice — 137

Multicultural Counseling 137
Professional Development 145
Answer Key 149

10 Ethics and Documentation 151

Documentation 151
Ethics 156
Answer Key 162

11 Practice Test 165

Answer Key 185

Online Resources

Trivium includes online resources with the purchase of this study guide to help you fully prepare for your exam.

Practice Test

In addition to the practice test included in this book, we also offer an online exam. Since many exams today are computer based, practicing your test-taking skills on the computer is a great way to prepare.

From Stress to Success

Watch "From Stress to Success," a brief but insightful YouTube video that offers the tips, tricks, and secrets experts use to score higher on the exam.

Reviews

Leave a review, send us helpful feedback, or sign up for Trivium promotions—including free books!

Access these materials at: www.triviumtestprep.com/addiction-counselor-online-resources

To access your SECOND practice test, follow the link below:
www.triviumtestprep.com/addiction-counselor-online-resources

Introduction

Congratulations on choosing a career as an addiction counselor. You are undertaking difficult, yet rewarding and necessary work that will make a difference in the lives of the people whom you help to treat every day.

This guide will provide you with a detailed overview of the IC&RC Alcohol and Drug Counselor examination, which is required for certification in several states. We'll take you through all of the concepts covered on the test and give you the opportunity to evaluate your knowledge with practice questions. Even if it's been a while since you last took a major exam, don't worry; we'll make sure you're more than ready!

What is the IC&RC ADC Examination?

The IC&RC Alcohol and Drug Counselor (ADC) examination is offered by the International Certification and Reciprocity Consortium (IC&RC). It is based on alcohol and drug counselor job descriptions and analyses. IC&RC contracts with Schroeder Management Technologies to develop, administer, and score the exam through ISO-Quality Testing (IQT).

As part of the credentialing process, candidates must also meet certain requirements in competence and ethical conduct, work experience, and education. Please consult with your state board for further details on eligibility.

What's on the IC&RC ADC Examination?

This test measures the knowledge and skills that are expected of credentialed addiction counselors. The certification examination will test you in four domains.

WHAT'S on the IC&RC ADC Examination?

DOMAIN	TOPICS	PERCENTAGE OF EXAM	APPROXIMATE NUMBER OF QUESTIONS
Domain I	Scientific Principles of Substance Use and Co-occurring Disorders	16%	38
Domain Ii	Evidence-based Screening and Assessment	44%	30
Domain III	Evidence-based Treatment, Counseling, and Referral	31%	45
Domain IV	Professional, Ethical, and Legal Responsibilities	9%	37
TOTAL	3 hours		150 questions (25 pretest questions)

Domain I: Scientific Principles of Substance Use and Co-occurring Disorders

Domain I (Scientific Principles of Substance Use and Co-occurring Disorders) comprises 25 percent of the exam. These questions will test your ability to recognize the effects that addiction has on the brain and may include questions on the disease model, reward pathways, tolerance, and cravings. You will be expected to be able to identify risk factors associated with developing a substance use disorder, such as family history or trauma. Your ability to identify the patterns, behaviors, and progressive stages of substance use disorders will also be tested. Knowing how to identify the signs and symptoms of co-occurring medical conditions, such as sexually transmitted infections and cirrhosis, will also be tested as part of this domain.

Finally, you must know how to differentiate some of the common substances that are abused and their characteristics:

- Pharmacology: drug classifications, interactions, and cross-tolerance
- symptoms and signs of intoxication and/or overdose
- the symptoms and stages of withdrawal
- social, physiological, and psychological effects

Domain II: Evidence-based Screening and Assessments

Domain II (Evidence-based Screening and Assessment) comprises 20 percent of the exam. You will be required to understand the following components of evidence-based screening and assessments:

- how to utilize established interviewing techniques, such as motivational interviewing, probing, and questioning
- how to utilize established screening and assessment methods and instruments
- how to identify methods and interpret results from drug and alcohol testing
- how to utilize established diagnostic criteria (i.e., DSM-5) for evaluating substance use
- how to assemble a comprehensive client biopsychosocial history that includes health, family, employment, and collateral sources
- how to determine the course of action to meet the individual's immediate and ongoing needs
- how to determine level of care based on placement criteria

Questions may involve assessing a client's current situation—including signs and symptoms of intoxication and withdrawal—by evaluating observed behavior and other available information to determine a client's immediate needs.

Prepare for questions about administering the appropriate screening and assessment instruments specific to the client's age, developmental level, culture, and gender in order to obtain objective data. There may also be questions about obtaining relevant history and related information from the client and other sources to establish eligibility and appropriateness to facilitate the assessment process. The test may also cover screening and assessing for physical, medical, and co-occurring disorders that may require additional assessment and referral.

You must also prepare to interpret data results in order to integrate all available information, formulate diagnostic impressions, and determine appropriate action. Finally, you will be expected to summarize assessment results in order to document and support the diagnostic impressions and treatment recommendations.

Domain III: Evidence-based Treatment, Counseling, and Referral

Domain III (Evidence-based Treatment, Counseling, and Referral) makes up 30 percent of the exam. These questions will require you to know how to practice and respond to verbal and nonverbal communication skills, learning styles, person-centered language, and various communication styles. You will also be expected to know how to recognize the opportunities and methods you can use to build rapport with clients as well as how to identify crisis events and respond to them (e.g., through de-escalation). Understanding how to review a client's patterns and use methods is also required as is recognizing how trauma and substance use are related and their effects on both the client and the counselor.

Expect questions that concern identifying available resources and understanding how to collaborate with other care providers. In addition to understanding when and how to refer clients, you must also know how to effectively collaborate with other professionals and client supports, including the client's family.

You must know the best practices for both developing and updating treatment plans, including goals, objectives, strategies, and interventions, such as coping skills and relapse prevention.

Your knowledge of specific populations and how to identify their concerns and respond to them will also be tested as will your knowledge of the various pathways of recovery, including medication-assisted treatment (MAT), holistic health, and support groups. Prepare to answer specific questions concerning support groups, such as counseling approaches that are specific to certain group sessions, structured curriculum and process, group dynamics, and cohesiveness.

Finally, you should anticipate questions concerning how to address clients who are resistant to change, the components of discharge planning, understanding when the counseling process should be terminated, and various feedback techniques, such as reflection, reframing, and clarification.

Domain IV: Professional, Ethical, and Legal Responsibilities

Questions about Domain IV (Professional, Ethical, and Legal Responsibilities) comprise 25 percent of the exam. These questions may concern adherence to established professional codes of ethics and standards of practice to promote the best interests of the client and the profession. Questions may also cover juris dictionally specific rules and regulations regarding best practices in substance use disorder treatment to protect and promote client rights.

Prepare to answer questions that demonstrate your understanding of conflicts of interest, professional boundaries, and self-awareness (e.g., dual relationships and self-disclosure) as well as how to recognize and address issues outside of the counselor's scope of practice. An understanding of how to develop and use multi-cultural perspectives within the counseling process will also be addressed. Additional questions in this domain test your knowledge of

- best practices for documentation;
- record keeping and storage;
- how to comply with privacy laws;
- how to comply with guidelines concerning informed consent;
- the grievance process;
- how to advocate for diversity, equity, and inclusion in the care setting; and
- how to adhere to the legal rights of clients.

How is the IC&RC ADC Administered?

The exam is administered by the IC&RC. It is a computer-based test offered throughout the nation on a continuous basis by ISO Quality Testing. Students must wait at least 90 days before retaking the exam. You may cancel or reschedule your exam up to five days prior to test day. You can register for the exam, pay the registration fee, and check exam locations and dates at www.iqttesting.com.

You will need to print your Candidate Admission Letter from your online account and bring it, along with your identification, to the testing site on exam day. You may not bring personal items with you into the testing center. No books, papers, or cell phones are allowed.

How is the IC&RC ADC Scored?

You will receive your preliminary scores immediately after the computer-based examination. Official scores become available two to three weeks after the exam and are reported by ISO to IC&RC.

Each multiple-choice question is worth one raw point. The total number of questions you answer correctly is added up to obtain your raw score. Raw scores are scaled from 200 – 800; a passing score is 500. The scaling takes question difficulty into account, so not every question is weighted equally.

There will be twenty-five pretest questions that are neither scored nor weighted; however, you will not know which ones these are, so you must answer every question to the best of your ability. Pretest questions are used to determine whether these new questions should be used for future exams.

About Trivium Test Prep

Trivium Test Prep uses industry professionals with decades' worth of knowledge in their fields, proven with degrees and honors in law, medicine, business, education, the military, and more, to produce high-quality study guides for students.

Our study guides are specifically designed to increase any student's score. Our books are also shorter and more concise than typical study guides, so you can increase your score while significantly decreasing your study time.

1 Psychoactive Substances and Their Effects

This section addresses the states of intoxication, stages of withdrawal, and psychological and physical effects of psychoactive substances.

What Is Substance Use Disorder?

Substance Use Disorders and Common Terminology

Substance use disorders are characterized by the excessive use of mind-altering substances to a degree that the user's life, relationships, and/or work are negatively impacted. People with substance use disorders, also known as addiction, cannot control their substance intake, even when they try to limit it or quit entirely.

People may be exposed to substances through recreational use. In other cases, habit-forming medications that have been prescribed by a doctor are misused. Some substances are easier to become addicted to than others. Common symptoms of substance use disorder include

- needing more of the substance to reach a euphoric state ("get high");
- withdrawal symptoms when trying to quit;
- an inability to quit despite trying to do so;
- having urges to use the drug or substance that cannot be ignored;
- spending more money than desired or can be afforded on the substance;
- neglecting work or family obligations due to substance use; and
- engaging in risky behaviors while on the substance or in an attempt to obtain the substance (for example, stealing or driving under the influence).

It is important to know the definition of some of the terms commonly used in addiction treatment; these are listed in Table 1.1.

 HELPFUL HINT

Illicit drugs present the greatest risk for people seeking opioids: they may be laced with other substances and not accurately measured, which can lead to emergent reactions and overdoses.

TABLE 1.1. Addiction Treatment: Commonly Used Terms

TERM	DEFINITION/DESCRIPTION
Drug	- a substance that has a physiological effect on the body when ingested - may or may not be addictive or produce a state of euphoria
Medicine	- a drug prescribed to a client to treat a medical condition - may have the potential for abuse and have its use monitored
Misuse	- using a drug in a manner or for a reason that differs from how it was prescribed - an unintentional type of use
Abuse	- using a drug in a manner other than prescribed with the intention of getting high (e.g., taking too much)
Dependence	- a state that occurs when drug or alcohol abuse persists for a prolonged time - can be both psychological and physical
Psychological dependence	- a strong mental urge to use a drug to experience effects considered pleasant - drug or alcohol use to reach a euphoric state of mind
Physical dependence	- when a person's body is accustomed to taking a drug - may include withdrawal symptoms when the drug is no longer present in the person's system
Cross dependence	- when another drug is used to lessen the withdrawal symptoms of the drug of choice and/or replace the drug of choice
Tolerance	- when the body adjusts to a drug over a prolonged time, altering its effects - often leads to taking larger amounts of the substance to try to achieve the same effects
Reverse tolerance	- can cause a person to become more sensitive (rather than less sensitive) to a drug over a period of time - causes the substance to have a higher level of impact on the person
Dose	- the amount of the substance taken at one time or over the course of twenty-four hours
Half-life	- the amount of time a drug stays present in the body - can be affected by metabolism and other factors, which differ from the specific half-life of the drug
Lethal dose	- a dose of a drug that is too potent and results in death

TERM	DEFINITION/DESCRIPTION
Therapeutic dose	• the amount of a drug needed to be effective
Drug interactions	• the way in which drugs interact with one another • includes interactions among street drugs, prescription drugs, and alcohol

QUICK REVIEW QUESTIONS

1. List TWO ways through which people frequently become exposed to misused substances.

2. What term describes when a person's body is accustomed to taking a drug, resulting in withdrawal symptoms when the drug is no longer present in the system?

Progression and Severity of Substance Use Disorders

People with substance use disorders (SUDs) commonly progress through several stages, with various levels of severity. It is therefore critical to understand the distinction between the terms *dependence*, *use*, *disorder*, and *addiction*:

- **Substance dependence** is a deep physical and/or psychological need to use a controlled substance to achieve a feeling of euphoria and/or calm.
- **Substance use** is the nonmedically warranted consumption of medications or substances, such as tobacco, alcohol, or illicit drugs.
- **Substance use disorder** is the continued use of a medication without medical reason, or the excessive and intentional use of a controlled substance (e.g., alcohol, opioids).
- **Addiction** is dependence on a substance or practice that is physically or psychologically habit-forming to the extent that it results in critical pain and damage.

People who misuse drugs and alcohol tend to exhibit common behavior changes that indicate that their use is becoming problematic; however, the misuse of drugs and alcohol does not necessarily signify an addiction or that a substance use disorder will develop.

Binge drinking is an example of alcohol misuse that can occur without the presence of a substance use concern. Other behavior changes observed when someone misuses substances can include

- experiencing hangovers or tiredness after heavy use;
- going to work hungover or sick; and/or
- not being able to remember events because of alcohol or drug use.

Overall, there is little impact on the day-to-day lives of people who misuse substances. People who misuse substances are often able to manage their responsibilities with no major noticeable changes to their behaviors.

When people move from misusing substances to developing a substance use disorder, their use has a larger impact on their day-to-day lives. Indications of this include

- a negative impact on their work performance;
- an inability to manage day-to-day responsibilities;
- interpersonal relationship struggles with family and friends;
- denial of the consequences and severity of their use;
- missing important events or withdrawing from usual hobbies;
- new financial concerns;
- new legal concerns (such as a DWI or possession charge);
- experiencing withdrawal symptoms;
- being defensive about their use behaviors;
- being irritable or angry more often;
- signs of dishonesty or manipulation;
- changes in their physical appearance (e.g., weight loss, changes in personal hygiene); and/or
- appearing impaired more often than not (e.g., slurred speech, changes in pupils).

There is no cookie-cutter presentation for substance use disorders. With that being said, some or all of the above concerns may be noticed in clients. Additionally, the time it takes to develop an addiction will vary from person to person. Individuals who struggle with a substance use disorder vary in age from adolescence to older adults.

There are a variety of tools that mental health professionals can use to assess the **severity** of a client's psychoactive substance use. Common assessments are discussed in depth in Chapter 3.

QUICK REVIEW QUESTIONS

3. What is the term used to describe a deep need to use a controlled substance to achieve a feeling of euphoria and/or calm?

4. What term describes the nonmedically warranted consumption of medications or substances such as tobacco, alcohol, or illicit drugs?

Models of Addiction Treatment

There are several **models** used to understand addiction and treatment. The model chosen by a counselor generally depends on the counselor's work experience and education and will have a direct impact on the theoretical approaches and interventions used with clients. An effective addiction model blends multidimensional aspects of addiction with various cultural and regional aspects, interpersonal preferences, and family concepts.

The **medical model** of addiction is well established among most rehabilitation centers. It is a descriptive model that does not lead to only one method of intervention. The medical model divides the process of addiction into stages, each of which can be viewed as a target for intervention.

This model helps counselors and medical professionals better judge the likelihood and severity of addiction in specific cases. Concepts integral to the medical model include those described in Table 1.2.

TABLE 1.2. Concepts Integral to the Medical Model of Addiction	
CONCEPT	DESCRIPTION
Genetic predisposition	• The client is genetically predisposed to addiction and has one or more family members who are also living with a substance use disorder. • This may explain why similar behavior leads to addiction in certain people.
Response to addictive chemicals	• The person has a specialized response to substances. • This explains why taking a drug is unpleasant or not a compulsion for some people.
Risk factors	• These include contexts. • Some contexts are social environment, preexisting mood disorders, drug availability, and life problems.
Practice	• The individual has undergone a trial-and-error process, experimenting or "learning" how to use the drug. • The person has become addicted in the trial-and-error process.
Change from use to addiction	• This is when behavior changes from occasional use to full-blown addiction. • It involves hyposensitization and hedonic dysregulation (the inability to feel good without the drug).

According to the **cultural belief model**, a client's cultural beliefs must be addressed when providing client care:

- Certain behaviors may be attributed to the culture of the client, and it would be unethical to disrupt any behaviors that are related to culture.
- Different cultural aspects must be considered when first assessing the client's drug addiction and then taken into consideration again when creating an effective treatment method for the client.

The **moral model** has fallen out of favor because the medical community identifies addiction as a real disease process with a true genetic component. The moral model encompasses the following:

- Historically, addiction has been seen as a moral failing in many societies.
- Today, some people still treat addiction as a character flaw, considering it a moral failing, although this taboo is changing.

HELPFUL HINT

The medical model does not apply to addictions that do not involve chemical substances.

- This is a dilemma for many people with substance use disorder who do not understand this process and feel as if their choices are the result of moral failings.
- Proponents of the moral model argue that addiction is either caused by a spiritual deficit or is the conscious choice of the addicted person.
- Suggested courses of treatment include clerical intervention and moral persuasion or, at the other end of the spectrum, imprisonment and other social consequences of drug use. These measures limit treatment workers to nonspecialists, such as clerical workers and law enforcement officials.

Often confused with the moral approach, the **temperance model** focuses on the substance itself rather than the client. The temperance model developed during the Prohibition movement in the United States during the early twentieth century. It condemns the addictive substance and its potential to harm people and social institutions.

The **cognitive model** of addiction focuses on cognition, the mental process that relates to judgment, perception, and reasoning. Counselors work to discover the core beliefs that allow the addicted person to engage in drug-using behavior, both conscious and unconscious:

- There is no one-size-fits-all approach with the cognitive model.
- The cognitive model of addiction became popular in 2005 and combines addiction treatment with behavioral therapy.
- This combination attacks false beliefs and teaches the addicted person skills to deal with stress in a positive manner.
- Interventions like cognitive behavioral therapy and dialectical behavior therapy may be used in conjunction with addiction treatment to help clients cope with emotions.

The **biopsychosocial (BPS) model** of addiction attempts to explain how addiction starts, continues, and persists:

- The BPS model helps counselors establish a treatment program.
- The biological factors of the BPS model involve genetics and chemical changes that occur from drug use and are viewed as the primary causes of the addiction.
- The BPS model expands to include emotional (psychological) and social aspects of addiction, such as
  - family matters;
  - poverty;
  - crime;
  - opportunity;
  - mental disorders; and
  - the influence of friends/peers.
- Critics of the BPS model feel that it is too broad and does not really identify a target to attack and treat.

- Practical addiction treatment blends the BPS model with the medical model. Along with medications, treatment is often more successful.

According to the **psychological model** (also known as the characterological model), addiction is caused by a psychological abnormality: the "addictive personality." So-called addictive personalities are characterized by

- self-centeredness;
- low self-esteem;
- impulsiveness;
- low tolerance for stress;
- tendencies toward manipulation; and
- a desire for power or control.

Treatment under the psychological model includes psychotherapy and social support. Treatment specialists help clients with SUD

- develop self-esteem and impulse control;
- learn how to set appropriate boundaries; and
- learn or improve interpersonal skills.

According to the **social education model**, addiction is a learned behavior. Based on principles of classical and operant conditioning, this integrative approach views addiction as the result of social influence or of the client imitating behavior, followed by ongoing cognitive processes:

- Proponents of the social education model believe that it identifies precursors to addiction—learned behaviors—followed by ongoing reinforcement of them through operant conditioning.
- This model cites causes of addiction, such as
  - poor socialization;
  - poor modeling; and
  - limited coping mechanisms and skills (or lack thereof).
- Treatment includes training in impulse control and other social skills, cognitive exercises and reconditioning, suitable and realistic goal setting, and appropriate behavioral modeling overseen by cognitive and behavioral counselors.
- Peer groups are often used in the social education model.

The **biological model** of addiction is based upon genetic factors that influence addiction. Genetics, biochemistry, and metabolism all play a role in biological addiction factors:

- Some people may be unable to tolerate alcohol and other drugs, even when consumed in small amounts.
- The bodies of some people will react adversely to the substance, and behavioral issues will occur.
- Women tend to have a lower alcohol tolerance than men.

HELPFUL HINT

Addictive personality is not recognized as a personality disorder in the DSM; however, the psychological model has been historically used in the treatment of SUD, and this model recognizes the concept of the addictive personality.

- People whose parents or siblings struggle with substance use are at a higher risk of developing an addiction; however, not all individuals with this circumstance will develop an addiction.
- There may be lower concentrations of certain enzymes in the brains of those who are susceptible to alcohol abuse due to their genetic disposition.

Genetics theory, or addictive inheritance theory, identifies the genetic factors of addiction separately from environmental factors:

- While there are many environmental components of addiction, studies have shown that the children of parents with alcohol use disorder (AUD) who are later adopted into families without this disorder have a greater risk of developing it than the general population.
- Certain populations are at a higher risk for addictive inheritance.
  - Due to a genetic predisposition to a deficiency in acetaldehyde production—the enzyme that degrades alcohol—they are hypersensitive to its effects.
  - Sons are more likely than daughters to inherit alcohol use disorder.

Exposure theory assumes that addiction will eventually occur after the regular use of a substance:

- Due to drug use, the body undergoes metabolic changes.
  - The drug is mimicking the body's natural painkillers (endorphins).
  - The substance reduces the body's ability to produce endorphins naturally, causing chemical dependency and, ultimately, addiction.
- To avoid withdrawal, the body demands higher and more frequent amounts of a drug.

Similarly, **conditioning theory** posits that addiction is reinforced by drug use itself. Given the rewarding effect of the drug, the substance controls the user's behavior: the user becomes conditioned—addicted—to use the substance due to its rewarding effect.

According to **adaptation theory**, environmental, social, and psychological factors influence addiction and contribute to its potential. These include beliefs about the drug, subjective emotional experiences, and other internal and external dynamics. Adaptation theorists have investigated the psychodynamics of drug reliance; they also believe that some causes of addiction are problems in childhood, low self-esteem, and other psychological challenges.

People with SUD continue to seek out and use drugs and alcohol despite negative life consequences. They may wish to stop using and even try to stop but are unable to do so. The **disease concept of addiction** identifies addiction as a brain disease. This model recognizes that a person's brain changes in the way it functions, which leads to an abnormal reaction to a substance to which most people would react differently. For example, someone without an alcohol use disorder could have one or two alcoholic beverages and easily stop drinking. On

DID YOU KNOW?

The term *alcohol use disorder (AUD)* is now preferred by behavioral experts over the term *alcoholic* to describe the progressive nature of addiction as concerns the misuse or abuse of alcohol.

the other hand, someone with an alcohol use disorder would feel compelled to continue drinking in a way the person without the disorder could never experience. It is thought that this compulsion is related to abnormalities concerning dopamine release and feedback in the brains of people who are addicted. Thus, people with an addiction may use more than one substance or seek out another substance if their drug of choice is not available.

QUICK REVIEW QUESTIONS

5. Which model of addiction treatment assumes that addiction is a learned behavior?

6. Which theory posits that addiction will eventually occur after the regular use of a substance?

Other Addiction Issues

Process addictions do not necessarily involve the consumption of mind-altering substances, but the signs and symptoms of addictive behavior are surprisingly similar. Some symptoms are

- lying about one's behavior;
- spending exorbitant amounts of money or time on the behavior;
- being unable to stop the behavior; and
- the behavior negatively impacting relationships.

Gambling addiction involves a compulsive need to gamble, often with increasing sums of money, property, or other items of value. Gambling addiction can include—but is not limited to—playing cards, buying lottery tickets, online gambling, and visiting casinos.

Shopping or spending addiction is the compulsive need to purchase items. Everyone shops, but it becomes a problem when the spending impacts one's life or when a person uses shopping to deal with or manage negative emotions or create positive emotions.

Unlike gambling or even shopping, **gaming addiction** does not typically involve the vast consumption of money, and, unlike gambling, winning a game is related to skill and practice, not luck. Nonetheless, some people game at such a high rate that it impacts their day-to-day lives and may negatively affect relationships or even their ability to hold down a job.

Work addiction is often not recognized because dedication to work is socially valuable and seen as a positive thing by society. However, things can go too far when work is the only thing people think about, when they let their work take precedence over their physical and mental health, and when they are overly emotionally tied to their work-related successes and failures.

Apart from gambling (which is listed as "gambling disorder" in the *DSM-5*), the addictive behaviors listed here are not clinically diagnosed disorders. Nonetheless, they are behavioral challenges that may negatively impact the daily lives of clients.

QUICK REVIEW QUESTIONS

7. A person exhibiting the signs and symptoms of addictive behavior without the consumption of mind-altering substances may have what?

8. Which process addiction is listed as a disorder in the *DSM-5*?

Cross Addiction

Cross addiction occurs when an individual is addicted to multiple substances or behaviors (e.g., gambling, sex, shopping, and/or other compulsive behaviors). Cross addiction is common among individuals with SUD. For example, medical providers may hesitate to prescribe controlled substances to someone who has reported actively misusing alcohol. One belief regarding the increased risk of developing a cross dependence is tied to the changes in a person's reward system when a substance use disorder develops:

- Many substances use the same pathways in our brains, including the reward pathway.
- These **reward pathways** contribute to the release of dopamine, which can induce the euphoric effect often associated with substances and other addictive behaviors.
- Over time, the use of alcohol and drugs can become more rewarding than other pleasurable activities.

When someone develops an addiction, the reward pathway develops too. It can be thought of as walking a trail in a forest: New foot trails become more visible and easier to use the more they are walked on. When the path is no longer used, weeds and brush may grow over it; still, the path remains, making it easier to use in the future. Similarly, individuals in recovery who relapse may find that their addiction progresses rapidly once the old reward pathways are reactivated.

In some cases, people with SUD misuse one substance to help with the short-term and long-term effects of another. As an example, individuals with alcohol dependence face depression and other mental health concerns. They may choose to use stimulants to boost their productivity and mood, thereby demonstrating cross addiction.

> **DID YOU KNOW?**
> Some people with SUD believe they only have an addiction to one substance and feel that they can safely use other substances. But other addictive substances can activate the same reward system, contributing to the development of cross dependence.

QUICK REVIEW QUESTIONS

9. When individuals are addicted to multiple substances or other behaviors, what are they demonstrating?

10. When a person develops an addiction, what is the pathway that develops in the brain?

Effects of Substance Use

Commonly Used Substances

Counselors should be aware of the short- and long-term effects of various substances. Familiarity with short-term effects helps the counselor recognize signs that a client may be impaired. If impairment is suspected, the counselor may need to address safety concerns. For instance, if the client drove to the appointment, the issue of safe transportation must be addressed.

Additionally, being familiar with the effects of various substances can help the counselor better understand how their use may be impacting a client's existing or new mental health concerns. For example, a client who has been struggling with depressive symptoms may believe using marijuana will relieve these symptoms. The counselor should educate the client about the negative impact of marijuana use on preexisting depressive symptoms (it causes more harm than good).

TABLE 1.3. Commonly Misused Substances

USES	SHORT-TERM EFFECTS	LONG-TERM EFFECTS
Alcohol		
• common uses: to relax, socialize, or lower inhibitions in social settings • risks: misused to cope with negative emotions or mental health issues	• lowered inhibitions • increased reaction time • diminished judgment • dehydration • nausea • dry mouth • disrupted sleep	• increased risk of severe organ damage, especially liver • memory problems • risk of withdrawal symptoms, including hallucinations and seizures • possibly fatal if heavy use is stopped without physician supervision
Opioids		
• common uses: prescribed analgesics (e.g., morphine, codeine, fentanyl, methadone, oxycodone) • risks: seeking out illicit opioids (heroin, manufactured pills), especially once prescriptions are completed	• endorphin release, invoking euphoria • muffling of pain receptors (analgesic effect)	• diminished ability for the body to create endorphins naturally, leading to greater dependence • possible to become addicted very quickly • may experience withdrawal symptoms very easily

Sedative-Hypnotics		
- common uses: prescribed antianxiety medications (e.g., alprazolam [Xanax], diazepam [Valium]); medications to treat insomnia (e.g., zolpidem [Ambien]) - risks: misused to cope with negative emotions or mental health issues	- drowsiness - confusion - sleepiness - slurred speech - memory problems - dyspnea	- risk of withdrawal symptoms, including seizures - could result in seizures or delirium if treatment is stopped without physician supervision
Stimulants		
- common uses: prescribed treatments for ADHD, narcolepsy (e.g., methylphenidate [Ritalin], dextroamphetamine [Adderall]) - risks: seeking out illicit stimulants (e.g., cocaine, methamphetamine)	- increased alertness - decreased appetite - insomnia - agitation - hypertension - irregular heartbeat	- tolerance (requiring more of the drug to feel the effects) - irrational behavior, especially when seeking out the substance - paranoia - hallucinations - skin picking - psychotic symptoms - angina and heart damage
Marijuana/Cannabis		
- common uses: increasingly socially acceptable and legal in many states; like alcohol, used to relax, socialize, or lower inhibitions in social settings - risks: similar to alcohol; misused to cope with negative emotions or mental health issues	- euphoria - increased appetite - memory impairment - paranoia - hallucinations	- withdrawal from activities - spending excessive amounts of money on the substance - behavioral changes - abandoning friendships - decreased motivation in life

QUICK REVIEW QUESTIONS

11. Withdrawal from which substances may cause seizures?

12. Which commonly misused substances may be prescribed for ADHD or narcolepsy?

Drug Administration

The way in which a drug is administered can affect its method of action. There are different forms of administration for each substance. Abuse of a substance can occur when the method that is traditionally used for the drug is altered. For example, if a prescribed oral medication is transformed into a liquid and injected with a syringe, it is being abused.

Oral administration occurs when a drug is consumed by mouth. The following drugs are generally administered orally:

- alcohol
- opioid, sedative-hypnotic, or stimulant medications
- some forms of cannabis
- LSD
- psilocybin

Certain drugs can be taken through **inhalation** methods. Tobacco is a commonly inhaled drug. Cannabis is frequently inhaled in the form of a marijuana cigarette or via vaporizer paraphernalia (e.g., pipes, "bongs"). **Vaporizers** (or "vapes"), through which users inhale vapor derived from oil extracts containing THC or nicotine, have also become popular.

Intranasal drug use is also called "snorting." Drugs in powder form (e.g., cocaine) may be snorted. Some oral medications are crushed and snorted when they are misused. Intranasal use is common among those who abuse oral medications, as this method of administration allows the drug to enter the bloodstream far more quickly than when it is taken orally. While the effects are fast-acting, the side effects can be extremely dangerous and, in some cases, deadly:

- Intranasal administration can cause severe damage within the sinus cavity.
- Brain damage can occur with both short-term and prolonged usage.

Some substances are administered rectally through a **suppository**. The mucus membranes in the rectum area can absorb some drugs quickly. Rectal administration can be risky because the sensitivity level of the membranes cannot be predicted, so the drug may be absorbed much faster, or to a greater extent, than through other forms of administration.

Intravenous (IV) administration refers to using a syringe to inject a substance. In IV administration, the drugs are injected into a vein and supplied directly into the bloodstream. The effects occur immediately. Over time, multiple injections can damage veins. As a result, some people with SUD turn to the **intramuscular** or **subcutaneous injection** method:

- Intramuscular injections administer the drug right into the muscle.
- Subcutaneous injections administer the drug into the soft tissue under the skin.

Intravenous administration presents additional risk to users:
- The risk of overdose increases.
- The risk of contracting a disease increases.
  - Non-sterile needles and paraphernalia can be vectors for infection.
  - A non-sterile environment can also cause infection.

QUICK REVIEW QUESTIONS

13. What is a negative health consequence of intranasal administration?

14. What are negative health consequences of intravenous or intramuscular administration?

Intoxication and Withdrawal

Working with clients who are seeking recovery from addiction requires boundaries. For example, a client who is intoxicated can be nonattentive, defiant, or dangerous. Sessions should be conducted while clients are sober. In addition, counselors should be alert for signs of **withdrawal** from substances, which can be a medical emergency. Symptoms of withdrawal include

- vomiting;
- tremors;
- increased heart rate (tachycardia);
- anxiety;
- sweating;
- insomnia;
- fatigue; and/or
- seizures and delirium tremens (in extreme cases).

While experiencing withdrawal, clients complaining of the symptoms listed above may benefit from—or require—medical assistance, such as a referral to a detox facility or inpatient treatment.

Blood alcohol content (BAC) describes the percentage of alcohol in a person's body after consuming alcohol. Ways to measure BAC include testing a person's blood, breath, saliva, or urine. Several factors impact a person's BAC:

- how quickly a person drinks
- body weight
- whether there is food in the stomach
- the sex of a person
- the type of alcohol being consumed
- the amount of alcohol that was consumed
- if the alcohol was mixed with another liquid
- any medications that a person is taking

TABLE 1.4. BAC Ranges and Effects on the Person

BAC RANGE	PRESENTATION	EXAMPLES
0.00 – 0.07	euphoria (feeling "buzzed")	• increased energy • improved self-confidence • feeling more social
0.08 – 0.10	impaired	• physical impairment • poor judgment • slurred speech
0.11 – 0.19	intoxicated (drunk)	• depressive symptoms • motor impairment (affecting ability to drive and talk) • vision impairment • nausea
0.20 and above	extremely intoxicated	• little to no awareness of time • confusion • insensitivity to pain • vomiting • alcohol-related blackout (amnesia without losing consciousness)
0.30	requires medical attention	• high risk of alcohol poisoning • dyspnea • risk of coma • possibly fatal

The **federal legal limit** to drive is a BAC of 0.08 for individuals who are legally allowed to drink. This is the standard across the United States. There are differences among the states regarding the "zero tolerance" limit established for individuals who are under the legal drinking age:

- A BAC of 0.02 is the zero tolerance limit in most US states and territories.
- Some states have a true zero tolerance of 0.00 for motorists who are under the legal drinking age.

An **alcohol overdose**, also known as alcohol poisoning, occurs when a person consumes alcohol faster than the liver can metabolize it. Similarly, when someone overdoses on other drugs, the person's body cannot adjust to the quantity of drugs in the system, which can be fatal. Symptoms associated with **overdose** include

- a blueish tint to lips and fingernails;
- cold and clammy skin;
- hypothermia;
- changes to pulse, heartbeat, or breathing;

 DID YOU KNOW?

Alaska, Arizona, the District of Columbia, Illinois, Maine, Minnesota, North Carolina, and Oregon all have a true zero-tolerance policy for underage drivers.

- incontinence;
- seizures;
- vomiting and/or choking; and
- unconsciousness.

People who have been using and are exhibiting any of the above symptoms will likely require medical attention. Medical treatment for alcohol poisoning can include receiving IV fluids; being given oxygen; pumping the stomach to remove toxins; and, in extreme cases, dialysis to remove alcohol from the individual's blood. When someone is suspected of having alcohol poisoning, emergency services should be called immediately:

- While waiting for first responders, try to talk to the individual who is intoxicated to keep the person conscious.
- If the person feels cold or clammy to the touch, try to keep the individual warm.
- Turn the unconscious individual onto the side to prevent choking in case the person vomits.

QUICK REVIEW QUESTIONS

15. What term describes the percentage of alcohol in a person's body after consuming alcohol?

16. What is the federal legal BAC limit to drive in the United States for people who are legally allowed to drink alcohol?

Relapse

A **relapse** occurs when an individual who has stopped using drugs or alcohol uses again. There are a variety of factors that can contribute to a relapse. The National Institute on Drug Abuse (NIDA) estimates that half of the individuals in recovery will experience a relapse. Some common factors that contribute to a relapse include the following:

- environment
  - A recovering person's daily environment can be a reminder of substance misuse (e.g., home, neighborhood, car, workplace).
  - For example, if a person habitually drank in the living room recliner after work, the individual may benefit from moving or removing the recliner.
- stress
  - Stress can come from any aspect of a person's life.
  - Relationships, finances, legal issues, work, and concern about managing sobriety can all trigger stress.
  - Finding healthy ways to manage stress can reduce the risk of relapse.

- emotional distress
  - Negative emotions such as sadness, anger, and loneliness are common emotions associated with relapse.
  - Learning to cope with challenging emotions is imperative to a healthy recovery.
- being around drugs or alcohol
  - Spending time with people who use, keeping substances in the home, or going places where substances will be present (e.g., bars and clubs) can put a person at higher risk for relapse.
  - People recovering from SUD should consider removing alcohol and other drugs from their homes and avoiding people, locations, and events that involve substance use.
- celebrating
  - Celebrations (e.g., weddings, holidays) often include alcohol and other substances.
  - Learning how to enjoy celebrations sober can be a challenging experience for many.

Counselors work with clients to develop relapse prevention plans. (See Chapter 6 for more on relapse prevention planning.)

QUICK REVIEW QUESTIONS

17. How common is relapse among people with SUD?

18. Why do celebrations present a risk of relapse?

Long-Term Consequences of Substance Abuse

Health Consequences of Substance Abuse

Substance abuse affects the physical body and body systems. Different substances have different effects. A person's sex, age, the length of time that a substance has been misused and/or abused, which substance is being abused, preexisting medical conditions, and whether safety is being practiced during the addiction all determine the impacts of addiction on a person's physical health.

Individuals who use drugs intravenously risk the transmission of

- HIV/AIDS;
- tuberculosis;
- hepatitis;
- sexually transmitted infections; and
- other infectious diseases.

Any of these diseases can be transmitted when individuals are not using sterile needles or are sharing other using equipment. A harm reduction approach related to this is needle exchange programs that are designed to decrease the transmission of these diseases.

Long-term substance misuse and abuse can lead to a variety of physical health concerns, including the following:

- type 2 diabetes
  - Alcohol abuse can damage the pancreas, an organ directly involved in releasing insulin.
  - Many substances cause cell damage, decrease antioxidant presence in cells, and impact glucose metabolism.
- heart disease
  - While there is some truth to the belief that drinking alcohol can have a positive impact on people's hearts, these benefits only occur when the individual's consumption is on a low-to-moderate scale.
  - Since it is still possible to experience other negative aspects of alcohol with low-to-moderate drinking, the overall benefits may not be as significant as one might hope.
  - Individuals who misuse and abuse alcohol experience an increased risk for cardiovascular health concerns.
- cirrhosis
  - When alcohol is consumed, the liver works to remove the poison from the person's body.
  - Consuming large amounts of alcohol, even for a short time, can cause fat to build up in the liver, which is the first stage of **alcohol-related liver disease (ARLD)**.
  - The second stage of ARLD is acute alcoholic hepatitis, which is associated with inflammation of the liver.
  - The final stage of ARLD is alcoholic liver cirrhosis.
  - Some illicit drugs, such as cocaine, also negatively impact a person's liver.
- brain damage
  - Individuals who misuse or abuse alcohol for an extended period of time are at an increased risk of experiencing permanent changes in the way their brains function. This, coupled with poor health (commonly associated with AUD), can negatively impact a person's overall health.
  - Individuals who abuse alcohol long term could develop **Wernicke-Korsakoff Syndrome (WKS)**, the symptoms of which include
    - mental confusion;
    - facial paralysis; and
    - poor muscle coordination.
  - Brain hypoxia can occur when a person does not get the needed amount of oxygen to the brain due to a drug overdose.
  - Prolonged illicit drug use can lead to

- headaches;
- neurological and cognitive disruptions;
- brain changes;
- loss of gray matter;
- a reduced hippocampal volume; and
- larger cerebral ventricles.

Table 1.5. lays out some of the general effects that all substances have on the various body systems when abused over the long term.

TABLE 1.5. Effects of Substance Use on Body Systems

SYSTEM	EFFECTS OF SUBSTANCE USE
Endocrine system	<ul><li>hormonal disturbances</li><li>reproductive difficulties</li><li>body growth concerns</li><li>thyroid concerns</li><li>certain cancers</li><li>bone disease</li></ul>
Immune system	<ul><li>autoimmune disorders</li><li>rheumatoid arthritis</li><li>polymyositis</li><li>dermatomyositis</li></ul>
Reproductive system	<ul><li>difficulty conceiving</li><li>miscarriage risk</li><li>fetal alcohol syndrome</li><li>loss of libido (opioid-induced)</li><li>Marijuana abuse specifically results in<ul><li>lower sperm count and motility,</li><li>abnormal menstrual cycle, and</li><li>the risk of premature birth.</li></ul></li></ul>
Musculoskeletal system	<ul><li>osteoporosis</li><li>arthritis</li><li>tooth decay</li><li>susceptibility to bone breaks</li><li>higher risk of injuries due to impairment</li><li>rhabdomyolysis</li><li>muscle wasting due to malnutrition</li></ul>
Neurological system	<ul><li>alterations to neural paths (e.g., reward pathways)</li><li>nerve damage</li><li>tissue damage</li><li>reduction in brain functioning</li></ul>

Respiratory system	• aspiration pneumonitis • pulmonary edema • pneumonia • respiratory cancers

Circulatory system	• Substance use is associated with
	  • coronary artery disease,
	  • hypertension,
	  • hypertension, and
	  • cardiomyopathy.
	• Alcohol abuse is particularly associated with
	  • heart disease,
	  • stroke,
	  • peripheral arterial disease, and
	  • cardiomyopathy.
	• Other drug abuse is particularly associated with
	  • cardiac arrest,
	  • dysrhythmias,
	  • atherosclerosis, and
	  • thrombosis.

Digestive system	• diarrhea • constipation • stomach discomfort • liver and GI tract inflammation • reduction of blood flow to the GI system

Prescribed medications have potential side effects. When medications are misused or abused, a person's risk of developing the associated side effects increases.

Individuals who use or abuse substances while taking prescribed medications are at a higher risk of developing damaging and uncomfortable side effects. As an example, the liver helps break down medications. When a person drinks alcohol while taking medication, the liver can become overwhelmed by having to break down both the medication and the alcohol, increasing the risk of liver damage. This concept of compounding damage can be applied to individuals who abuse other substances while taking medications as well as individuals who abuse more than one substance.

 DID YOU KNOW?

Tobacco use can contribute to a woman's inability to conceive, double her risk of being infertile, and reduce the hormones needed for pregnancy. Men who smoke tobacco or marijuana may have a lower sperm count.

QUICK REVIEW QUESTIONS

19. List TWO risks of IV drug abuse.

20. List TWO chronic health conditions associated with alcohol abuse.

Psychosocial Consequences of Substance Abuse

People with SUD typically focus on their substance of choice; as a result, they step back from interests and activities. The **psychosocial consequences** of substance use include negative impacts on

- spirituality and/or religion;
- employment status;
- mental health; and/or
- relationships.

Negative impacts of substance use on a person's career include

- missing shifts/having unexcused absences;
- going to work impaired;
- attending work while sick from earlier use; and
- decreased productivity.

Experiencing employment consequences can contribute to continued use and struggles since substance use also has **emotional consequences**. People self-medicate by using substances to cope with challenging emotions and other mental health concerns.

For example, someone who has had a stressful day may drink alcohol to relieve symptoms of distress. In this case, alcohol is masking the individual's emotional distress rather than allowing it to be processed. When this is done repeatedly, emotions can intensify and lead to even more distress.

Another common experience is the use of alcohol and drugs to cope with an undiagnosed or untreated mental health disorder. Mental health symptoms commonly worsen as a result. Mental health concerns among individuals who struggle with a substance use disorder include

- depressive symptoms;
- anxiety symptoms;
- suicidal ideation;
- hopelessness;
- feeling worthless;
- insomnia; and
- anger.

The **cognitive effects** of drugs and alcohol can be observed in individuals who use or drink recreationally, and among those who have a mild, moderate, or severe substance use disorder. Using even a limited quantity of substances can impact thinking patterns, motor skills, and judgment.

HELPFUL HINT

Many addiction treatment programs tie spirituality into their recovery programs. This can help individuals feel connected to something other than themselves.

Individuals undergoing withdrawal may experience cognitive impairments. For many, these symptoms decrease as a person ends the withdrawal period. Withdrawal-related cognitive impairments include

- poor concentration;
- poor impulse control;
- poor memory; and
- lack of cognitive flexibility.

Individuals who misuse and abuse substances long term are at risk for other cognitive impairments. The potential consequences a person faces will depend on the substance being used, genetics, and the person's environment:

- Individuals who misuse and abuse marijuana long term can experience hardship in learning, problems with memory retention, long- and short-term memory loss, and difficulty with time estimation.
- Individuals who misuse and abuse amphetamines and opiates can experience difficulty with their verbal skills, pattern recognition, planning, and impairment in their decision-making abilities.
- Those who misuse and abuse methamphetamine may experience motor function impairments, poor memory for spoken words, and difficulty with other neuropsychological tasks.
- Those who misuse and abuse MDMA and ecstasy can struggle with recall of spoken words for up to two years of maintained abstinence.

Individuals with SUD often demonstrate **behavior changes**, including

- changes to their hygiene routine;
- distancing and/or withdrawing from family and friends;
- being dishonest;
- not meeting previous work standards;
- increase in risky behaviors (e.g., driving under the influence);
- being focused on their next use;
- failing to meet all responsibilities; and
- not engaging in previously enjoyed activities or hobbies.

Sociological effects of substance use include impacts on the person's family, friends, and other support systems. Relationships can be damaged by dishonesty, manipulation, and denial. Problematic behaviors related to SUD affect the broader community. Examples include impaired driving and other criminal behaviors related to obtaining substances (e.g., theft).

An example of an **environmental effect** of substance use would be the loss of housing, which can be the result of eviction or not making scheduled payments. This can also be applied to a person's vehicle payments, which impact the ability to travel.

Individuals who live in an environment where substances are in the home and/or others in the home are actively using substances often find recovery more challenging. This can contribute to an increase in cravings and relapses.

DID YOU KNOW?

The US Surgeon General estimates that alcohol misuse costs the United States $249 billion a year; consequences of illicit drug use cost $193 billion a year.

QUICK REVIEW QUESTIONS

21. What are TWO cognitive impairments related to withdrawal?

22. Use and misuse of which drug causes hardship in learning, problems with memory retention, long- and short-term memory loss, and difficulty with time estimation?

Answer Key

1. People frequently become exposed to misused substances through recreational use and prescribed habit-forming medications.

2. The term *physical dependence* describes when a person's body is accustomed to taking a drug. This can result in withdrawal symptoms when the drug is no longer present in the system.

3. The term *substance dependence* describes a deep need to use a controlled substance to achieve a feeling of euphoria and/or calm.

4. The term *substance use* describes the nonmedically warranted consumption of medications or substances such as tobacco, alcohol, or illicit drugs.

5. The social education model assumes that addiction is a learned behavior.

6. Exposure theory posits that addiction will eventually occur after the regular use of a substance.

7. A person who exhibits the signs and symptoms of addictive behavior but does not consume mind-altering substances may have process addiction.

8. Gambling addiction is a process addiction that is listed as a disorder in the *DSM-5*.

9. Individuals who are addicted to multiple substances or other behaviors are demonstrating cross addiction.

10. When a person develops an addiction, the reward pathway develops in the brain.

11. Withdrawal from alcohol and sedative-hypnotics may cause seizures.

12. Stimulants are commonly misused substances that may be prescribed for ADHD or narcolepsy.

13. Sinus damage and brain damage are negative health consequences of intranasal administration.

14. The risk of overdose increases; needles, paraphernalia, and/or environments that are not sterile may cause infection.

15. The term *blood alcohol content (BAC)* describes the percentage of alcohol in a person's body after consuming alcohol.

16. A blood alcohol content (BAC) reading of 0.08 is the federal legal limit to drive in the United States for people who are legally allowed to drink alcohol.

17. The National Institute on Drug Abuse (NIDA) estimates that half of the individuals in recovery will experience a relapse.

18. Celebrations often include alcohol and other substances.

19. Tuberculosis, HIV/AIDS, hepatitis, sexually transmitted infections, and other infectious diseases are all risks of IV drug abuse.

20. Wernicke-Korsakoff Syndrome (WKS), alcohol-related liver disease (ARLD), cirrhosis, heart disease, stroke, peripheral arterial disease, and cardiomyopathy are all chronic health conditions associated with alcohol abuse.

21. Poor concentration, poor impulse control, poor memory, and lack of cognitive flexibility are all cognitive impairments related to withdrawal.

22. Use and misuse of marijuana causes hardship in learning, problems with memory retention, long- and short-term memory loss, and difficulty with time estimation.

2 Screening and Interviewing the Client

Clinical Screening

Screening and assessment are not the same thing. During **screening**, a counselor determines the following:

- whether a problem is present
- the nature and severity of the problem
- a proper diagnosis

Counselors use screening to determine whether someone who uses a substance (or substances) requires assessment. Finally, screening establishes rapport, provides a framework for the management of crises, and determines the need for additional professional assistance.

Establishing Rapport

A counselor who actively listens and delivers on guarantees builds trust with the client. While building trust can take time, it makes the therapeutic process easier for all involved.

The basic elements of communication and active listening form the foundation of a counselor's **rapport** and relationship with the client. To build a strong rapport with a client, the counselor must

- be engaging,
- be an active listener, and
- avoid interrupting the client.

Counselors who actively listen deliver on guarantees, establish and maintain boundaries, and build trust with their clients. When a strong rapport is built, clients will trust that the counselor cares about their issues and advocates for their well-being. Building trust can take time, but doing so helps the counselor manage the client's condition and makes the process easier for all involved.

QUICK REVIEW QUESTIONS

1. How does screening differ from assessment?

2. How can a counselor build a strong rapport with a client?

Verbal and Nonverbal Communication

Communication includes both verbal and nonverbal components:

- **Verbal communication** is the use of language to convey information. Characteristics of verbal communication include tone, volume, and word choice.
- **Nonverbal communication** includes behavior, gestures, posture, and other nonlanguage elements of communication that transmit information or meaning.

The theory of basic communication is made up of several components:

- **sender**: the individual or entity sending the message
- **channel**: the method by which the sender transmits the message
- **receiver**: the individual or entity translating the message
- **destination**: the individual or entity for whom the message is targeted
- **message**: the information transferred from the sender to the recipient

Without even realizing that they are doing so, people use these communication components in everyday conversations. The sender will transfer information through the channel to the receiver, who interprets or translates the message to the destination. In recent times, oral conversation has given way to texting, emailing, and using social media; without aural cues, sometimes the intended tone of the message is lost.

Active listening means paying attention to speakers, not just hearing their words. The listener makes eye contact with the speaker to indicate interest in what is being said. An active listener repeats important points the speaker has made to ensure understanding, asks follow-up questions, and does not interrupt. The goal is twofold: improved understanding and making the speaker aware that the listener cares about what the speaker is saying.

TABLE 2.1. Dos and Don'ts of Client Communication

DO...	DON'T...
• make eye contact with the client, • introduce yourself and use the client's name, • speak directly to the client when possible, • ask open-ended questions, • speak slowly and clearly, • show empathy for the client, and • be silent when appropriate to allow the client time to think and process emotions.	• use medical jargon, • threaten or intimidate the client, • lie or provide false hope, • interrupt the client, • show frustration or anger, and/or • make judgmental statements.

In addition to active listening, a variety of techniques are used for therapeutic communication:

- **Sharing observations** may open up the conversation to how the client is feeling.
- **Using touch**, such as a gentle hand on the shoulder or arm—when appropriate or welcome—can offer comfort.
- **Silence** allows the client a moment to absorb or process any information that is given.
- **Summarizing and paraphrasing** information back to a client helps ensure or confirm understanding.
- Asking relevant questions that pertain to the situation helps the counselor gather information for decision-making.
    - **Closed-ended questions** can be answered with a "yes" or "no" and are useful for obtaining basic information.
    - **Open-ended questions** cannot be answered with a simple "yes" or "no" and instead encourage clients to elaborate on their points.

QUICK REVIEW QUESTIONS

3. What are some characteristics of verbal communication?

4. What are some aspects of active listening?

Diversity in Communication

As part of developing tailored treatment plans, counselors must be sensitive to the backgrounds and experiences of clients and be willing to learn about their cultures, beliefs, behaviors, and attitudes. Some strategies follow:

- Instruments and tools should be adapted for people of specific cultural groups and populations.

- Interviews should be conducted in the client's language by a trained staff member.
- Thorough discussion facilitates full understanding of substance use.

Culture and gender affect the way people see the world. To effectively communicate with people from different backgrounds, it is important to understand how diversity affects the way information is transmitted and received.

The counselor should expect diverse communication styles depending on the client demographic. **Indirect communication** values how a message is conveyed and its context. Nonverbal cues may be of more importance to indirect communicators. **High-context cultures** communicate heavily through relationships, context, and nonverbal cues. High-context cultures can be found in the Middle East, Asia, Africa, and South America.

Direct communicators say what they mean without using too much context or background information. They may make more eye contact than indirect communicators, and they may more easily express disagreement. **Low-context cultures** generally rely more on direct communication. North America and parts of Europe are typically considered low-context cultures.

In the same way that culture affects communication style, gender also plays a role in how people communicate. It is important to note that not all students communicate according to gender types, but awareness of variations in the way people communicate reduces potential conflicts. Typically, men are more direct, authoritative, and confrontational. Conversation for men is usually geared toward finding solutions rather than venting or sharing. Women are more likely to be vulnerable, take turns talking, ask for help, and discuss their feelings.

Counselors should be aware of perceptions and prejudgments that are based on **socioeconomic status**. False perceptions could lead to a failure to detect drug use in certain client populations. For instance, health care providers often forget to ask middle- to upper-level-income clients about substance use. There is also bias regarding substance use and appearance. If people don't look like they are using—if they do not fit the stereotypical image of someone with an addiction—the assumption is that they are not using. However, substance use may be an issue among people who do not display the expected physical signs; this is especially the case with the widespread misuse of prescription medication.

Finally, counselors should keep in mind that clients may have had poor experiences with social service workers or programs in the past and are therefore distrustful of encounters with counselors and treatment programs. Ultimately, no two people are exactly alike. Although culture, gender, and socioeconomic background can be used to make generalizations about expectations or communication styles, knowing and understanding each individual client is most effective.

QUICK REVIEW QUESTIONS

5. Which style of communication values the context of a message and how it is conveyed?

6. Which type of cultures generally rely on direct communication?

Self-Awareness

As objective participants guiding a therapeutic process with clients, counselors must be able to practice clinical detachment while conveying empathy. This requires awareness of self. **Awareness of self** is a practice of reflection and observation both in the moment and outside of the moment.

Awareness of self in the moment is a skill whereby counselors notice their own thoughts, beliefs, emotions, and behaviors without judgment and recognize how they impact the client. By noticing and evaluating these, counselors can adjust based on the client's reactions. For example, a counselor may react emotionally to a client by crying:

- The client's reaction may be one of surprise.
- The counselor can then choose what to do about the situation without judging his own emotional reaction.
- Sharing an emotional reaction with a client may contribute to the client trusting the counselor more.
- On the other hand, a counselor may find herself reacting negatively to a client's disclosure.
- In practicing self-awareness, the counselor can recognize that negativity, evaluate it, and put it aside so as not to make the client feel judged.

The counselor may also use the situation for therapeutic benefit by sharing the process of self-awareness and inviting the client to do the same. Another aspect of self-awareness is the practice of self-reflection on one's own or in consultation with others. Perhaps a counselor is going to meet a client of a significantly different cultural background. Before meeting that client, the counselor might reflect on his values and beliefs about the client's culture and how those beliefs could impact the client in the session. By practicing self-reflection beforehand, counselors can

- check whatever bias they may have;
- educate themselves about the culture; and
- meet the client without bringing bias into the session.

The counselor's verbal and nonverbal communication impacts clients in both positive and negative ways. Clients can tell if something is not right with the counselor, and that may interfere with building a therapeutic relationship. Therefore, the counselor needs to remain self-aware in sessions and be able to read the cues from the client to understand the client's reaction and make adjustments as needed.

 HELPFUL HINT
Self-reflection can also be done in consultation with a supervisor or other colleague to help the counselor bring into awareness any bias or prejudice that could adversely affect the relationship with the client.

QUICK REVIEW QUESTIONS

7. How can counselors practice awareness of self in the moment?

8. Why should counselors practice self-awareness?

Intake and Screening Tools

Intake Forms

When meeting with clients for the first time, counselors conduct an intake assessment to get to know them. Clients are often asked to complete intake forms before their appointment and bring them to discuss with the counselor. **Intake forms** are kept in the client's chart and enable clients to explain—in their own words—why they are seeking counseling.

Several versions of intake forms can be used. Standard intake forms are specific to the location where treatment is being offered. The general categories of information on these forms can include

- personal contact information;
- emergency contact information;
- relevant insurance information;
- list of current symptoms;
- medical concerns and medications;
- current substance use;

WELLNESS CENTER
COUNSELING INTAKE FORM

Today's date: _____ Student ID #: _____ Gender: _____

Name: _____ Date of birth: _____

Ethnicity: _____ Education Level: _____ Major: _____

Campus address: _____ City: _____ State: _____ Zip: _____

Home address: _____ City: _____ State: _____ Zip: _____

Phone (h): _____ (email): _____ (cell): _____

Emergency Contact Person: _____ Phone: _____

Relationship to you: _____ Referred by: _____

Do you work: _____ Where: _____ Position: _____

Counseling History

Have you had previous counseling: _____ Dates: _____

Name of counselor: _____

Explain why: _____

Reason for this appointment request today: _____

List any concerns you have: _____

Are you currently taking any medications: What: _____ Why: _____

Have you ever thought about, or attempted suicide: _____

Has anyone in your family, or friends committed, or attempted suicide: _____

If yes who: _____

What are your positives: _____

Figure 2.1. Sample Intake Form

- history of mental illness including trauma, suicidal ideation, suicide attempts, and homicidal ideation; and
- privacy consents, including consents for prescribing doctors, if relevant.

Some treatment centers provide intake documentation for the counselor to complete that serves as a guide for the initial interview. In other cases, the counselor begins by reviewing the categories listed on the client's intake form and expanding on any items that need clarification. Common issues are

- mental health history;
- history of trauma and abuse;
- current substance use;
- suicidal ideation; and
- homicidal ideation.

QUICK REVIEW QUESTIONS

9. Why are intake forms useful for clients and counselors?
10. Where are intake forms kept?

Readiness to Change

Most people come to counseling because they want to change something in their lives. The **transtheoretical model (TTM)**, developed by researchers James Prochaska and Carlo DiClemente, offers a useful perspective on the birth and growth of behavioral change. It defines a five-step process that is determined by an individual's readiness or willingness to change:

1. precontemplation stage (not ready to change)
2. contemplation stage (getting ready to change)
3. preparation stage (ready to change)
4. action stage (performing the action that will bring about change)
5. maintenance stage (integrating the action into one's lifestyle and making it habit)

CONTINUE

A counselor must determine readiness and willingness to change in all clients. The willingness of clients shows how successful they will be in self-managing their condition(s).

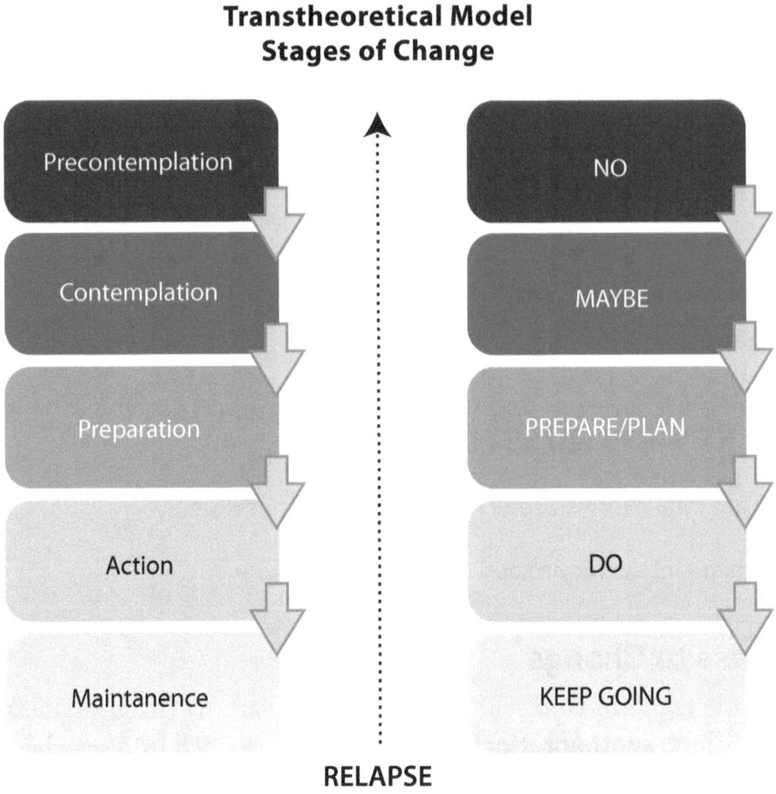

Transtheoretical Model Stages of Change

Precontemplation → NO

Contemplation → MAYBE

Preparation → PREPARE/PLAN

Action → DO

Maintanence → KEEP GOING

RELAPSE

Figure 2.2. Stages of Change

QUICK REVIEW QUESTIONS

11. What happens to the client in the contemplation stage?

12. What happens to the client in the action stage?

Screening Tools

Some common screening tools available to the counselor during intake are described in Table 2.2.

TABLE 2.2. Common Intake Screening Tools
Tobacco, Alcohol, Prescription medication, and other Substance use (TAPS) Tool
• a four-question screening tool for adults that determines if the client is using tobacco, alcohol, prescription medications, or other substances, and at what frequency in the previous twelve months • can be self-administered or administered by the clinician

National Institute on Drug Abuse (NIDA)-modified Alcohol, Smoking, and Substance Involvement Screening Test (NM-ASSIST)
• a clinician-administered online assessment • asks the client about lifetime prescription and illegal drug, alcohol, or tobacco use • if indications of usage, questions progress to frequency and degree to which use has negatively impacted the client's life
Brief Screener for Alcohol, Tobacco, and other Drugs (BSTAD)
• administered online or by a clinician • four questions about the frequency of use in the past year for substances most used by adolescents • provides clinician direction regarding the need for further substance use evaluation
The Alcohol Use Disorders Identification Test (AUDIT)
• identifies heavy drinking • a ten-question, self-administered test
The Texas Christian University Drug Screen II (TCU Drug Screen II or TCUDS II)
• widely used in the criminal justice setting • a fifteen-item, self-administered substance use test • takes around ten minutes to complete
CAGE and CAGE-AID
• questionnaires involving simple tests that screen for drug and alcohol consumption
Mini-International Neuropsychiatric Interview (MINI)
• a brief, structured interview used for major substance use disorders • takes around thirty minutes to complete

QUICK REVIEW QUESTIONS

13. What ten-question test is self-administered to identify heavy drinking?

14. What screening tool has four questions, is used for adults, and may be self-administered or administered by the clinician?

Interviewing the Client

Counselors conduct a clinical assessment interview, which requires sensitivity and a considerable amount of time. This is the start of the therapeutic relationship for the client and the counselor.

Interview Techniques

The purpose of a client interview is to collect relevant information to determine the correct treatment plan. A counselor who is preparing to interview a client must review the following to get the clearest possible picture of the client's health status:

- alcohol or substance use history
- health history
- recent hospitalizations and emergency department visits
- current medication list

To develop a rapport with the client during the initial interview, the counselor must be engaging; this includes active listening and matching the client's communication style. Establishing a rapport with clients is important in making them feel more comfortable and will create a relationship in which the client is willing to share more information.

At the end of the interview, the counselor should summarize the gathered information and highlight important points for the client to ensure that nothing was missed. The counselor should also allow the client to ask questions.

Some clients may have an intellectual disability that hinders or prevents productive interviewing. In such cases, a family member or guardian may assist in obtaining all pertinent information in order to establish a care plan. The care plan will be the foundation to develop a treatment strategy with achievable goals for the client.

Sometimes **concerned others** are part of the assessment process either because the client needs their support or because they are a good source of information. For example, many adolescents are brought to counseling by their parents. While parents may be good sources of information, the client must consent to their involvement in the assessment because of confidentiality. In the case of adolescents, obtaining their assent for their parents to be involved in the assessment helps establish trust with them as clients.

During the interview process, a counselor can gain information about the importance of the relationship between the client and the concerned other(s), including whether the concerned other may be a positive or negative resource for the client. The counselor should

- observe the nonverbal communication between the two; and
- listen to what each person says during the assessment and how these things are said.

QUICK REVIEW QUESTIONS

15. What is the purpose of a client interview?

16. What must the counselor do during the initial interview?

Initial Interview and Interviewing Techniques

For the **initial interview**, the counselor will meet with the client individually. Before beginning, the counselor should discuss confidentiality and situations during which confidentiality might be broken. The underlying goal of any interview is to assess the client's concerns and work toward developing an appropriate treatment plan.

A key reason to conduct the initial interview is for the counselor to establish a rapport with the client. Establishing a rapport means building trust and understanding. A strong counselor-client rapport means the client will feel more comfortable with the counselor and offer more information.

Asking **open-ended questions** allows clients to lead the conversation in a way that is specific to them and their experiences. Open-ended questions teach counselors more about clients than do "yes" and "no" questions. For example, saying, "Tell me about your family," to a client will reveal more information than "Do you have any children?" Thoughtful open-ended questions start a conversation.

Motivational interviewing (MI) strategies can be used with clients who are resistant and unsure about engaging in treatment. MI skills include

- open-ended questions;
- reflective listening; and
- summarizing statements.

Using these strategies can help create an environment where clients feel more comfortable talking about their concerns.

At the end of the interview, the counselor should summarize the gathered information and highlight important points for the client to ensure that nothing was missed. The client should be informed of the next steps, offered an opportunity to ask questions, and given the counselor's contact information.

In behavioral health interviewing, the client may have a mental disability that prevents productive interviewing. A family member or guardian may assist in obtaining all pertinent information to establish a care plan. This can also include children who need mental health treatment. The care plan will be the foundation to develop a treatment strategy with achievable goals for the client.

 HELPFUL HINT
Counselors should be mindful of their body language while clients are sharing. If clients feel uncomfortable or as though they are being judged, they are less likely to share openly.

QUICK REVIEW QUESTIONS

17. What type of questions are helpful for the counselor to ask in the initial interview?

18. What technique can be used with clients who are resistant and unsure about engaging in treatment?

Structured Clinical Interview

A structured clinical interview is part of a client's initial intake exam. It is conducted primarily through **client self-report**, when the client describes to the counselor the symptoms being experienced based on questions the counselor asks.

There are some standardized structured clinical interviews, like the **Structured Clinical Interview for *DSM-5* (SCID-5)**. The SCID-5 is most commonly used in research settings to screen participants for certain diagnoses that would disqualify them from participating in a study. There are four main reasons to use the SCID-5:

1. to evaluate for all the major *DSM-5* diagnoses
2. to select the population for a study
3. to identify current and past mental health concerns within a study's population
4. to help students and new mental health professionals improve their clinical interviewing skills

Currently, the SCID-5 is only approved for use with adults over the age of eighteen. Some clinics use the SCID-5 as part of their clinical intake; others use their own version of structured questions, or even use an unstructured format. In either case, the goal is to provide a set list of questions (some open-ended) that can be used to screen for and rule out diagnoses and presenting issues in clients.

There are ten core diagnoses covered in the SCID-5:

1. mood episodes, cyclothymic disorder, persistent depressive disorder, and premenstrual dysphoric disorder
2. psychotic disorders and associated symptoms
3. differential diagnosis of psychotic disorders
4. differential diagnosis of mood disorders
5. substance use disorders
6. anxiety disorder
7. obsessive-compulsive and related disorders
8. feeding and eating disorders
9. externalizing disorders
10. trauma- and stressor-related disorders

The SCID-5 is a comprehensive assessment that can take anywhere from fifteen minutes to several hours. Because it relies primarily on self-report, it may not be an appropriate assessment tool for individuals with significant intellectual issues or an inability to self-report for other reasons (such as poor language ability or highly disorganized thought).

During a structured clinical interview, the counselor relies on both formal and informal observations. A **formal observation** includes items such as the content of the client's responses to questions.

Informal observations include the client's body language, affect, and the emotive quality of the client's behavior. Interactional dynamics are an important

HELPFUL HINT

In general, it is not considered best practice to diagnose from only one meeting or assessment. Diagnosis can be ongoing, especially with more complex cases. A diagnosis can change if new information emerges.

part of informal observations. **Interactional dynamics** can include not only how clients interact with family members during a session but also how they speak about friends, colleagues, family members, and even how they interact with the counselor. The goal of a structured clinical interview is not to determine a firm diagnosis but rather to have a working diagnostic theory, a good understanding of the client's presenting problem and any environmental factors contributing to the problem, and the foundations for building a treatment plan with the client.

Cultural competence is a key concern in structured clinical interviews. A client who has visions or hears voices that are related to religion or culture should not be diagnosed with hallucinations, especially when these are corroborated by the client's community. Knowing diagnostic standards for cultural differences and having a strong understanding of the client's background are essential for effective structured clinical interviewing.

QUICK REVIEW QUESTIONS

19. What is client self-report?

20 What are examples of informal observations?

Other Types of Interviews

There are several specific types of interviews counselors can conduct, including

- a biopsychosocial interview;
- a diagnostic interview;
- a cultural formulation interview.

Templates for guiding the interview and creating documentation exist for all these types of interviews.

A **biopsychosocial interview** studies the relationship among the client's biological, psychological, and social health. A biopsychosocial interview shows the counselor how these three areas intertwine and impact the client's distress.

- Biological effects can include
  - medical health concerns;
  - disabilities; and
  - the effects of substance use.
- Psychological health refers to the client's mental health concerns and coping skills.
- Social health includes clients' relationships with others and their families.

A **diagnostic interview** assesses specifically for potential mental health diagnoses. These interviews tend to be more structured to ensure that the necessary information is covered to make an accurate diagnosis.

The **cultural formulation interview (CFI)** asks sixteen questions to recognize the cultural impacts on a client while assessing for an appropriate diagnosis. The

HELPFUL HINT

During an initial interview, counselors can use any interview type.

CFI uses open-ended questions to give the client space to talk about concerns regarding the cultural norms being experienced.

An **unstructured interview** has no standardized questions, which enables counselors to guide the interview in ways that they believe will lead to the most relevant information. An unstructured interview often allows for a more open discussion about the client's concerns, goals, and motivations. The main topics covered in an unstructured clinical interview include

- age and sex;
- the reason for seeking counseling;
- work and education history;
- current social activities;
- physical and mental health concerns, past and present;
- current medications and any drug and/or alcohol use;
- family history of mental health and physical health concerns; and
- the counselor's observations of client behavior during the session (e.g., anxious, detached, euthymic).

QUICK REVIEW QUESTIONS

21. What type of interview assesses specifically for potential mental health diagnoses?

22. What type of interview has no standardized questions and allows the counselor to guide the interview?

Evaluating Substance Use

The first time a counselor meets a client is usually during intake and screening—a therapeutic relationship is not yet established. The client may not feel comfortable being entirely truthful about substance use; therefore, the counselor should look for indications of substance use according to the following criteria:

- use patterns
  - When did the client first use; how and what was used?
  - How long has the client used?
  - How have the client's use patterns changed since starting to use?
  - Has the client changed substances or added more substances?
  - Have there been changes in methods of administration (e.g., moving from swallowing pills to crushing pills and smoking them)?
- tolerance
  - Does the client have to use more of a substance to achieve the same effects?
  - Does the client "need" the substance to function?
- withdrawal

- Does the client experience physical symptoms after not using?
- Does the client experience cravings when not using?
- Do thoughts of the substance use occur at inappropriate times?
- attempts to quit
  - Has the client tried to quit and failed?
  - If so, how many times? How long did the abstinence last?
  - Have concerned others encouraged the client to quit?
  - What were the reasons the client wanted to quit?
- continued use despite problems
  - Has the client gotten into arguments with loved ones over substance use?
  - Has the client experienced changes in school or work, such as missing days or declining performance?
  - Has the client gotten into legal trouble?
  - Is the client experiencing financial problems because of use?
- level of functioning
  - Does the client participate in regular hygiene activities?
  - Does the client go to work and/or school?
  - How are the client's family and social relationships?
- reasons for use
  - Does the substance serve a purpose (e.g., emotional numbing, helping to forget, boosting social prowess)?
  - Does the client have co-occurring mental health issues?
  - Does the client have a history of trauma?

A client may not be completely honest during the intake and screening, but positive indications of these criteria give the counselor more information about which formal assessments are appropriate and which issues to explore more thoroughly with the client once rapport is established.

Diagnostic reports from lab tests can show which substances are in the body and at which levels. Lab tests may include urinalysis and blood testing. For example, if a client says she only drinks alcohol, but the urinalysis shows high levels of other substances, the client is not being truthful. The counselor can then use this data to inspire honesty from the client or to determine if there is another explanation for the presence of the substances in the lab reports.

Substance use disorders are progressive, usually starting with casual, social use or a desire to experiment. Depending on biology, psychology, and social environment, a person may progress to more serious addiction and dependence.

QUICK REVIEW QUESTION

23. Why are lab tests useful in addiction counseling?

Co-Occurring Disorders

The term *co-occurring* refers to the presence of a mental health diagnosis in addition to a substance-related disorder. Some people use alcohol and drugs to cope with symptoms resulting from a mental health condition; as a result, individuals who have co-occurring disorders require treatment for both concerns for the best treatment outcomes.

Dual diagnosis refers to an individual who meets the criteria for two separate diagnoses:

- Symptoms for both diagnoses must be present at the same time.
- The term is typically used to describe the presence of a mental health diagnosis and a substance use disorder, but it can refer to other disorders.
- Dual diagnoses can be two mental health conditions, two medical health conditions, or one of each.

Comorbidity is similar to dual diagnosis, but it refers to the presence of more than one health condition. These can be medical or mental health conditions. Each diagnosis section in the *DSM-5* ends with a paragraph explaining the common comorbidities found with that particular diagnosis.

💡 **HELPFUL HINT**
Counselors may come across dual diagnoses referred to as "co-occurring disorders."

QUICK REVIEW QUESTIONS

24. What does the term *co-occurring* mean?

25. What does the term *comorbidity* mean?

Answer Key

1. Counselors use screening to determine whether a substance user requires assessment.

2. The counselor should be engaging, practice active listening, and avoid interrupting the client.

3. Characteristics of verbal communication include tone, volume, and word choice.

4. Active listening involves making eye contact with the speaker, repeating important points the speaker has made, asking follow-up questions, and not interrupting.

5. Indirect communication values the context of a message and how it is conveyed.

6. Low-context cultures generally rely on direct communication.

7. Counselors can notice their own thoughts, beliefs, emotions, and behaviors without judgment and recognize how they impact the client.

8. Self-awareness helps counselors practice clinical detachment while conveying empathy.

9. Intake forms enable clients to explain in their own words why they are seeking counseling.

10. Intake forms are kept in the client's chart.

11. The client is getting ready to change.

12. The client is performing the action that will bring about change.

13. The Alcohol Use Disorders Identification Test (AUDIT) identifies heavy drinking through a self-administered, ten-question test.

14. The Tobacco, Alcohol, Prescription medication, and other Substance use (TAPS) tool can be self-administered or administered by the clinician. It is a four-question screening tool for adults that determines if the client is using substances and at what frequency in the previous twelve months.

15. The purpose of a client interview is to collect relevant information to determine the correct treatment plan.

16. The counselor must develop a rapport with the client during the initial interview.

17. Open-ended questions reveal more about the client and allow the client to lead the conversation.

18. Motivational interviewing (MI) can be used with clients who are resistant and unsure about engaging in treatment.

19. Client self-report is when clients describe their symptoms to the counselor based on questions the counselor asks.

20. Informal observations include the client's body language, affect, and the emotive quality of the client's behavior.

21. A diagnostic interview assesses specifically for potential mental health diagnoses.

22. An unstructured interview has no standardized questions and allows the counselor to guide the interview.

23. Lab tests are useful in addiction counseling because they can show which substances are in the body and at which levels. The counselor can use this data to inspire honesty from the client or to determine if there is another explanation for the presence of substances.

24. The term *co-occurring* refers to the presence of a mental health diagnosis in addition to a substance-related disorder.

25. The term *comorbidity* refers to the presence of more than one health condition—medical or mental health conditions.

3 Assessments

Counselors cannot advocate for clients without first assessing their needs. The answers to the assessment questions will provide the counselor with a clearer picture of the plan that needs to be formulated to assist clients in achieving their goals.

Conducting Assessments

What is an Assessment?

During an **assessment**, counselors obtain more detailed information about clients and their circumstances in order to design a treatment plan tailored to the client's needs. There are six key areas of assessment:

1. Determine client behaviors, values, and frequency of use.
2. Identify why substance use is a problem.
3. Determine how that patient's life is affected by the substance use.
4. Identify the location, time frame, and method of treatment.
5. Recognize any reinforcement for change needed by the patient.
6. Examine factors that are specific to culture and spirituality-related issues.

Useful initial assessment tools include the following:

- client reports
  - Get reports from clients on when they are active or nonactive in their substance use.
- empathy
  - Use empathy when discussing the substance use test results with clients who receive treatment.
- biomarkers
  - Use biomarkers to evaluate clients' progress.

The alcohol and drug counselor assesses demographics, financial status, social needs, some psychological needs, the caregivers used, and medical information. The client will provide all medical information as well as a list of prescribed medications. Any legal documents related to care will also be discussed. In addition, the counselor should ask about wellness exams and financial concerns.

QUICK REVIEW QUESTIONS

1. What is the purpose of assessment?

2. What are three useful tools in assessing SUD?

Clinical Assessment

The **clinical interview** is a basic but integral component of any psychological testing. Also known as an "intake" or "admission interview," the clinical interview is generally a comprehensive assessment to collect information about an individual's background and family relationships. Only a licensed clinician may perform a clinical interview.

During the assessment, counselors work with the client and other stakeholders to collect and interpret more detailed information than what is used in the screening. Assessment is a necessary, ongoing process to plan treatment and evaluate a client's progress. The counselor leads the client through a comprehensive assessment process that accounts for age, race, gender identity, cultural background, disabilities, and other factors. Some areas explored in the assessment process include the following:

- history of alcohol and other drug use
- physical health, mental health, and substance use treatment history
- psychological, emotional, and worldview concerns
- current status of physical health, mental health, and substance use
- family issues
- work history and career issues
- history of criminality
- spirituality
- education and basic life skills
- socioeconomic characteristics and lifestyle
- current legal status
- use of community resources

QUICK REVIEW QUESTIONS

3. A comprehensive assessment to collect information about an individual's background and family relationships is called what?

4. Who performs clinical interviews?

The Psychosocial History

The interviewer should initially explain the reason for obtaining the psychosocial history. In addition, the counselor needs to make appropriate referrals within and outside the facility during this time. During the interview, the counselor should

- determine the goals of the assessment process;
- decide what resources are needed to administer and score the assessment instrument, interpret the results, and establish appropriate services;
- decide what screening measures are required for this client; and
- use a standardized formal assessment tool that offers uniformity and consistency.

A psychosocial history reviews several aspects of a client's life, history, and circumstances. These are outlined below.

Medical history and physical health: It is important to review any **medical conditions** with a client during an assessment. Counselors should especially discuss conditions for which people with SUD are at high risk, including

- a client's HIV/AIDS status and risk behavior;
- history of infectious diseases, like hepatitis C;
- history of sexually transmitted infections;
- use of hormone replacement therapy;
- use of birth control;
- the relationship between gynecological problems and substance abuse;
- history of pregnancies, abortions, miscarriages, and substance abuse during pregnancy; and
- any need for prenatal care.

Substance abuse history: Counselors should review the ways and reasons clients began using drugs and continued to abuse substances. Counselors should also review any history of substance abuse in the client's family of origin and in current or previous significant relationships. Finally, counselors should explore any history of clients using substances with their significant others and family members.

Mental health and treatment history: Counselors should discuss any history of previous treatment and the nature of the client's relationship with those providers, as well as the consequences of treatment. Any diagnoses of anxiety or mood disorders, history of traumatic events and PTSD, and eating disorders should also be discussed with the client. In addition, counselors must determine the severity of any threats to the safety of the client and/or others, including suicidal ideation (SI) and parasuicidal behaviors, threats of suicide, and history of violence and abuse (including sexual violence and abuse). The counselor should also discuss any history of mental illness in the client's family of origin. The client's personal strengths and history of coping strategies should also be discussed at this stage of the psychosocial history review.

Interpersonal and family history: Determine the extent of substance abuse in the client's current significant relationship (if any). Discuss the level of acceptance toward the client's addiction among the client's family, friends, or significant relationships and any support in receiving treatment that these people have provided the client. Finally, review any childcare needs with the client.

Family, parenting, and caregiver history: If applicable, discuss any parenting or caregiver roles the client has held in the past or present.

Children's developmental and educational history: Here, the counselor should assess any child safety needs. The counselor should also determine the child/children's medical, developmental, or emotional needs, if any.

Sociocultural history: Counselors must assess the client's social support system, including isolation before treatment and support for recovery. Review the client's culture, including attitudes toward substance abuse and recovery, especially beliefs and taboos relating to women and substance abuse. Furthermore, counselors should explore any cultural conflicts or stressors the client is currently experiencing or has experienced in the past. Determine the need for bilingual services or services in other languages. Finally, discuss the client's current spiritual beliefs and practices (if any).

Vocational, educational, and military history: Determine if the client is employed and whether the client's employer supports recovery. Likewise, assess the client's military history (if any), including history of traumatic events during military service and any substance abuse during that time. Finally, determine whether the client is financially independent and to what extent.

Legal history: Assess the client's history of involvement and current relationship with child protective services, if any, as well as custody disputes. Gather details regarding the client's arrest record, history of incarceration, and history of restraining orders, if any. In the case of single parents, ascertain their history of child placement during periods of incarceration (past and present).

Barriers to treatment and related services: Assess the client's needs regarding childcare, health insurance, transportation, finances, and case management. Review other potential barriers to treatment.

Strengths and coping strategies: Review how the client has managed challenges in the past, previous attempts at recovery and failed strategies, and assess successful coping mechanisms practiced by the client in managing life challenges.

QUICK REVIEW QUESTIONS

5. Why is it important for counselors to review medical history with a client who has SUD?

6. Discussing the client's social support system and culture is part of what?

7. What are some common barriers to treatment?

Reliability and Validity

It is important to understand if the data are reliable and valid. **Reliability** refers to the consistency of the measurement. Take, for example, a performance-scoring system. To be reliable, the system must measure employees in the same manner. Though their scores may be different, *how* they are measured is consistent.

Validity refers to what is being measured and whether it is relevant. In the example of a performance review, if an employee's performance on a non-work-related issue is being measured, that item is not valid. It may be a reliable measurement, but it is not accurate or relevant to the actual review.

 **HELPFUL HINT**

The concept of reliability can be thought of in the same way as a person who is reliable. A reliable person behaves as expected every time. A reliable assessment instrument does too.

QUICK REVIEW QUESTIONS

8. What term refers to the consistency of a measurement?

9. What term describes what is being measured and whether it is relevant?

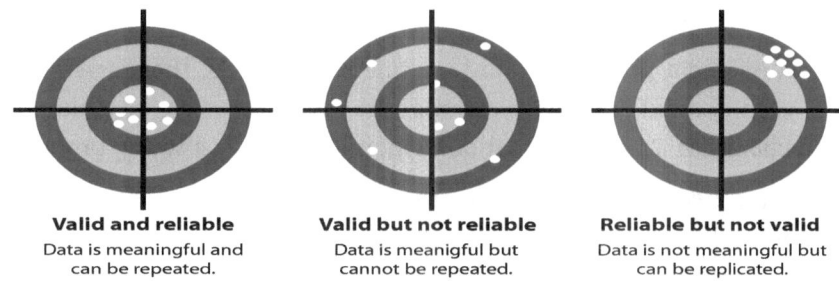

Figure 3.1. Reliability and Validity

Assessment Instruments

An important part of being an effective counselor is understanding how to choose a good assessment. Considering whether the assessment has been tested and approved for a client's age, ethnicity, language, or presenting problem can help a counselor determine what is the best choice to make when assessing a client.

Statistical analysis of large groups of clients and how accurately the assessment measures their symptoms can help the counselor determine the assessment's efficacy.

Substance Use Disorder Assessment Instruments

To assess substance use, several evidence-based assessment instruments are available to the counselor. Addiction professionals are expected to understand and administer SUD assessment instruments. A discussion of their limitations and strengths follows.

The **Addiction Severity Index (ASI)** is the most widely used assessment tool. It assesses seven domains of the client's life:

1. physical health
2. employment
3. drug use
4. alcohol use
5. social support
6. psychiatric status
7. legal status

This assessment is most suitable for adult clients who present with co-occurring substance use and mental health disorders. A clinician can administer the assessment, but it is often given via computer if clients are able to read and answer the questions on their own. The ASI illustrates the client's current status in various domains and drives treatment planning priorities.

The ASI can also be administered every thirty or sixty days to provide information on client progress toward treatment plan goals. The assessment is scored on each domain and yields a composite score from zero to nine. Zero means the client has no issue in that domain; nine suggests a severe problem.

HELPFUL HINT

The ASI-F expanded the ASI by accounting for familial, social, and psychiatric elements of a client's life experience.

The **Tobacco, Alcohol, Prescription medication, and other Substance use (TAPS) Tool** is a four-question screening tool for adults that determines if the client is using tobacco, alcohol, prescription medications, or other substances, and at what frequency in the previous twelve months. It can be self-administered or administered by the clinician.

The **Drug Abuse Screening Test (DAST-10)** is a ten-question assessment to determine drug abuse. It has been approved for adults and older young adults (ages sixteen and up). It can be administered by the counselor or the client.

The **Screening, Brief Intervention, and Referral to Treatment (SBIRT)** is used by clinicians to determine alcohol use. It can be used with adolescents and adults. The client's reported alcohol consumption is placed into different danger levels depending on the amount consumed weekly. This is then discussed with the client, and possible motivation for change is assessed. If the client is amenable, the final part of the SBIRT involves referral to treatment.

The **National Institute on Drug Abuse (NIDA)-modified Alcohol, Smoking, and Substance Involvement Screening Test (NM-ASSIST)** is a clinician-administered online assessment that asks the client about lifetime prescription and illegal drug, alcohol, or tobacco use. If the client indicates any usage, the questions progress to frequency and the degree to which use has negatively impacted the client's life.

The **Clinical Opiate Withdrawal Scale (COWS)** is an eleven-item screening tool administered by clinicians. It measures objective symptoms of opiate withdrawal, such as heart rate, joint pain, stomach issues, goose bumps, sweating, and more. The assessment is used to help clinicians understand the level of opiate dependence and the severity of a client's withdrawal symptoms.

The **Car, Relax, Alone, Forget, Friends, Trouble (CRAFFT)** is a screening tool approved for youth ages twelve to twenty-one to determine substance use. It can be administered by a counselor or through self-assessment. It begins with three questions to determine any level of drug or alcohol use in the previous twelve months. If the client affirms any usage, screening moves on to query about six situations. The final portion is a brief intervention.

The **Drug Abuse Screening Test for Adolescents (DAST-A)** is a modified version of the DAST. It is a twenty-eight-question screening tool to determine adolescent abuse of prescription or illegal drugs, tobacco, and/or alcohol. It can be self-administered or administered by the counselor.

The **CAGE questionnaire** consists of four questions that can be worked into an intake assessment or an individual session. CAGE is an acronym for "**c**ut down, **a**nnoyed, **g**uilt, and **e**ye-opener." The questions for the CAGE are as follows:

1. Have you ever felt the need to cut down on your drinking?
2. Have you been annoyed by others criticizing your drinking?
3. Have you ever felt bad or guilty about your drinking?
4. Have you ever had a drink first thing in the morning to steady your nerves?

The **Alcohol Use Disorders Identification Test (AUDIT)** is a ten-item tool that helps counselors recognize when drinking behaviors have become dangerous to a client's health. Once the questions have been answered, the points will score into one of the following areas: sensible drinking, hazardous drinking, harmful drinking, and possible dependence.

The **Michigan Alcohol Screening Test (MAST)** is a twenty-five-item assessment that helps counselors better understand the lifetime severity of a client's alcohol use. The MAST is often used to help guide treatment plans.

The **Texas Christian University Brief Intake** assesses drug and alcohol use as well as psychological, legal, medical, and family aspects of the client's life. This assessment is delivered via interview by a clinician with adults entering a drug or alcohol treatment program. The assessment takes approximately thirty minutes and indicates the client's immediate treatment needs and areas for further assessment.

The **Drinker Inventory of Consequences (DrInC)** is self-administered. It assesses the negative consequences of drinking in five domains and illustrates which areas of the client's life are most impacted by alcohol. Subscales measure physical, social, intrapersonal, impulsivity, and interpersonal consequences. Clients take approximately ten minutes to complete the DrInC. A score sheet identifies a numerical value for each subscale of consequences; the values are then added to yield a total score. Scores are compared to norms based on age and gender to determine a decile ranking of the client's subscale and total scores.

The **Religious Practices and Beliefs Measurement** is a self-assessment tool that reviews religious practices and beliefs. It is filled out by an adult client and takes approximately five minutes. The assessment provides a view of the client's current and lifetime religious beliefs and practices. The assessment is scored by adding the points associated with each circled response, yielding a total score that indicates a number associated with the client's level of religiosity.

The **Multidimensional Measure of Religiousness/Spirituality** examines domains of religious and spiritual activity, such as values and beliefs, framed in a way that is appropriate for those outside of Judeo-Christian traditions. The assessment is for adults and is completed by the client or through an interview format. The total assessment can be used, or each domain can be assessed separately. Domains include daily spiritual experiences, meaning, values, beliefs, forgiveness, private and organizational religious practices, religious/spiritual coping and support, and commitment to spirituality. Each domain is scored separately. The assessment illustrates areas of spirituality that could be problematic for the client as well as areas of strengths.

QUICK REVIEW QUESTIONS

10. What is the most widely used assessment tool in treating SUD?

11. Which assessment tool specifically measures symptoms of opiate withdrawal?

12. Which assessments are appropriate for youth and adolescents?

Toxicology Testing and Laboratory Data

Biomarkers allow counselors to track a client's recovery process and can detect occasional or heavy use. There are different testing methods that collect information on the type, amount, and last use of a drug. The four most common toxicology testing methods include

- urine testing;
- blood testing;
- saliva testing; and
- hair follicle testing.

In rare cases, sweat or the contents of the stomach can be tested; however, these types of toxicology tests are rarely used with addiction.

A **urine sample** is collected in a sterilized container. Some containers have a built-in testing device. If additional screening is required, the sample can be sent to a laboratory, which will provide more accurate testing results. Results will indicate the amount of the drug present in the urine and the last time the drug was used.

Saliva samples are obtained from the mouth with a cotton swab. The mucus membranes in the mouth will have traces of the drug; these traces are present in the saliva. The swab is rubbed on the inside of the cheek to obtain a sample. The swab is then enclosed in a sterilized container that is sent to a lab for testing.

To perform **blood testing**, a blood sample is taken from the client with a syringe. Blood testing is highly effective because drugs stay in the blood for

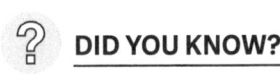

DID YOU KNOW?

Urine testing must be done within five days of collecting the sample. The drug begins to leave the urine after five days, and an accurate test cannot be conducted.

longer periods of time and can be detected in the blood much faster than in urine and saliva. Only one blood sample is needed, regardless of the quantity of drugs being assessed.

In **hair follicle testing**, a piece of hair is removed and tested for the presence of drugs. Hair follicle testing can show evidence of use from up to three months in the past and can indicate the presence of several drugs in the body. This form of drug testing can be used to detect patterns of use over time.

Drug testing in any of these forms can be done to check for one specific drug or for up to thirty drugs at one time. The testing method used depends upon the reason for testing. For example, if the test is taken for legal purposes, the examiner will look for a variety of drugs. In the treatment context, one specific drug or those in a similar class may be the focus.

QUICK REVIEW QUESTIONS

13. Which form of testing uses containers with a built-in testing device?

14. Which form of testing can provide more information about patterns of use over time?

Assessing Other At-Risk Behaviors

Counselors have an ethical duty to conduct ongoing assessments for **suicidal** and **homicidal** behavior, **self-injury**, and **relationship violence**. Counselors are legally required to report any serious threats of suicide or homicide to the police for intervention. Self-injury with no suicidal intent and relationship violence are not reportable events, but responsible counseling involves ongoing monitoring and assessment of these aspects of a client's life to ensure safety.

As part of ongoing assessment, counselors have a responsibility to screen for **suicidal** or **homicidal ideation (SI/HI)**—thoughts of harming oneself or others:

- Frequency and duration: How often does the client think about harming herself or others, and for how long?
- Intensity: Are the thoughts fleeting and easy to ignore, or are they pressing and disturbing?
- Plan: Does the client have a plan for how he would kill himself or others, or is it more of a vague wish to be dead?
- Means: If the client has a plan, does she have the means to carry it out? For example, if the client has contemplated shooting herself, does she have access to a gun?
- Intent: How seriously is the client considering enacting his plan? Does he have a specific time and date that he is planning on; does he deny any intent; is it something in between?

Nonsuicidal self-injury (NSSI) is any form of self-injury without intent to kill oneself. The most common forms of NSSI include cutting, burning, and head banging or hitting. Other forms include scratching, hitting oneself or other objects, ingesting harmful substances, and more.

 HELPFUL HINT

Some people are afraid that asking about suicidal ideation can make a person suicidal. Research shows that this is not true and that assessing for SI can be lifesaving.

It is important to refrain from judgment or reacting emotionally when assessing for NSSI. Although cutting is the most common form of NSSI, it is important to screen for other types of NSSI behaviors, as counselors can easily miss them. The **SOARS model** is a brief assessment used in clinics to screen for NSSI:

- **S**uicidal ideation: Is the NSSI motivated by or paired with suicidal ideation?

- **O**nset, frequency, methods: When did the NSSI begin; when was the most recent time; how often does it happen; what methods are/were used?

- **A**ftercare: How are the wounds cared for; has medical attention for the wounds ever been required?

- **R**easons: What prompts or motivates the client's self-harm (emotional release, anger, self-hatred, and so forth)?

- **S**tages of change: Does the client think about stopping; does the client want to stop?

Relationship violence, also known as "domestic violence" or "intimate partner violence," occurs when one or both partners are enacting physical, emotional, financial, and/or psychological abuse on the other partner. Intimate

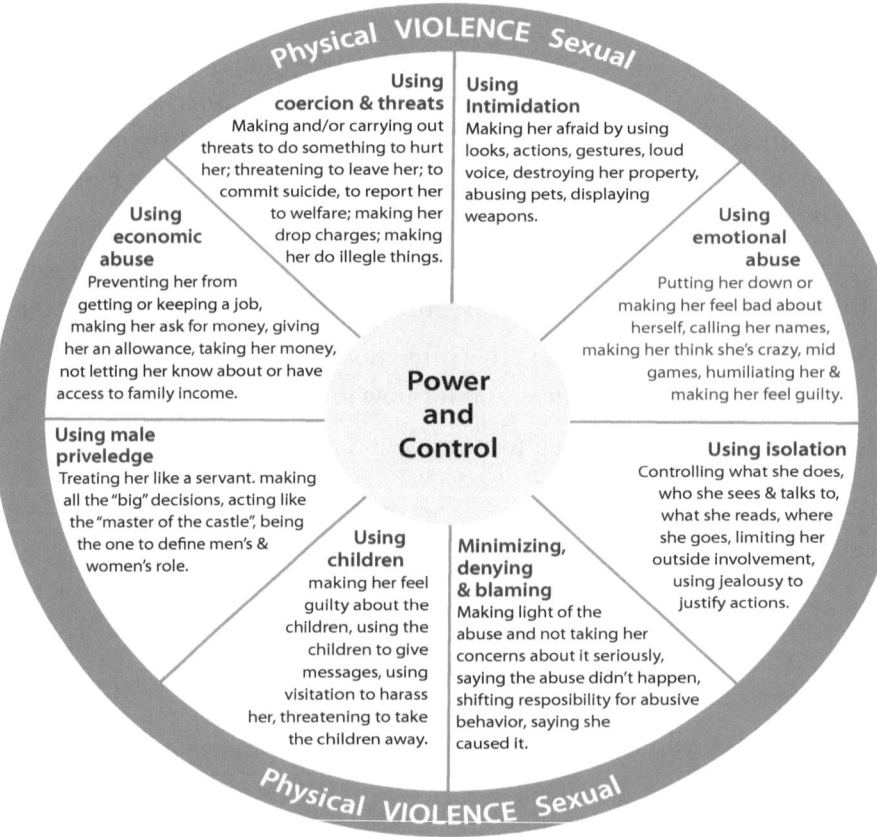

Figure 3.2. The Power and Control Wheel

partner violence is dangerous and can be life-threatening. Despite this, it is not reportable except in cases where children witness the abuse or if the abuse is aimed at an older adult. Important areas of assessment for people who have experienced domestic violence include

- the frequency and duration of attacks (can be helpful to use a calendar);
- the type of attack (whether a weapon was used, level of injury);
- partner stability (employment, drug/alcohol use, mental health concerns, suicide threats);
- controlling behavior (money, stalking, controlling whom the partner sees); and
- attacks on others (children, pets, family members).

Safety planning is of paramount importance for clients who experience relationship violence. It often takes a long time for them to leave their abusers. Planning where to go, saving enough money, and childcare are all crucial elements of treatment planning for clients who experience relationship violence.

QUICK REVIEW QUESTIONS

15. What term describes self-injury without suicidal intent?

16. Which assessment screens for self-injury without suicidal intent?

Assessing Trauma

Trauma is an emotional response or reaction to distressing events. Some common exposure events include natural disasters, war, witnessing or experiencing violence, witnessing or experiencing abuse, witnessing or experiencing rape or sexual assault, or being in an accident that leads to hospitalization.

Clients with SUD may exhibit signs of trauma. There are four main domains of trauma symptoms:

1. **Intrusion** includes intrusive memories, nightmares, flashbacks, or reactions to triggers.
2. **Avoidance** involves changing one's behavior to avoid certain thoughts, memories, or external reminders.
3. **Negative changes in mood and affect** include memory issues, low self-worth, thoughts that the event was their fault, consistent negative emotions, a sense of detachment, or difficulty feeling positive emotions.
4. **Increased reactivity** includes symptoms like irritability, hypervigilance, elevated startle response, attention issues, sleep issues, and self-destructive behavior.

In order to be diagnosed with **post-traumatic stress disorder (PTSD)**, clients must have had exposure to a traumatic experience, exhibit symptoms across all four domains, and experience those symptoms for at least one month.

QUICK REVIEW QUESTIONS

17. What are the four main domains of trauma symptoms?

18. A client has disturbing dreams about a traumatic experience but does not exhibit intrusion, avoidance, or other negative changes. Does the client have PTSD?

Interpreting Results and Acting on the Assessment

Diagnostic Criteria

A **diagnosis** is an identified health condition that is based on an assessment by a trained professional. In some states, determining a diagnosis is beyond the scope of practice of SUD counselors. Still, understanding the different diagnostic criteria will help the ADC serve the client.

The *Diagnostic and Statistical Manual of Mental Disorders (DSM-5)* contains criteria for diagnoses. Each diagnosis has different requirements, all of which are explained in the "Diagnostic Criteria" section for the diagnosis. Determining a diagnosis for a substance use disorder according to *DSM-5* criteria involves evaluating a client's use and functioning patterns along a continuum of severity within four groups of symptoms.

The counselor must first determine if the client is in a state of intoxication or withdrawal and then identify the substance or substances that caused the intoxication or withdrawal. If the client is not in either state, then the counselor evaluates according to the following four criteria for each substance reportedly used by the client:

1. impaired control
2. social impairment
3. risky use
4. pharmacological criteria

Impaired control refers to clients' ability—or inability—to control their use of the substance. Signs include

- using more than originally intended or for longer than originally intended,
- unsuccessful attempts to stop or cut down using,
- excessive time spent obtaining the substance or recovering from use, and
- cravings for the substance when not using.

Social impairment refers to a disruption in the performance of various roles in the client's life, such as

- failing to fulfill responsibilities at home, work, or school;

- continuing to use the substance despite disruptions in obligations and social relationships; and/or
- discontinuing participation in former responsibilities or disengaging from social relationships because of substance use.

Risky use refers to the potential harm involved in substance use, including

- continuing to use in dangerous situations; and/or
- continuing to use the substance despite knowing it is the cause of physical or psychological problems.

Pharmacological criteria refer to the way the substance affects the body, including

- tolerance, or requiring more of the substance to obtain the same effects; and
- withdrawal, or the physical symptoms that arise as a result of not using the substance.

Levels of severity apply to substance use disorder diagnoses and are based on how many of the above-described symptoms a client exhibits. The *DSM-5* highlights the progression by qualifying substance use as **mild**, **moderate**, or **severe** based on the number of diagnostic criteria met:

- If the client has three symptoms or fewer, the disorder is **mild**.
- If the client has four or five symptoms, the disorder is **moderate**.
- If the client has six or more symptoms, the disorder is **severe**.

 DID YOU KNOW?

Contrary to previous versions of the *DSM*, tolerance and withdrawal are NOT required to meet the diagnostic criteria for a substance use disorder.

This is explained in the "Coding and Recording Procedures" section for each diagnosis in the *DSM-5*. Diagnoses may also have additional specifiers that would be listed in the same section. A counselor can detect the progressive stages of substance use by looking for any of the following cues:

- started with social or casual use but now uses more and more often
- uses substances while alone or regardless of social environment
- finding and using substances start interfering with other aspects of life
    - changes in friends and social activities
    - changes in grades, school performance and attendance, or changes in work attendance and performance
    - financial problems due to spending too much money on substances, such as not being able to pay the bills
    - isolation from people in the client's life who do not use substances
- substance becoming the focus of life with previously mentioned changes worsening
- significant, observable changes in behaviors and appearance
- substance use becoming dangerous to health and life, such as overdosing, using needles, and neglecting health issues
- engagement in dangerous or criminal activity to obtain substances or money for substances

ASSESSMENTS 55

Substance use disorder diagnoses also have **specifiers** that may apply to the client:

- A client in a treatment facility where there is no access to substances is considered to be in a **controlled environment**.
- A client who has not met diagnostic criteria for the substance use disorder for three to twelve months is in **early remission**.
- A client who has not met diagnostic criteria for the substance use disorder for more than twelve months is in **sustained remission**.

Treatment plans allow for further specification and can include goals specific to a diagnosis. Treatment plans should be in place after the initial interview and adjusted continually to reflect the client's progress. See Chapter 4 for more on treatment planning.

> **HELPFUL HINT**
>
> Cravings are the only symptom exempt from the remission specifiers. This is because cravings can be present for many years once someone stops using. The presence of cravings alone does not count as a diagnostic symptom when no other symptoms are present.

QUICK REVIEW QUESTIONS

19. What term describes an identified health condition based on an assessment by a trained professional?

20. A client has not met diagnostic criteria for SUD for six months. How would this client be described?

Discussing Results with the Client

The counselor should balance information obtained from the client with the information in assessments. Some clients may lie about themselves, their situation, or their substance use. Many of the assessments used in substance use counseling are based on the client's responses; some clients may exhibit dishonesty on the assessments.

However, when working with clients, assessment answers and scores can be used therapeutically to explore discrepancies between what clients say in session and what they answer on the assessment. A counselor can also use an assessment to explore issues clients have not yet brought up in counseling. When discussing results with clients, it may also be appropriate to ask them if they agree with the scored results of the assessment and then process how they respond.

Toxicology testing will determine quantitatively whether there are substances in the client's body. If there is a discrepancy between what the client says and what the test results show, the counselor can discuss these with the client by asking the client to explain and then talk about the importance of honesty in treatment.

Clients may show ambivalence regarding readiness to change. Ambivalence can be revealed by comparing what the client says and what the client does.

- Clients may use "yes, but" language.
  - This suggests that they acknowledge that substance use has become problematic, but they do not see a reason to stop using just yet.
- Clients may avoid talking about the negative consequences of using the substance.

- Clients may enjoy using the substance, or they may get something from the substance and its use that they are not ready to give up.
- Clients may discuss the costs associated with stopping substance use and determine it is not worth the work.
  - Costs may include going through pain or other types of hardship.

Behavioral indicators that clients are ambivalent toward change include

- missed appointments,
- rescheduling appointments,
- continued substance use while in treatment, and
- telling the counselor they will not use and then use anyway.

QUICK REVIEW QUESTIONS

21. Should a counselor tell a client who claims to have thirty days sober that indications of substance use appeared in a urinalysis?

22. A client expresses interest in treatment and getting sober, but she misses appointments and continues to use marijuana. What is the client showing?

Answer Key

1. Assessment allows the counselor to obtain more detailed information about the client and design a treatment plan.
2. Counselors should use client reports, empathy, and biomarkers when assessing substance use disorder (SUD).
3. A clinical interview is a comprehensive assessment to collect information about an individual's background and family relationships.
4. Only a licensed clinician may perform clinical interviews.
5. Clients with substance use disorder (SUD) are at higher risk for some medical conditions.
6. Social support system and culture are discussed as part of the sociocultural history.
7. Barriers to treatment include lack of child care, health insurance, transportation, and financial resources.
8. The term *reliability* refers to the consistency of a measurement.
9. The term *validity* refers to what is being measured and whether it is relevant.
10. The Addiction Severity Index (ASI) is the most widely used assessment tool to treat substance use disorder (SUD).
11. The Clinical Opiate Withdrawal Scale (COWS) specifically measures objective symptoms of opiate withdrawal.

12. The Car, Relax, Alone, Forget, Friends, Trouble (CRAFFT) is a screening tool approved for youth ages twelve to twenty-one to determine substance use; the Drug Abuse Screening Test for Adolescents (DAST-A) is a modified version of the Drug Abuse Screening Test (DAST-10).

13. Urine testing uses containers with a built-in testing device.

14. Hair follicle testing can provide more information about patterns of use over time.

15. The term *nonsuicidal self-injury* (NSSI) describes any form of self-injury without intent to kill oneself.

16. The SOARS model is a brief assessment used in clinics to screen for nonsuicidal self-injury (NSSI). SOARS stands for **s**uicidal ideation; **o**nset, frequency, methods; **a**ftercare, **r**easons, and **s**tages of change.

17. Intrusion, avoidance, negative changes in mood and affect, and increased reactivity are the four domains of trauma symptoms.

18. For clients to be diagnosed with post-traumatic stress disorder (PTSD), they must have had exposure to a traumatic experience, exhibit symptoms across all four domains, and experience those symptoms for at least one month. In the situation described, the client may not have PTSD.

19. The term *diagnosis* describes an identified health condition that is based on an assessment by a trained professional.

20. A client who has not met diagnostic criteria for substance use disorder (SUD) for three to twelve months is described as being in early remission.

21. Yes. The counselor should discuss the discrepancy by asking the client to explain it. Counselors should emphasize the importance of honesty in treatment.

22. The client is demonstrating behavioral indicators that she is ambivalent to treatment and change.

4 Treatment Planning

Developing a Treatment Plan

Planning Treatment Strategies

Planning a treatment strategy is vital for achieving the client's goals. To create a care plan, the counselor will use the list of needs discovered during the client assessment. A good **care plan** will include

- the problem noted,
- the goal to be achieved,
- objectives for achieving the goal,
- interventions the counselor will use,
- the timeline for achieving objectives and goals, and
- an evaluation of the intervention.

The **main components** of a treatment plan include

- brief client background,
- diagnosis,
- problem list,
- treatment goals,
- objectives,
- interventions,
- timeline,
- method of evaluation, and
- tracking progress.

The following **strategies** draw on the main components of a treatment plan and drive treatment planning:

1. The **diagnosis** acts as the anchor for the treatment plan. Every step in the treatment plan must address the diagnosis.

2. The **problem list** details the problems described by the client that are related to the diagnosis. There will likely be more than one, and there may even be multiple problems for each diagnosis. The problem list must follow the diagnosis.

3. **Treatment goals** are the broad statements of what the client wants to achieve in treatment; they must relate to the diagnosis.

4. **Objectives** are the steps taken to achieve the goals. Just as the goals directly relate to the diagnosis, so too do the objectives.

5. **Interventions** are the clinical therapeutic techniques the counselor plans to use with the client. These must be evidence-based interventions appropriate for the diagnosis. The counselor must be adequately trained to provide any chosen interventions.

6. **Timeline** refers to the projected amount of time expected to meet the objectives.

7. **Method of evaluation** details how the client's progress will be measured.

8. **Tracking progress** includes keeping notes related to the client's achievement of the objectives and goals in the treatment plan. If the client does not show progress, the counselor and client may consider adjusting the treatment plan.

The treatment plan should be reviewed and revised regularly; the schedule and frequency for review depend on both the agency and state regulations. Some states require that agencies providing mental health services review and revise treatment plans formally every thirty days or every four to six sessions. Those reviews must be documented in the client's file. Additionally, some states require an agency's program directors to regularly review client files, sometimes as often as quarterly. This varies based on state law and the type of service provider.

If a state or agency does not provide these guidelines, it is up to the counselor to determine the review schedule based on the frequency of sessions and client needs. It is generally appropriate to review and revise every four to six sessions. Other circumstances may inspire a review and revision of the treatment plan, including

- if the client experiences a crisis;
- a change in diagnosis;
- if a new problem arises;
- if the client solves a stated problem outside of therapy; and/or
- if the client is not making progress with current interventions.

QUICK REVIEW QUESTIONS

1. What are objectives?

2. How often should the treatment plans be reviewed and revised?

Goal Setting

By engaging in thorough assessments, counselors form neutral concepts of what their clients experience. Assessments that focus on substance use, such as the Addiction Severity Index (ASI) evaluate not only domains of substance use but also other aspects in a client's life that act as risk and protective factors.

Once each domain has been assessed, the client's treatment plan focuses on the domains with the highest severity levels. Counselors can help clients sift through the symptoms and their presentations in each domain and set priorities pertaining to each domain's relationship to the substance use issues. This process may include identifying

- which domains are priority treatment categories (e.g., substance use, family, employment, legal, medical, social);
- the purpose of the substance use or the need it fulfills (e.g., forgetting trauma, emotional numbing, escaping from pain, reducing inhibitions to improve social life, helping with sleep);
- mental health issues that exacerbate the substance use;
- risk factors and triggers for substance use (personal, family, social, environmental);
- sources of social support and other recovery capital;
- required steps to satisfy the conditions of mandated treatment;
- what works for making mental health symptoms subside;
- how best to reduce or eliminate substance use (past or present);
- what might be a cause for substance use and co-occurring mental health issues; and
- client strengths.

Breaking down the problem into meaningful parts helps demystify what the clients experience and gives them hope that the problem can be solved.

Finally, the counselor guides clients in formulating a road map of where they are now and where they would like to be in the future. That road map becomes the client's goals. There are four main reasons to establish goals:

1. Goals offer hope to clients by creating a plan for what they want to achieve.
2. Goal setting complies with the medical model of care.
3. Goals demonstrate how therapy will help a client with a presenting problem.
4. Goals break the recovery journey into manageable parts.

Within the goal-setting process, counselors helps clients identify **strengths** and resources that can help them attain their goals. Strengths are found at the individual, relational, social, and environmental levels.

TABLE 4.1. Client Strengths

INDIVIDUAL	RELATIONAL	SOCIAL	ENVIRONMENTAL
positive self-esteem	supportive parent	belongs to a religious organization	lives close to services
willing to work hard	supportive significant other or friend	makes friends easily	access to the beach

Identifying strengths in the goal-setting process reminds clients of the resources that can help them achieve their goals. Some clients forget about these resources as they become overwhelmed by the presenting problem.

Goals should be **SMART**: **S**pecific, **M**easurable, **A**ttainable, **R**ealistic, and **T**ime-restricted. SMART goals are useful for clients for several reasons:

- They break problems into manageable pieces.
- Each goal includes actions to be taken.
- They set a client up for success.
- Success fuels hope, so as clients achieve each SMART goal, they feel empowered to pursue the next.
- They help clients track their progress.

Common client goals include the following:

- coping skills (exercise instead of substances, journaling)
- functional status (financial stability, employment)
- lifestyle factors (diet, exercise)
- relationships (improve communication, establish boundaries)
- changing thought patterns (gratitude journals, identifying cognitive distortions)
- managing emotions (controlling anger, allowing oneself to feel sad)

TABLE 4.2. Example of a SMART Goal

Situation	A client uses marijuana whenever she gets bored.
Diagnosis	cannabis use disorder
SMART goal	The client will choose from a previously created list of activities to do when bored and will participate in that activity instead of using marijuana for five of the next seven days. She will then journal about the experience in her recovery journal.

QUICK REVIEW QUESTIONS

3. What are four important kinds of strengths that counselors help clients identify?

4. What are SMART goals?

Types of Goals

Short-term goals fall within a time frame of up to thirty days and build toward long-term goals. A short-term goal might be to download a mindfulness meditation app and use it once per day for a week to manage anxiety symptoms.

Long-term goals have an extended time frame of three months and beyond. For example, if someone has the aforementioned short-term goal, a long-term goal might be to reduce anxiety symptoms by 50 percent within six months based on the Beck Anxiety Inventory scores.

Short-term goals stack up to help the client achieve long-term goals, and all goals must be directly related to the diagnosis. The intake and assessment inform the counselor's collaborative process with the client to establish goals consistent with the diagnosis. For example, a client might commit to abstaining from alcohol use and attending thirty meetings in thirty days as a short-term goal.

QUICK REVIEW QUESTION

5. Which type of goal should be met within thirty days?

Reviewing Progress

Counselors understand that assessment and the **review of progress** of treatment goals occur at multiple levels:

- During the session, the counselor checks regularly to make sure the client is comfortable with the intervention.
    - Client feedback will inform the counselor about the usefulness and appropriateness of the intervention as well as the client's reaction to it.
- At the end of each session, the counselor checks in with the client to determine
    - what the client got out of the session,
    - whether it was helpful, and
    - what the client might do between sessions to continue the work.
- Every four to six sessions, or every thirty days, the counselor reviews the full treatment plan with the client to determine and document progress.
- Each quarter or preauthorization period, the counselor reviews the full treatment plan with the client to determine and document progress.

- At the end of the counseling relationship, the counselor and the client review progress and celebrate successes.

Multiple **barriers** can affect the attainment of client goals:

- The client is mandated to treatment and resistant to change.
- The client lied about the problem and/or symptoms.
- The client is ambivalent about making changes to current behaviors.
- The client presents for one problem and does not want help with any others that may contribute to the presenting problem.
- Goals are too broad, vague, or unrealistic.
- Goals are not achievable or coordinated to help the client succeed.
- External factors in the client's life can interfere.
- The wrong intervention is used to help the client achieve the goals.

QUICK REVIEW QUESTION

6. When should progress be reviewed?

Collaborating with the Client and Other Entities

Client Feedback and Ambivalence

Offering client feedback will enhance treatment. The counselor can

- offer positive feedback about the client's actions related to recovery thus far,
- explain that coming to treatment indicates that the client is working toward a positive goal,
- point out client strengths observed during the session, and
- recognize positive efforts the client has made to move toward change.

There are many reasons a client displays **ambivalence**. Common reasons for ambivalence include

- lack of trust in the counselor or the treatment process,
- being mandated to attend treatment, and/or
- fear of and discomfort with the recovery journey.

Counselors can address ambivalence by

- explaining the assessment process and how it is used in treatment,
- getting to know clients on their terms before the assessment starts, and
- answering client questions.

It may also be helpful to differentiate the counselor and treatment services from those of the entity that mandated a client to treatment. This can be done by stressing the client-focused nature of recovery.

 **HELPFUL HINT**

Offering feedback is important because clients do not often recognize their strengths or their positive choices when the problems of substance use are prominent in their lives.

QUICK REVIEW QUESTION

7. Clients mandated to treatment by the court might display what characteristic?

Collaborative Care

Collaboration means working with clients, families, colleagues, and other care providers to support clients in meeting their goals. The goal of **care coordination**, or **collaborative care**, is to achieve safe, effective care through the deliberate organization of client care activities within the interdisciplinary team. Counselors may collaborate with medical staff or other professionals in contexts such as

- inpatient treatment settings,
- outpatient programs,
- schools,
- child protective services,
- the criminal justice system,
- drug courts,
- mental health courts,
- disability services,
- housing case management, and
- veterans' services.

Some examples of care coordination include

- sharing knowledge within the health care team (in a clinical setting);
- aligning resources with clients' emotional and social needs;
- setting clients up with community resources;
- reporting on program compliance;
- sharing client progress related to stated goals; and
- reporting effects of other interventions, such as medications or case management, that are reported in counseling.

Collaboration with other care providers requires a client's written consent. Ethical conduct requires a counselor to be transparent about what is shared with other providers. Ideally, clients will be involved in any care collaboration meetings, but if they are not, the counselor should tell the clients what information was shared about them. Counselors should also collaborate with other providers and client support systems. A collaborative counselor

- is willing to be mentored, coached, or taught;
- is open to team members' contributions;
- participates in health care meetings to discuss practice issues/care activities;

- reaches out to mentor others and continues self-learning by a willingness to be taught;
- facilitates care delivery discussions and practice decisions;
- optimizes diverse resources and promotes client/family outcomes through inclusivity;
- cooperates in maintaining documentation and reporting;
- participates in discussions regarding ethics and cultural competence; and
- educates other providers about the counseling process and the role of the counselor.

During this process, the counselor should collaborate with the client to establish treatment goals and objectives—clients should be involved in all care decisions. The counselor begins with the end in mind. Important questions to ask the client include the following:

- "How will you know when you are better?"
- "How will you know when the issue is no longer a problem for you?"

These questions give the counselor insight into what the client considers to be the goal and how the client will measure progress. As goals are discussed, the counselor should also outline other services or resources that could help the client achieve the goals.

When determining the treatment plan goals and objectives, an important topic is the integration and maintenance of therapeutic progress. In other words, how will the client and the counselor know that the client is making progress, and what steps can the client take to maintain that progress? Again, this should be an ongoing process.

QUICK REVIEW QUESTIONS

8. What term describes a counselor who displays a willingness to learn?

9. Setting clients up with community resources is an example of what?

10. Which care decisions should clients be involved with?

Behavioral Management and Medical Intervention

Counselors may encounter clients who are impaired and require behavioral management or even medical intervention. Each agency or organization will have policies and procedures in place for the safety of the client, employees, and counselors. In general, the goal of **behavioral management** of people who are impaired is twofold:

- get them to a safe space
- determine whether medical help is necessary

Getting people who are impaired to a **safe space** may mean taking them to a private room or office where they cannot cause a disturbance in front of others that could be distressing or physically unsafe. Moving people who are impaired to a private area can also save them from embarrassing situations in public. Once the person is in a safe space, the counselor should

- help the person remain calm, and
- obtain any information that can shed light on what caused the person's impairment.

Based on the cause of the impairment and its severity, a person may require medical attention. Typical situations requiring medical intervention include the following:

- The impaired person is presenting with the physical symptoms of overdose.
- The impaired person is unconscious.

In these cases, medical personnel should be called immediately. If medical intervention is not required, the counselor should determine whom to call to get the person home safely. This may involve calling an emergency contact or asking the person who is impaired whom to call on their behalf.

Confidentiality also applies to people who are impaired. Information provided to either the emergency contact or medical personnel should be limited to what is needed to establish the client's safety. Any disclosure should be documented in the client's records and discussed with the client after the crisis has passed.

QUICK REVIEW QUESTIONS

11. What are the two goals of managing someone who is impaired?

12. When is medical intervention typically required?

Answer Key

1. Objectives are the steps taken to achieve the goals.

2. It is generally appropriate to review and revise treatment plans every four to six sessions.

3. Counselors help clients identify individual, relational, social, and environmental strengths.

4. SMART goals are those that are specific, measurable, attainable, realistic, and time-restricted.

5. Short-term goals fall within a thirty-day time frame.

6. Progress should be reviewed on an ongoing basis; treatment plans should be reviewed according to state requirements. If no state requirements exist, treatment plans should be reviewed every four to six sessions.

7. Clients mandated to treatment might display ambivalence.

8. The term *collaborative counselor* describes a counselor who displays a willingness to learn.

9. Setting clients up with community resources is an example of care coordination.

10. Clients should be involved in all care decisions.

11. Getting the person to a safe space and determining whether medical assistance is needed are the two goals of managing someone who is impaired.

12. Medical intervention is typically required when the person who is impaired is unconscious or suspected of overdosing.

5 Referrals and Service Coordination

Scope of Practice and Referrals

Scope of Practice

Although the scope of practice for a substance use disorder (SUD) counselor varies by state, some similarities exist throughout the US. In general, SUD counselors

- do not prescribe medication;
- understand the services available to family members and concerned others as they affect treatment and the recovery process;
- understand the continuum of care;
- assess the need for referral to outside services and provide referrals when appropriate;
- protect and communicate client rights;
- identify appropriate resources for specific client needs;
- collaborate with outside resources;
- work with clients to develop an effective and realistic relapse prevention plan;
- develop a treatment plan, in collaboration with clients, that will be modified routinely throughout treatment;
- educate clients about the physical components of addiction;
- collaborate with other mental health and medical health professionals for holistic care (e.g., social workers, physicians, psychiatrists);
- provide individual counseling sessions;
- offer process group sessions;
- provide psychoeducational group sessions;
- offer education to family members about addiction and recovery; and
- help clients understand the role that other mental health concerns can have on addiction and the recovery process.

A client's recovery may be impacted by factors that require concurrent treatment. As a counselor completes a thorough assessment, problems will be identified, including some that are not appropriate for a counselor to address but that impact a client's well-being. **Concurrent treatment** needs may include

- psychiatric medication;
- physical therapy;
- vocational training;
- occupational therapy;
- housing counseling;
- case management; and
- medical care.

QUICK REVIEW QUESTIONS

1. Can a SUD counselor prescribe medication to help treat addiction?

2. Occupational therapy and psychiatric medication are examples of what kind of treatment?

What Are Referrals?

During the clinical evaluation and/or treatment planning, the counselor and client identify the client's needs. As a result, the counselor may provide a **referral**, which is a way to guide the client to other available resources and support systems to meet those needs.

Counselors determine whether a referral is appropriate by interpreting assessment, treatment planning, evaluation, and client feedback data. Referrals address client needs and service gaps by connecting clients with

- agencies,
- governmental bodies,
- civic groups, and
- other treatment professionals.

Like other elements of care, referrals should be collaborative. Counselors should work with clients regarding decision-making and respect their capabilities in taking ownership of the referral (initiating and following up). Maintaining an attitude of collaboration and respect promotes the client's needs and positive self-determination. Counselors should educate clients on the referral process and motivate them to initiate the referral process and follow through with recommendations and commitments:

- **Readiness and education** include motivating clients to actively participate in the referral process.
- In **active participation**, the client is responsible for following through on the referral and following up.

When making a referral, counselors should keep the client's cultural influences, appearance, presentation abilities, and defenses in mind. All of these factors can affect follow-through on referrals. Some examples to consider include the following:

- If clients are legally obligated to participate in treatment, they may present with limited engagement and have difficulty developing therapeutic rapport. Additionally, they may struggle to find sources of intrinsic motivation.
- There may be a language barrier among clients whose second language is the counselor's native language; this can impact the ability of clients to communicate their thoughts and experiences effectively.
- Some clients may not have a working knowledge of different emotions and feelings. This can make it difficult for them to communicate how their emotions, thoughts, and feelings impact their use and recovery.
- Clients who relied on substance use as a primary coping skill may not have the tools necessary to deal with emotional distress in their recovery, which can be a contributing factor to relapses.
- The socioeconomic status of clients can impact their grooming patterns. It is important to differentiate this reason for changes in grooming patterns from those that result from clients' addiction or other mental health concerns, such as a major depressive episode.
- Clients who had treatment previously might already have an understanding of addiction and recovery, allowing the counselor to focus on their relapse or current use.
- Clients who had a negative experience in a previous treatment setting may be hesitant to participate and engage, and may struggle to develop a therapeutic rapport with their counselor.

The counselor must ensure that the client has the necessary access and logistics to follow through on referrals. For instance, a client who has no phone or internet access will need assistance to make medical appointments.

Counselors measure follow-up with the client by using specific processes and instruments, and reporting information accurately. Counselors must be able to understand how referrals relate and contribute to progress in the overall treatment plan.

QUICK REVIEW QUESTIONS

3. What term describes guiding clients to other available resources and support systems to meet their needs?

4. What term describes the responsibility of clients to follow through and follow up on a referral?

Referral Best Practices

Not every client is appropriate for every counselor, and vice versa. A counselor should provide a referral in certain situations:

- The counselor does not have adequate training to work with the client's issues.
- The counselor and client cannot establish a productive therapeutic relationship.
- An ethical issue (e.g., a dual relationship) precludes a counselor from working with a client.
- The counselor experiences an issue that would disrupt the client's treatment.
- The counselor is resigning, retiring, or otherwise leaving the organization or profession.

When providing referrals, there are several **best practices** recommended for counselors:

- Give the client plenty of notice, if possible.
- Provide the client with several choices for other providers and offer to facilitate the transfer.
- Ask if the client wants a joint session or a phone introduction with the new provider.
- Ask if the client wants the counselor to share information about her with the provider; if so, discuss what information to share.

Counselors must know and adhere to local, state, and federal confidentiality regulations, client consent procedures, and other standards guiding the exchange of information. Still, a counselor should **provide information to third parties** as required by law. These generally include

- insurance companies,
- health care professionals, and
- legal guardians.

Counselors should remain aware of their own potential **biases** toward or against referral resources. Examples of biases that counselors could unintentionally experience include the following:

- Counselors who do not have a spiritual or religious foundation in their lives may have a hard time encouraging religious and spiritual aspects of recovery.
  - Peer support groups such as Alcoholics Anonymous and Narcotics Anonymous have a spiritual component to their recovery programs.
  - Without personal experience, it is important for counselors to educate themselves about the role that spirituality and religion can have in a person's recovery so that they can provide support to clients who could benefit from having a spiritual or religious component in their recovery.

- Counselors who grew up in a home environment with a parent or guardian who struggled with an addiction may have unintentional bias toward clients who are parents or guardians.
  - Counselors are often drawn to this career path from a desire to help others, which can be a result of a history of personal challenges.
  - Being mindful of the role that past experiences have in their motivation can help counselors understand more about their personal biases.
  - Clinical supervision can help the counselor provide nonjudgmental and empathetic care.
- Similarly, counselors who are in recovery may have unintentional bias toward or against clients who are struggling.
  - Such biases could impact the counselor's ability to provide empathetic support and the quality of care needed.
  - Supervision is a useful tool to keep counselors' biases in check.

QUICK REVIEW QUESTIONS

5. Can a counselor ever provide any information to third parties?

6. What tool can help counselors check their biases?

Levels of Care

One of the functions of screening, interview, and assessment is to determine which **level of care** is appropriate for clients and their presenting concerns. There are a variety of options, each with its own benefits.

Residential inpatient care programs typically occur within a hospital setting. The goal is to stabilize clients so they can begin receiving treatment for their mental health concerns at a different location.

- Clients receive treatment that can include
  - psychoeducation,
  - individual therapy,
  - crisis intervention, and
  - medication management.
- Inpatient programs are appropriate for individuals who have safety risks, such as
  - recent suicide gestures or attempts, and/or
  - homicidal attempts.
- Inpatient programs are also suitable for clients who need a high level of care, including
  - medication management, and/or
  - drug/alcohol detox and treatment.

In **partial hospitalization programs (PHPs)**, the client attends a structured day program at a treatment facility:

- The program's structure resembles an inpatient program, but the client goes home at night.
- PHPs typically run five days a week for six to eight hours per day.
- PHPs provide clients with safety and structure for most of their day.
- PHPs are appropriate for clients who can safely live at home but still need a thorough treatment program.
- Typical clients might have a severe mental illness, be compliant with medication, and be learning how to manage symptoms behaviorally.

In **intensive outpatient programs (IOPs)**, the client attends structured programming for a few hours per day:

- IOPs usually treat addiction, eating disorders, and depressive disorders.
- IOPs typically have a psychoeducational component in addition to group treatment.
- IOPs are appropriate for
  - clients with mild disorders, and
  - clients with mild or severe use disorders who have already completed residential treatment programs.

Outpatient treatment (outpatient therapy) is usually recommended to build on what clients learned in other, more intensive programs:

- The duration of an outpatient program varies depending on the presenting concern.
- Outpatient treatment typically follows the successful completion of an IOP or PHP.
- Outpatient treatment is usually fewer hours per day than an IOP or PHP.
- Outpatient activities include
  - group therapy,
  - individual therapy,
  - medication management,
  - specialized treatment,
  - psychoeducation, and
  - family therapy.
- Outpatient treatment programs address various mental health concerns, including
  - addiction,
  - childhood behavioral and emotional concerns, and
  - mood disorders.

Psychotherapy is individual counseling between a client and a counselor that

- is appropriate for individuals with a mild mental health concern,
- allows clients with a complex diagnosis to maintain a connection to a supportive professional after more intensive treatment,
- includes high-functioning clients, and
- usually consists of weekly or biweekly individual sessions.

Self-help programs generally refer to support groups run by peers rather than mental health professionals:

- Many self-help programs address addiction, but some address other concerns:
    - twelve-step programs (e.g., Alcoholics Anonymous, Narcotics Anonymous);
    - support for families of people with an addiction (Al-Anon, Nar-Anon);
    - eating and weight management groups (Overeaters Anonymous, Weight Watchers); and
    - grief support groups.
- Activity and attendance rate depend on the client.
- Self-help groups can be used at every level of care.

Treatment programs offer guidelines that can help the counselor decide which level of care to recommend to the client.

QUICK REVIEW QUESTIONS

7. What term describes a program where a client attends structured programming for a few hours per day?

8. At which level of care can self-help groups be used?

Community-Based Prevention

Recovery-Oriented Systems of Care

Recovery-oriented systems of care (ROSC) refer to the variety of community-based resources designed to help individuals who are living with a substance use disorder. These community-based resources can provide individuals with a continuum of care that supports them during every stage of their journey through addiction and recovery. Some of the resources included in ROSC are

- prevention,
- early intervention,
- treatment, and
- continuing care options.

These resources are simple to understand and accessible to individuals in the community. The options provided by ROSC can help individuals with SUD and their loved ones.

Counselors can be active in all stages of ROSC and can participate in preventive psychoeducation efforts within their community. **Early intervention** can include early screening, education, and outreach. Counselors can be involved in inpatient and some outpatient treatment options, in addition to family therapy services. Continuing care options can include check-ins with clients who have established recovery, self-monitoring, and recovery support services.

QUICK REVIEW QUESTIONS

9. What are four resources included in ROSC?

10. How can counselors contribute to prevention efforts?

Agencies and Community Resources

Counselors must understand the mission, function, resources, and quality of services offered by community-based organizations. Community-based organizations include

- civic groups,
- community groups/neighborhood organizations,
- religious organizations,
- governmental entities,
- health and allied health care systems (managed care),
- criminal justice systems,
- housing authorities,
- employment and vocational rehabilitation services,
- child care facilities,
- crisis intervention programs,
- programs for people who have been abused,
- mutual and self-help groups,
- cultural enhancement organizations,
- advocacy groups, and
- other agencies.

Community resources exist to enhance the quality of life of community residents. Community resources include people, community services, and businesses. Older adult care services, for example, can provide meals to people over age sixty-five, help them maintain the structural integrity of their homes, and bring trusted professionals and community volunteers to their homes to perform chores. Other community resources include the following:

- **Religious organizations**, such as missions and youth groups, serve the community through meal programs, clothing/toy donation drives, and projects that may involve building houses for the homeless or providing medical care.

- **Government programs** often provide financial aid for communities. Just a few of these programs include
  - Medicare and Medicaid,
  - housing assistance through the US Department of Housing and Urban Development (HUD), and
  - grants and scholarships.
- **Meal delivery programs** such as Meals on Wheels and Nurture Life deliver meals to older adults and children.
- **Pharmacy assistance programs** offer medication prescriptions at discounted rates and are an excellent resource for people with multiple prescriptions who are on a fixed budget.
- **Psychiatric assistance** and **hospitalization** may be appropriate for individuals who need detoxification, medication-assisted treatment, and/or prescribed psychiatric medications.
- **Psychological assistance and counseling** services in a hospital setting help to stabilize clients' mental health so that they can continue engaging with care on an outpatient basis.
- The **Substance Abuse and Mental Health Services Administration (SAMHSA)** helps people find treatment; provides grants for substance use prevention and treatment programs; and offers training, education, and research on behavioral health.
- **State and community health agencies** provide outpatient treatment services for individuals who use government programs like Medicare and Medicaid, increasing access to care for those in low-income and rural areas.
- **College and university health agencies** often offer students prevention education, intervention strategies that address student substance use and misuse, and counseling services, which increase access to care.
  - These programs are not designed to provide treatment for individuals who have a substance use disorder, but they can help students locate appropriate treatment providers.
- **State and local departments of family services** (e.g., child and adult protective services) can help individuals who are dependent on someone who is struggling with a substance use disorder.
- The **National Council on Alcoholism and Drug Dependence, Inc. (NCADD)** provides education and information to local communities, individuals in recovery, and concerned loved ones about addiction.
  - Additionally, the NCADD offers assessment and referral resources to individuals who are interested in treatment services.
- The **National Institute on Alcohol Abuse and Alcoholism (NIAAA)** is an independent institute within the Alcohol, Drug Abuse, and Mental Health Administration (ADAMHA).

HELPFUL HINT

Some clients may resist inpatient treatment programs due to a negative stigma associated with being in a mental health hospital setting. Additionally, many individuals are concerned about their ability to pay for inpatient treatment programs.

- The NIAAA researches alcohol use and its impact on public health and well-being.
- NIAAA findings provide guidance in prevention and outreach efforts across the community.

QUICK REVIEW QUESTIONS

11. What programs help clients on a budget who may need to fill multiple prescriptions?

12. Where might a counselor find reputable data on behavioral health in the United States?

Other Health Care Providers

The counselor may collaborate with many different health care providers. This section describes the roles of these providers in treating clients.

Physicians include general (family) practitioners and specialists. Physicians spend a minimum of ten to twelve years in medical school and training/residency to earn a degree in medicine; then they must take certification exams to legally practice medicine. They can diagnose conditions, order procedures, and treat and write medication prescriptions for illnesses. Physicians usually see clients in their office.

Physician assistants (PAs) assist a physician. They can operate within the same scope of practice as a physician but with limitations contingent on their education and professional experience, state regulations, office policies and procedures, and clients' needs. Physician assistants may collect a comprehensive medical history, perform a physical head-to-toe assessment, diagnose illnesses, prescribe medications, and establish care plans.

Nurse practitioners (NPs) possess a master's (or higher) degree in nursing and function in a similar capacity as that of a physician. They may diagnose and treat illnesses; they can also write prescriptions.

Clinical nurse specialists (CNSs) have advanced education and training in a specialized field, such as psychiatric care, women's health, or critical care. Clinical nurse specialists have graduated from an accredited school of nursing, earned a master's or doctoral degree in nursing, and passed a specialized certification exam. They can make diagnoses, develop treatment plans, and provide care and are often in leadership roles in which they supervise other nurses.

Registered nurses (RNs) and **licensed vocational/practical nurses (LVNs/LPNs)** typically do not have advanced degrees. They will carry out orders from a physician, physician's assistant, or nurse practitioner; collect medical histories; perform assessments; develop a nursing diagnosis and treatment plan; implement the treatment plan; and evaluate client outcomes.

Nurse technicians provide care for patients under the supervision of an RN or other more credentialed health care provider. There is no official certification or scope of practice for nurse technicians, but some nursing coursework is usually required. Nursing techs are often students working toward a nursing degree or recent graduates looking to gain work experience.

Behavioral health care providers dedicate their lives to supporting and preserving the mental/emotional health and well-being of individuals with a mental illness. A **psychiatrist** is a physician who has attended medical school, earned a degree in medicine, and chosen to specialize in psychiatry. Psychiatrists can write prescriptions for anti-anxiety medications and antidepressants, among other medications.

Psychiatrists are not to be confused with **psychologists**, who must undergo training and an internship to secure an advanced degree in psychology. While psychologists may have a doctoral degree, they are not medical doctors and therefore cannot prescribe medications. They offer focused counseling services that can assist in the diagnosis and treatment of medical and mental health issues.

Licensed professional counselors (LPCs) possess a master's or doctoral degree in counseling and will, within their scope of practice, offer collaborative, therapeutic counseling to individuals who seek professional guidance to promote emotional, behavioral, and mental health well-being.

Licensed clinical social workers (LCSWs) are licensed to practice in a clinical or counseling setting and work directly with clients to diagnose and treat mental, emotional, and behavioral issues. These professionals will also often focus on public health and develop or implement new and advanced measures to facilitate and promote communication within the community.

Community vendors provide goods and services to the entire community. One such example is a **community health fair**. During the fair, health care professionals will talk to individuals about their health and ways to promote a healthy lifestyle. They will also often record vital signs and weight.

Another type of community vendor is a **community-based day program**. Community-based day programs include after-school activities for children and outpatient behavioral management programs.

QUICK REVIEW QUESTIONS

13. Can nurse practitioners write prescriptions?

14. What is an important difference between a psychologist and a psychiatrist?

Service Coordination

Case Consultation and Working Relationships

The counselor's role is to advocate for clients' interests. As a **client advocate**, the counselor's attitude should be one of professional concern. When consulting with other providers, counselors should appreciate incremental changes and recognize relapse as an opportunity for growth rather than as a failure.

 DID YOU KNOW?

While the overarching goal of all health care providers is to promote a healthy lifestyle and healthy outcomes, each provider's scope of practice is very different. Counselors should consider which medical professional is appropriate to meet the client's needs.

In **case consultation**, counselors consult with service providers and other relevant stakeholders to monitor assessments, develop or modify treatment plans, or review client progress. **Working relationships** with other providers, such as physicians, psychiatrists, case managers, and social workers, can enhance quality of care for the client.

Consultants and service providers should always maintain respect for clients, their right to privacy, and the privacy of the information shared by them and their significant others. When interacting with service providers on behalf of the client, counselors should maintain a respectful and nonjudgmental attitude. **Consultation** with other professionals helps secure a high quality of care by ensuring a review of

- the treatment plan;
- the client's progress; and
- any problems that inhibit progress.

Consultation enables the counselor to gather feedback and adjust the treatment plan as appropriate. Consulting counselors must have a strong knowledge of assessment procedures and the following methodologies:

- assessing the client's biopsychosocial status (both past and present)
- social systems that may affect the client's progress
- methods for ongoing assessment of the treatment plan and modification if necessary

Consulting demands a deep understanding of teamwork and appropriate behaviors within a professional group setting. Counselors must be knowledgeable about related disciplines, including

- their various functions and any unique language/terminology used; and
- the primary roles of other team members within their own disciplines.

In the collaborative professional setting, counselors must always demonstrate respect for the interdisciplinary nature of consulting work by showing interest in professional collaboration with partners. Counselors should be at ease sharing information and asking questions. They should always remain appreciative of the contributions of other team members and respect their professional roles and backgrounds.

QUICK REVIEW QUESTIONS

15. What is the counselor's role in case consultation?

16. What attitude should the counselor exhibit when discussing a client with service providers?

Referrals and Confidentiality

It is imperative to understand and follow **confidentiality** procedures concerning referrals and consulting. Counselors and consultants must know and understand all local, state, and federal confidentiality laws and regulations and know how to apply them when sharing information and documentation regarding clients. They must also be aware of client rights and responsibilities; furthermore, they should know the ethical and professional standards applicable to confidentiality.

Information provided to insurance companies and other health care professionals is regulated under state law and the Health Insurance Portability and Accountability Act (HIPAA), with those policies outlined in the informed consent. A counselor should share the minimum amount of information necessary to honor the confidentiality of the client. For example, to get reimbursement for services rendered, the counselor may need to disclose the diagnosis and treatment plan objectives to an insurance company; however, the counselor should not include process notes that contain intimate details of the client's session. Those are not required to secure payment and should therefore remain confidential.

Within the comprehensive care model, organizations often encourage counselors to consult with a client's physician or case manager. This should be discussed with the client and included in the informed consent discussion. When counselors share information with other members of the care team, they should let the client know when and what information was disclosed. For example, the court usually requests progress reports for clients who are in court-mandated treatment. These reports may include attendance records and progress toward goals, but they should be limited to the required information only.

When the counselor provides services to a client with a legal guardian, some information may need to be disclosed to the guardian. Again, that information should be limited. The counselor should discuss the disclosure of other information with the client and get permission to disclose it; then the information can be shared in the client's presence.

For example, an adolescent client may not want the full extent of her substance use shared with her parents. The counselor is not required by law to tell the parents but feels it would be therapeutic for both the client and the family. The counselor may rehearse the disclosure with the client and then facilitate a family session in which the adolescent discloses the substance use to her parents. It is not the counselor's responsibility to tell the parents unless required by law to do so. Disclosing this information without the client's consent could damage the therapeutic relationship and harm the client.

QUICK REVIEW QUESTIONS

17. How much information may the counselor share about the client with third parties?

18. Does the client have a role when the counselor shares information with third parties?

Answer Key

1. No, substance use disorder (SUD) counselors may not prescribe medication.

2. Occupational therapy and psychiatric medication are examples of concurrent treatment.

3. The term *referral* describes guiding clients to other resources and support systems to meet their needs.

4. The term *active participation* describes the responsibility of clients to follow through and follow up on referrals.

5. Yes, in some cases, the counselor must provide information to insurance companies, health care professionals, and/or legal guardians.

6. Clinical supervision is helpful to check counselor biases.

7. The term *intensive outpatient program (IOP)* describes structured programming that the client attends for a few hours per day.

8. Self-help groups can be used at every level of care.

9. Four resources included in recovery-oriented systems of care (ROSC) include prevention, early intervention, treatment, and continuing care options.

10. Counselors can offer psychoeducation in the community as part of prevention.

11. Pharmacy assistance programs offer medication prescriptions at discounted rates.

12. The Substance Abuse and Mental Health Services Administration (SAMHSA) publishes research and data on behavioral health.

13. Yes, nurse practitioners can write prescriptions, and diagnose and treat illnesses.

14. Unlike psychiatrists, psychologists are not medical doctors and therefore cannot prescribe medications.

15. The counselor's role in case consultation is to advocate for clients' interests.

16. Counselors should maintain a respectful and nonjudgmental attitude regarding the client.

17. To respect the client's confidentiality, a counselor may share the minimum amount of information necessary.

18. Yes, counselors should let the client know when and what information was disclosed. In some cases, the counselor may rehearse the disclosure of information with the client.

6 Recovery Beyond Primary Treatment

Discharge Planning for Ongoing Recovery

The counselor should help clients plan for recovery beyond primary treatment.

Discharge Planning

Discharge planning includes referrals and aftercare options. It should be discussed from the beginning of treatment and start during a counselor's first session with a client. Discharges can occur unexpectedly, and discharge planning can help identify treatment goals and treatment expectations.

Depending on the circumstances for discharge, discharge planning for addiction counseling will vary. For example, clients who are discharged with a referral for a higher level of care will have a discharge plan that focuses on the steps needed to get them from the treatment program to the appropriate level of care. These steps include

- completing an initial screening over the phone;
- getting an admission date; and
- identifying their transportation to the facility.

When developing a discharge plan for a client whose treatment goals and subsequent program have been completed, the counselor will focus the plan on what the client can do to maintain recovery. This can include attending support groups, such as Alcoholics Anonymous or Narcotics Anonymous, or engaging in individual therapy. Clients should be able to reflect on their discharge plan as a guide for behaviors that will help them in their recovery.

Discharge criteria depend on the different levels of care. For instance, discharge criteria for a detoxification program may include the absence of withdrawal symptoms. On the other hand, discharge criteria for an inpatient rehab program might require the successful completion of all treatment goals. **Treatment goals** typically include

- achieving a set length of sobriety;

- having a working knowledge of addiction and recovery;
- developing a relapse prevention plan;
- identifying support groups; and
- identifying other sober supports at home.

Since discharge planning begins in the initial session, discharge criteria can be part of a client's treatment plan. The counselor should review client progress toward the expected discharge criteria throughout treatment; this way, the counselor can modify the discharge criteria if the client's circumstances change during treatment.

Counselors review the client's discharge plan and referral services in the final session. Referrals offered should be tailored to the needs of the client:

- Clients who are discharged because they have successfully completed their treatment goals may receive referrals for individual therapy.
- Clients who have been receiving medications may be referred to a medication-assisted treatment (MAT) provider.
- When clients are being discharged because they require a higher level of care, the discharge plan may vary.
  - The counselor can help these clients identify an appropriate program.
  - The counselor can help these clients take steps toward admission to an appropriate program.
- Clients who are not willing to go to a higher level of care should still receive
  - appropriate referrals;
  - emergency hotline numbers; and
  - requirements to reengage in the treatment program (e.g., completing a higher level of care or a period of sobriety).

All clients should receive a physical copy of their discharge plan for their benefit. If the discharge is due to loss of contact, the counselor can mail the discharge plan to the address on file per organization procedures.

QUICK REVIEW QUESTIONS

1. When should discharge planning begin?
2. When should the counselor review client progress toward discharge criteria?

Developmental Stages of Recovery

Terence Gorski created the **Developmental Model of Recovery (DMR)**. According to DMR, there are six stages of recovery:

1. transition stage
2. stabilization
3. early recovery

4. middle recovery
5. late recovery
6. maintenance

TABLE 6.1. Developmental Model of Recovery	
STAGE	**CLIENT EXPERIENCES/ACTIVITIES**
Transition	• recognizes that substance use is a problem • is unable to control the use of substances • motivating problems develop (e.g., legal or employment repercussions) • understands the need to stop using • realizes powerlessness over the addiction
Stabilization	• experiences discomfort and withdrawal • begins learning tactics to keep from using substances (e.g., avoiding people, places, and things that contribute to cravings and triggers) • learns new stress management and coping skills to deal with cravings, triggers, and uncomfortable emotions • begins to feel hopeful and identify motivation for recovery and abstinence
Early recovery	• fully accepts having a substance use disorder (accepts powerlessness over addiction) • begins internal work on the addiction • moves past any denial • addresses feelings of shame, guilt, and remorse (common challenges among individuals in recovery that can contribute to subsequent relapses if not managed appropriately) • begins to identify and establish new boundaries that support recovery (e.g., avoiding substances or situations where substances may be present)
Middle recovery	• begins to address consequences of the addiction • may begin making amends for prior behaviors • understands which behaviors must be incorporated into daily routines to maintain sobriety and abstinence • begins finding a healthy life balance (e.g., family life, social life, mental health, physical health, employment, spiritual health, and recovery needs)
Late recovery	• works to recognize learned dysfunctions that contributed to the substance use disorder • applies healthy changes to these learned concerns to support a healthy recovery • makes broader lifestyle changes (e.g., in friendships, romantic relationships, and relationships with family members)

Maintenance	- focuses on maintaining sobriety and daily personal growth
- uses healthy coping skills to deal with natural life distress and discomforts
- continues to establish and maintain healthy boundaries
- recognizes recovery as a lifelong process that requires constant attention and work

Withdrawal has serious risks. For example, unsupervised detox from alcohol or benzodiazepines can lead to seizures and death. Individuals experiencing withdrawal are therefore encouraged to seek medical attention.

QUICK REVIEW QUESTIONS

3. At which stage of the DMR do clients recognize that their use of substances is a problem?

4. In which stage of the DMR do clients begin making amends for their prior behaviors?

Developing a Recovery Plan

Addiction is a unique and personal experience. As such, there is no cookie-cutter approach to addiction counseling. Factors that contribute to individual differences in a recovery plan include

- the severity of a person's addiction;
- the presence of other mental health concerns;
- relationship concerns;
- physical health concerns;
- the presence of multiple addictions; and
- having a history of relapse.

Individual **recovery plans** provide guidance as clients recover from substance use disorder. Recovery plans should be tailored to each client to address the client's personal needs for recovery. Consider the following when developing an individual recovery plan:

- The recovery plan should be developed in collaboration with the client.
  - The client can address their concerns, goals, and motivations.
  - The recovery plan should be realistic and include the client's perspective and concerns.
- Recovery plans should be created as soon as the counselor begins meeting with the client.
  - Initial client goals commonly include attaining and maintaining sobriety.
  - Once initial goals have been met, the client's recovery plan may be modified to address personalized goals for recovery.
  - Counselors should continually monitor the client's progress regarding the recovery plan.

- Monitoring should be discussed with the client so that the client and counselor maintain their collaborative relationship.
- Counselors should remain vigilant in recognizing the signs of addiction substitution.
  - Counselors and clients should be aware of the misuse of other substances, medications, or behaviors (e.g., shopping, sex, or gambling).
  - Individuals in recovery may consume more sugar than they did previously, which could act as an addiction substitution.
- Counselors must maintain confidentiality and best practices when working with clients.
  - Rules, regulations, and expectations differ among states.
  - Counselors must familiarize themselves with local legislation.
- Recovery plans should work to help clients learn **self-directed support**, including
  - stress management skills;
  - effective coping skills;
  - mindfulness skills; and
  - new life skills that support abstinence.
- Recovery plans should work to help clients be aware of recovery support in their community, such as
  - nonprofit organizations;
  - peer support groups (e.g., twelve-step groups);
  - mental health professionals (e.g., counselors, psychiatrists);
  - primary care physicians; and
  - 24/7 support hotlines.
- The counselor should use reflection and clarification to ensure that the client's treatment plan meets the current treatment needs.
  - Counselors should not rely on interpretation, which can contribute to miscommunications.
  - Maintaining a collaborative relationship throughout the client's treatment is imperative for optimal outcomes.
- To ensure care coordination, the counselor should maintain contact with any other providers with whom the client is working (e.g., mental or physical health professionals).
  - For instance, if a client with bipolar disorder is working with a psychiatrist, changes in medication could be relevant.
  - Any information received regarding the client should be reviewed in a timely manner and documented appropriately.

As treatment continues for a client, the recovery plan should be modified and discussed. Clients should be open to client **feedback** when counselors discuss progress and concerns with them. If a client presents as angry or upset, the counselor should maintain composure and model effective communication patterns. De-escalation skills may be necessary for some situations.

Being open about discharge and aftercare options can help with anxiety or separation concerns that a client may have. If a client's concerns continue, the counselor can facilitate the care transition in a way that makes the client more comfortable. For example, counselors can sit with clients who are calling to schedule or speak with their new care provider.

QUICK REVIEW QUESTIONS

5. Who has input into the recovery plan: the counselor or the client?

6. What forms of self-directed support should recovery plans offer?

Relapse Prevention

People with SUD who are in addiction treatment receive psychoeducation about relapses and relapse prevention. Counselors and other staff work with individuals to develop a relapse prevention plan that can help them maintain abstinence when they return home. A **relapse prevention plan** can include the following:

- making changes to their environment
- avoiding people who use and places where they would use
- learning to manage emotional distress
- establishing healthy boundaries
- identifying social supports
- encouraging self-help groups
- continuing in addiction treatment
- receiving mental health treatment

Clients with a dual diagnosis may be at an increased risk of relapsing if they do not receive the treatment they need. Research has shown that clients with a dual diagnosis have a better chance of a healthy recovery when they are engaged in treatment for both substance use disorder and their mental health condition. To this end, many addiction treatment providers—both inpatient and outpatient—offer various forms of treatment for mental health.

Common dual-diagnosis concerns include depression, anxiety, a history of trauma, PTSD, and bipolar disorder. Some mental health concerns, such as bipolar disorder, require long-term medication-assisted therapy.

QUICK REVIEW QUESTIONS

7. What kind of plan helps clients maintain abstinence?

8. What clients may be at an increased risk of relapse?

Multiple Pathways and Continuum of Care

Understanding Multiple Pathways

The counselor should use multiple pathways of recovery in treatment planning and referral. According to the Recovery Research Institute, **multiple pathways** that can be used in addiction recovery include

- clinical pathways;
- nonclinical pathways; and
- self-management pathways.

TABLE 6.2. Multiple Pathways for Recovery

PATHWAY	DEFINING ASPECTS AND EXAMPLES
Clinical pathways	- various therapeutic approaches (e.g., acceptance and commitment therapy, cognitive behavioral therapy, dialectical behavior therapy) - inpatient treatment programs - outpatient treatment programs - holistic-based recovery services - medication-assisted treatment - contingency management - relapse prevention measures
Nonclinical pathways	- sober houses - recovery community centers - peer-led support groups - education-based programs - employment-based programs - faith-based support
Self-management pathways	- also known as natural recovery - does not involve clinical or nonclinical services - occurs when a person ceases substance misuse voluntarily without clinical or nonclinical support - cycles of abstinence and substance misuse; causes unknown

A **continuum of care** for addiction refers to the levels of care available. For example, many individuals begin treatment in a detoxification program. From there, clients progress to an inpatient rehab program, then a partial hospitalization program, then an intensive outpatient program (IOP), and finally an aftercare program. Depending on the needs of clients, some may remain at one level of the continuum or skip levels (e.g., transitioning from detox to outpatient care, or returning to inpatient care from IOP). Different treatment options offer clients access to the appropriate level of care for their stage of functioning.

All levels of care should work to educate clients about intervention services, treatment options, and recovery. This can occur in psychoeducational groups, group therapy, and individual sessions. Prevention efforts are offered within a community and can include

- access to educational materials;
- naloxone (Narcan) training; and
- Q&A nights for parents and families.

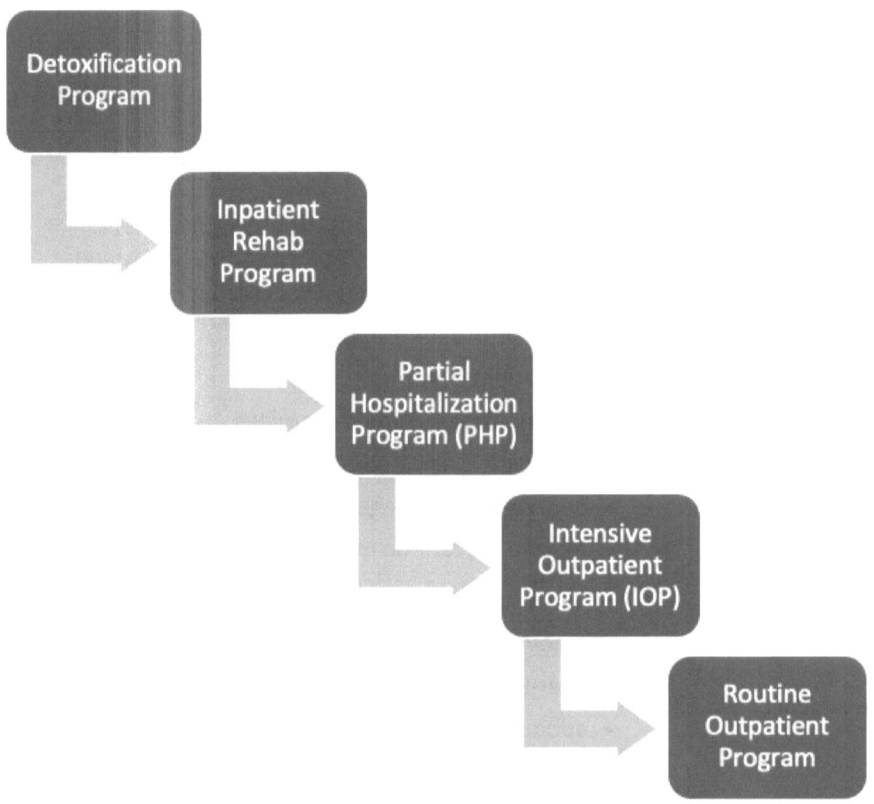

Figure 6.1. Typical Levels of Care

QUICK REVIEW QUESTIONS

9. An intensive outpatient program is an example of what kind of pathway?

10. A peer support group is an example of what kind of pathway?

What Are Support Programs?

Support programs provide aid to people living with challenging conditions and who are in need of comfort and guidance. These programs are not isolated to addiction recovery, and people in recovery from addiction may benefit from more than one support program.

Support programs often take the form of discussion groups. They are typically facilitated by counselors or by other individuals who have directly experienced the situation that the support group addresses. For example, Alcoholics Anonymous meetings are conducted by people in recovery from alcohol use disorder. Support groups are conducted this way for several reasons:

1. It is more effective to have a facilitator whose wisdom and experience can benefit others.
2. The facilitator can also defuse controversy and make sure everyone gets a turn to speak.
3. This arrangement provides a judgment-free environment because everyone in attendance has had similar experiences.
4. Support groups are generally voluntary; members attend for their own benefit.

While attending support groups is usually voluntary, in some cases it is legally mandated. For instance, attending a certain number of Alcoholics Anonymous or Narcotics Anonymous meetings might be part of an offender's sentence. Common support groups include

- Alcoholics Anonymous (AA);
- Narcotics Anonymous (NA);
- Gamblers Anonymous (GA);
- grief and bereavement counseling groups;
- groups for people who have experienced abuse and/or sexual violence;
- groups that support members who have chronic illnesses (e.g., diabetes, cancer).

DID YOU KNOW?

Support groups also exist for the families and friends of people in recovery, and for people who have lost loved ones to violence or suicide.

QUICK REVIEW QUESTIONS

11. Who leads support groups?
12. Is it voluntary or mandatory to attend support groups?

Mutual Support Groups

Individuals who participate in **mutual support groups** have access to a community of like-minded individuals who are working on their own recovery programs:

- Twelve-step groups are well-known mutual support groups, but not all mutual support groups follow the philosophy of the Twelve Steps.
- Mutual support groups are led by volunteers within the group rather than professionals.
- Participants attend meetings, embrace positive lifestyle changes, and may read literature.
- Participation can decrease loneliness, increase personal support, and provide guidance for behaviors.

The **twelve-step program** was developed in the 1930s by financier Bill Wilson and physician Bob Smith. Known as Bill W. and Dr. Bob, both men found recovery from alcohol use disorder through mutual aid that developed into the Alcoholics Anonymous program. Core components of the twelve-step program include

- anonymity;
- believing in a higher power;
- attending meetings;
- working the Twelve Steps;
- helping others; and
- sponsorship.

Common twelve-step groups include Alcoholics Anonymous (AA), Narcotics Anonymous (NA), Cocaine Anonymous (CA), Crystal Meth Anonymous (CMA), and more. These groups are considered **fellowships** in that they are not hierarchical. Meetings are organized and led by people in recovery, with service positions (like leading meetings) rotating among members. Fellowships solicit donations from members but do not profit monetarily: donations are used to purchase literature and rent space for meetings.

- Alcoholics Anonymous, the largest twelve-step fellowship, focuses on recovering from alcohol abuse; today, many AA groups welcome members who struggle with other substances as well.
- Narcotics Anonymous focuses on recovering from substance abuse.
  - NA emerged when people who abused drugs other than alcohol sought an alternative to AA.
  - NA adapted the Twelve Steps and Twelve Traditions from AA.
  - NA considers alcohol a drug and welcomes members who struggle with alcohol.

The **Twelve Steps** are a list of twelve actions that an individual can take to work toward a healthy recovery. Individuals who participate in a twelve-step program learn to recognize their strengths and weaknesses, work through any shame and guilt, and repair damaged relationships:

- The Twelve Steps embrace introspection, faith in a higher power, self-inventory, making amends, and helping others.
- The steps are intended to be completed in order and with the guidance of a sponsor.
- The length of time it takes to complete the Twelve Steps will vary for individuals.

The **Twelve Traditions** are guidelines for meetings and provide consistency and accountability regarding fellowship operations. Key components are anonymity, belief in a higher power, attraction rather than promotion, and the nonhierarchical voluntary nature of service in the fellowship.

Sponsorship refers to the helping relationship between a member in early recovery (a sponsee) and someone who has been in recovery for some time (a sponsor). It is a mutually beneficial and nonprofessional arrangement. Sponsors typically have some time in recovery and have worked the Twelve Steps. Sponsors act as mentors and provide guidance to their sponsee(s) regarding the Twelve Steps.

A key difference between twelve-step groups and other mutual support groups is the programmatic emphasis on spirituality and believing in a higher power. Members are encouraged to develop their own concept of a higher power, which need not be religious. Membership in twelve-step groups is open to people regardless of their religious beliefs (or lack thereof).

Several non-twelve-step mutual support programs exist as alternatives to the twelve-step concept. They also have meetings and philosophies of recovery:

- **Self-Management and Recovery Training (SMART)** recovery is a mutual support group that works to help members overcome their addiction in a self-empowering way.
  - SMART recovery is based on science and is not a twelve-step program.
  - Some limitations of SMART recovery are viewing addiction as bad habits, discouraging the use of MAT, and not addressing feelings of guilt that individuals struggle with.
- **Women for Sobriety (WFS)** is a nonprofit organization that works to help women with SUD find a new life, free from the use of substances.
  - WFS embraces thirteen Acceptance Statements and the New Life Program.
  - WFS is for individuals who have expressions of female identity and welcomes people from the LGBTQIA+ community.
- **Refuge Recovery** is a Buddhist-oriented mutual aid support program for people in recovery from SUD.
  - Buddhist beliefs and teachings are used to help individuals overcome their struggles with addiction.
  - Refuge Recovery embraces the four truths, the Eightfold Path, and regular meditation practice.

Frequent meeting attendance at mutual support groups is recommended at the beginning of recovery and whenever individuals find themselves struggling. For example, attendance of ninety meetings in ninety days is often suggested to newcomers. This helps to develop a habit of attending meetings and gives people enough time to start noticing personal gains.

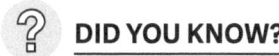

DID YOU KNOW?

Individuals who benefit the most from mutual support groups are active participants in the group, work with a sponsor, engage in the Twelve Steps, and work daily on their recovery.

QUICK REVIEW QUESTIONS

13. Do members of twelve-step programs need to be religious?

14. What are some alternatives to twelve-step programs?

Harm Reduction

Due to the significant presence of addiction across the United States, there has been an increase in public safety measures aimed at helping those who are struggling. **Harm reduction** is an approach to combat the concerns associated with addiction without focusing on abstinence. Harm reduction approaches include

- syringe exchange programs;
- providing fentanyl testing strips;
- overdose prevention centers;
- increasing access to naloxone and overdose education; and
- increased education about addiction, recovery, and relapses.

Harm reduction strategies are controversial. These strategies strive to improve safety for individuals who are using drugs and alcohol but are not intended to provide addiction treatment, although education and access to treatment may be offered to participants.

Harm reduction strategies can help reduce the risk of transmitting infections caused by using soiled equipment, decreasing injection-related dangers, and reducing the risk of overdose. These practices can be helpful for individuals who are at high risk due to being in active addiction. Additionally, harm reduction locations provide an opportunity to offer education about addiction, safety-related topics, and available treatment options in the local community.

Individuals who are against the use of harm reduction approaches see these strategies as a way to enable those in active addiction. Providing a safe environment and access to clean utensils is believed to prolong a person's addiction. It has been argued that without access to harm reduction approaches, individuals will reach rock bottom faster, which can lead to them seeking and engaging in addiction treatment. Additionally, there can be safety concerns in a community regarding harm reduction sites due to the negative stigmas associated with individuals who are actively using drugs and alcohol.

QUICK REVIEW QUESTIONS

15. What is the purpose of harm reduction strategies?

16. What is a concern associated with harm reduction programs?

Medical Follow-Up

Counselors should provide clients with a referral for **medical consultation** at the beginning of their treatment to check for common health concerns that appear among people with SUD. Even moderate and short-term use of drugs and alcohol can negatively impact a person's physical health. Furthermore, SUD makes clients vulnerable to health concerns like vitamin deficiencies, injuries, and sexually transmitted infections.

Some chronic illnesses are associated with SUD (e.g., HIV/AIDS, hepatitis C). Clients may have left chronic illnesses (e.g., diabetes) untreated while in their addiction. The counselor should provide unbiased information about medical treatment and help clients choose what is best for them. If a client is reluctant to have a medical consultation, the counselor should process the concerns and identify steps that can help encourage the client to attend the appointment.

In some cases, clients may exhibit symptoms associated with health concerns (e.g., jaundice, wounds). Receiving a medical consultation allows the client to discuss these experiences with a medical professional who can investigate the concerns.

Medical treatment can help reduce the stress and discomfort that can contribute to cravings and triggers for the use that would have a direct impact on the client's sobriety. A healthy recovery should include working toward optimal physical health. Optimal health will vary for each client.

Medical treatment can also help clients learn if any unknown medical conditions contributed to their addiction. For example, thyroid malfunction may cause depressive symptoms. Treating the thyroid can help improve depressive symptoms and strengthen recovery.

Medication-assisted treatment (MAT) refers to the use of psychopharmacology with other behavioral treatment approaches. This can be an effective treatment intervention at various stages of recovery, including detoxification; early recovery; and, in some cases, late recovery.

Medications used will vary based on the client's needs. While counselors must understand the different options available for MAT, they cannot prescribe medications. A medical professional must prescribe medications. Common medications used in MAT are methadone, buprenorphine (Suboxone), naltrexone, and naloxone (Narcan).

- Methadone and buprenorphine are controlled substances; counselors must be mindful of their potential for abuse.
- Urine screens are commonly used to ensure that these medications are being taken as prescribed.

TABLE 6.3. Common Medications Used in Medication-Assisted Treatment

MEDICATION	PURPOSE AND DOSAGE	OTHER ASPECTS
Methadone	<ul><li>treats opioid use disorder</li><li>taken daily</li><li>dispensed at a clinic under medical supervision</li><li>clients usually expected to engage in outpatient treatment and test negative for all other substances</li></ul>	<ul><li>long-acting opioid agonist</li><li>reduces cravings and withdrawal symptoms</li><li>can block euphoric effects of opioids</li><li>has potential for addiction</li></ul>

Buprenorphine (Suboxone)	• treats opioid use disorder • dosage and frequency tailored to address client needs • not necessarily taken under medical supervision (may be taken at home)	• prescribed in addition to regular behavioral treatment • can block euphoric effects of opioids • has potential for addiction
Naltrexone	• treats alcohol use disorder and opioid use disorder • taken in a daily oral dose or a monthly intravenous injection	• reduces cravings associated with alcohol use disorder • can block the euphoric and sedative effects of opioids
Naloxone (Narcan)	• temporarily reverses the effects of an opioid overdose • effectiveness depends on opioid taken • administered intranasally or injected	• may be administered outside the health care setting (e.g., by peers, first responders) • training available from health care professionals • available for free or without a prescription in some states

DID YOU KNOW?

In some methadone clinics, after a period of sobriety, an individual may be eligible to get two days' worth of medication at a time rather than going to the clinic daily.

QUICK REVIEW QUESTIONS

17. When should a client receive a referral for medical consultation?

18. What medication is used to reverse the effects of an opioid overdose?

Answer Key

1. Discharge planning should begin during the first session with a client.

2. The counselor should review client progress toward discharge criteria throughout treatment.

3. Clients recognize that their use of substances is a problem in the transition stage of the Developmental Model of Recovery (DMR).

4. Clients usually begin making amends for prior behaviors during the middle recovery stage of the Developmental Model of Recovery (DMR).

5. Recovery plans should be developed in collaboration with the client: both the counselor and the client have input.

6. Self-directed support includes stress management skills, coping skills, mindfulness skills, and other life skills that support abstinence.

7. A relapse prevention plan helps clients maintain abstinence.

8. Clients with a dual diagnosis may be at an increased risk of relapsing if they do not receive the treatment they need.

9. An intensive outpatient program (IOP) is an example of a clinical pathway.

10. A peer support group is an example of a nonclinical pathway.

11. Support groups are typically facilitated by counselors or individuals who have directly experienced the situation the support group addresses.

12. Attending support groups is usually voluntary, but in some cases it is legally mandated.

13. No. Twelve-step programs encourage spirituality and the development of a higher power, but they are open to all people regardless of religion or lack thereof.

14. Self-Management and Recovery Training (SMART) recovery, Women for Sobriety (WFS), and Refuge Recovery are alternatives to twelve-step programs.

15. Harm reduction strategies offer safety measures for people who are using drugs and alcohol.

16. Some argue that harm reduction programs enable people in active addiction.

17. Clients should receive a referral for medical consultation at the beginning of their treatment.

18. Naloxone (Narcan) can temporarily reverse the effects of an opioid overdose in some cases.

7 Counseling

The Therapeutic Relationship

The importance of the therapeutic relationship cannot be understated. The counseling relationship is the most important factor when predicting treatment outcomes. For clients to accept the proposed treatments, they must first trust the counselor enough to be honest about their experiences and issues:

- Without trust, the client may not feel comfortable sharing everything with the counselor.
- If the client does not share openly, the counselor may make an inaccurate diagnosis and devise the wrong treatment plan.

The foundation of the counseling relationship is the therapeutic alliance. The **therapeutic alliance** is an unwritten agreement between the client and the counselor based on trust, boundaries, and mutual respect. It is not a friendship but rather a formal treatment relationship.

In the therapeutic alliance, clients feel safe to explore issues and be vulnerable with the counselor. At the same time, they know that the counselor will hold them accountable and maintain professional boundaries. Clients need assurance that the counselor will not judge them.

The therapeutic alliance also creates an equalization of power between the client and the counselor. Clients often begin treatment viewing the counselor as a person of authority, much like many people regard physicians. According to that view, clients may expect the counselor to tell them what to do to get better. Unlike the client-physician relationship, however, the counselor in the therapeutic alliance

- makes it clear that clients lead the way and establish their own goals; and
- uses therapeutic techniques—not force or coercion—to help clients achieve their goals.

Empathy is the ability to understand and accurately perceive the feelings and experiences of others from their perspective. Psychologist Carl Rogers viewed empathy as a state of being for counselors that facilitates being non-judgmental and accepting.

Empathy differs significantly from sympathy. Although both involve emotions, empathy does not involve the counselor's personal experience, nor does it involve judgment. Sympathy, on the other hand, is the process of pitying or feeling bad for someone without really understanding that person's perspective; this means it includes judgment.

Sympathy is a surface-level intellectual understanding based on personal experience. Empathy is a deeper understanding and sharing of emotions based on each person's perspective. Empathy builds connection; sympathy does not:

- **Empathetic attunement** combines empathy with attending skills. When using empathetic attunement, counselors are aware of both their and the client's emotions:
    - Counselors communicate verbally and nonverbally that they recognize the client's emotions.
    - For example, if a client starts to cry in a session, the counselor can demonstrate empathetic attunement by staying silent and relaxed, being present with the client, and allowing the client to experience that emotion without judgment or comment.
- **Empathetic responding** is a verbal response from the counselor that conveys an understanding of what clients are feeling and why they feel that way.
    - This skill shows clients that the counselor respects and understands their emotions and the reasons for them.
    - Using the example of a client who feels like hitting someone during a family conflict, the counselor might empathetically respond by saying, "You feel intense anger because you feel that person is not listening to you."

QUICK REVIEW QUESTIONS

1. What is the therapeutic alliance based on?

2. What term describes a verbal response from a counselor that conveys an understanding of what a client is feeling and why the client is feeling that way?

Counseling Strategies for Substance Use Disorder

Communicating the Structure, Expectations, and Purpose of Counseling

Every client has a first counseling session. Clients might feel uncomfortable or uncertain about what they can expect from the counseling relationship. Concerns like these are common, and counselors can offer comfort and reassurance.

Before beginning an initial assessment, the alcohol and drug counselor (ADC) can explain what the layout for the session entails. This can include learning about the client's history and background, completing necessary consent and release forms, and conducting assessments. Knowing what to expect can help a client feel some relief during the session.

A strengths-based approach is useful when working with individuals who are struggling with a substance use disorder. This method uses a **strengths-based assessment** to investigate the strengths and supports clients have that can help them in their recovery. Other elements of a strengths-based approach include

- allowing clients to set their own goals; and
- searching for resources in clients' environments that can support them.

A strengths-based approach offers clients hope. The ADC helps clients recognize and use supports in their environment, such as sober support and members of support groups (e.g., Alcoholics Anonymous [AA]). Allowing clients to identify their own goals will also enhance their motivation.

Person-centered recovery planning (PCRP) refers to a partnership between the client and the counselor that uses a holistic approach to the client's treatment plan. An individualized treatment plan will address a client's personal struggles, strengths, and goals for recovery:

- The PCRP process involves developing a treatment plan that addresses the client's values, cultural beliefs, personal goals, and language.
- Counselors who use PCRP should update the plan continuously to reflect a client's progress and setbacks.

Different clients have different needs when it comes to addiction treatment. For instance, individuals with a mild substance use disorder may require an intensive outpatient program (IOP), whereas clients with a severe substance use disorder may require inpatient treatment.

Counselors can encourage **recovery-oriented behavior** at all stages of treatment. These behaviors are known to support clients' recovery and can include

- attending peer support groups, such as AA or NA;
- avoiding individuals who are actively struggling with addiction;
- avoiding situations where substances could be present;
- using healthy coping skills to manage uncomfortable emotions; and
- removing objects from their environment that have been used during active addiction.

QUICK REVIEW QUESTIONS

3. What type of assessment investigates strengths and supports that can help clients in their recovery?

4. What type of recovery planning takes a holistic approach and refers to a partnership between the client and the counselor?

Motivation to Change

Motivation is the driving force behind people's actions. Counselors should assess clients' sources of motivation in the context of managing their recovery to better educate, encourage, and advocate for them:

- **Intrinsic motivation** is driven by the enjoyment and personal satisfaction of achieving a goal, seeking challenges, or completing a task (e.g., exercising because it is enjoyable). Motivation comes from within the client.
  - People who are intrinsically motivated to pursue change are more likely to follow through with counseling.
  - For example, someone who struggles with depression and irritability and who is intrinsically motivated may come to counseling with a goal of becoming a happier person.
- **Extrinsic motivation** is driven by the external rewards (or punishments) of accomplishing a goal (e.g., exercising to improve health). Extrinsic motivation comes from forces outside the client.
  - People who are extrinsically motivated may follow through with counseling, but they are less likely to do so than those who are intrinsically motivated.
  - For example, an adolescent forced into therapy by his parents may only come to counseling to avoid punishment. This will impact the level at which the client engages in the process.
  - Another example is a client referred to therapy by a drug court proceeding whereby her success in therapy will determine whether or not she goes to jail for a drug offense. In this case, extrinsic motivation may positively influence the client.

Counselors should consider clients' motivation for change as it pertains to their recovery from SUD. In other words, a client may have an intrinsic motivation to stop using a substance but may not be ready to make the behavioral changes necessary to do so.

In these cases, the counselor should help clients discover and tap into their motivations to change. This will move them from the stages of change talk to change action. The **transtheoretical model** allows counselors to identify which stage of change clients are in and how to guide them to a stage of change where they are motivated to engage in change behavior:

- Clients with an **external locus of control** will attribute their successes or failures to outside forces. These clients tend to blame others for

what they experience and feel there is little to nothing they can do to change these experiences.
  - Some of these clients will feel helpless and hopeless that anything can change.
  - Others recognize that even if those outside forces impact their success or failure, there are options to counter them.
- Clients with an **internal locus of control** will attribute their success or failure to themselves.
  - Some of these clients will unrealistically take the blame and responsibility for everything that happens to them.
  - Others use their strengths to overcome adversity.

> **HELPFUL HINT**
> See Chapter 2 for more on the transtheoretical model.

QUICK REVIEW QUESTIONS

5. What type of motivation is driven by enjoyment and personal satisfaction?

6. Clients who attribute their success or failure to themselves have which locus of control?

Stages of Treatment

Counselors should be aware of the various **stages of treatment**, as this can help them understand the appropriate and effective techniques and strategies they should be using. Research has broken the stages of treatment into the following three categories:

- early stage
- middle stage
- late stage

Individuals in the **early stage of treatment** can be in varying levels of the stages of change (precontemplation, contemplation, preparation, and early action):

- People can struggle with maintaining sobriety at this stage, even with a sincere intention of remaining sober.
- Clients are more likely to be impacted by the current use of substances and/or withdrawal symptoms.
- Individuals commonly have external motivations for sobriety, including
  - health concerns,
  - family pressure, and
  - current legal concerns.
- Some clients may believe that they will be able to use substances recreationally in the future.
- Counselors can work toward addressing clients' denial and resistance regarding recovery.

COUNSELING 103

> **DID YOU KNOW?**
>
> Cognitive impairment related to substance use begins to resolve for clients during the middle stage of treatment. This cognitive impairment contributes to the challenges clients can face in the early stage of treatment regarding decisions about their recovery.

During the **middle stage of treatment**, clients can begin to experience stability in their recovery and other aspects of their lives:

- Counselors should help clients focus on their motivation for recovery.
- Clients whose source of motivation is external should work toward finding internal sources of motivation.
- Counselors should be mindful of any emotions or decisions that can contribute to relapse, and provide the necessary support.
- For example, if a counselor knows that a client struggles with the holiday season, the counselor should focus on the potential challenges the client can experience as that time of year approaches.

During the **late stage of treatment**, clients are often in the maintenance stage of change, which involves focusing on maintaining their progress in treatment:

- Clients work to avoid known triggers and challenging situations.
- Clients can experience a relapse at any stage of treatment, including the late stage.
- In the event of relapse, clients return to their recovery with new knowledge that can strengthen their recovery.
- The late stage of treatment is a time to focus on other concerns. Common issues include
    - relationship concerns,
    - self-image concerns,
    - trauma, and
    - other interpersonal struggles.

QUICK REVIEW QUESTIONS

7. In what stage of treatment are clients more likely to be impacted by the current use of substances and/or withdrawal symptoms?

8. When are clients in the maintenance stage of change?

Meeting Psychosocial Needs

There are a variety of tools and assessments to help counselors recognize therapeutic techniques that would benefit their clients. Assessments can be used during an initial interview and throughout the counseling relationship to highlight other mental health concerns. Individuals with a dual diagnosis are more likely to have a successful recovery when receiving treatment for both concerns at the same time.

Counselors should be mindful of their clients' level of treatment since it can guide how their needs are addressed. Additionally, being aware of the stages of change can provide guidance for clients' needs at that time. For example, a counselor working with a client in the early stage of treatment while in the precontemplation stage of change will likely be focusing on the client's sources of motivation and avoidance of triggers.

Clients with limited intrinsic motivation for treatment often show some level of resistance toward recovery. Because their motivation for recovery is extrinsic (e.g., for legal or family purposes), these clients lack a deeper motivation to maintain sobriety.

Motivational interviewing (MI) is a therapeutic technique that can help clients find internal motivation and strengthen existing motivation. In MI, counselors first focus on building rapport and trust within the therapeutic relationship before addressing any ambivalence clients are experiencing. Strategies associated with MI include

- expressing empathy,
- avoiding arguments,
- rolling with clients' resistance, and
- supporting self-efficacy.

Certain aspects of MI that can be used during all stages of treatment include

- asking open-ended questions,
- offering affirmations,
- using reflective listening, and
- summarizing at the end of the session.

Counselors can use MI skills to encourage engagement from clients who may resist treatment. Resistance is common among clients who are in treatment due to external pressures such as family, work, and legal systems.

Other strategies depend on which stages of treatment and change the client is in. Knowing the client's current motivation for recovery and readiness to change allows the ADC to identify effective strategies (see Table 7.1.).

TABLE 7.1. Strategies Based on Stage of Treatment		
EARLY STAGE OF TREATMENT	**MIDDLE STAGE OF TREATMENT**	**LATE STAGE OF TREATMENT**
• instilling hope • psychoeducation • learning new social skills • learning from others in similar stages of recovery	• recognizing the impact that substance use has had on all aspects of life • learning effective coping strategies • exploring emotions • learning to cope with emotions	• processing uncomfortable, painful realities • processing any history of trauma • improving current relationships • learning life skills that support recovery

Reflective listening is a skill counselors can use to give clients space to express themselves, which is more effective than telling them what they should do. Reflective listening helps clients develop their own ideas for change without the influence of others. This will provide them with a stronger sense of motivation than if they were told to do the same thing by a third party.

Summarizing can be used at the end of a session to recap important topics that were covered and provide the client with time to correct any misunderstandings that may have occurred. Summarizing can also be used to draw connections between the client's current situation and identified goals.

 HELPFUL HINT
Using open-ended questions can reveal new details that the counselor may not have known.

QUICK REVIEW QUESTIONS

9. What therapeutic technique can help clients find internal motivation and strengthen existing motivation?

10. What are two factors a counselor should take into account when considering therapeutic techniques?

Monitoring and Evaluation

Counselors must continually evaluate the client's safety, relapse potential, and need for crisis intervention.

Assessing Risk and Managing Crisis

Individuals who struggle with a substance use disorder can experience a multitude of consequences. When an individual faces a crisis, ADCs can use this experience to facilitate the recovery process:

1. Tie the crisis to the client's values.

   If a client places high value on family, he may find motivation if his family establishes new boundaries that limit their relationship with him due to his substance use.

2. Explore how the crisis impacts the individual's personal goals.

   If an individual wishes to advance in her career, she might look at how her substance use affects her work performance and attendance and how that directly impacts her career.

The examples described in Table 7.2. fall into a person-centered approach that can be tailored to each individual's characteristics.

TABLE 7.2. Typical Crisis Situations Faced by Individuals in Treatment for SUD

RELATIONAL	FINANCIAL	LEGAL	HEALTH
• loss of friendships • family members distancing themselves • damaged relationship with children • new or worsening cases with child protective services	• loss of employment • loss of home or living environment • loss of vehicle • new or worsening financial concerns • inability to meet or satisfy responsibilities	• new legal concerns, such as a DWI/DUI • worsening legal concerns due to continued use	• nonfatal overdose • new or worsening mental health concerns • new or worsening physical health concerns

The ADC needs to assess for both mental health and substance use risks. When clients are actively using, counselors should be assessing them for risk factors. **Risk factors** include being aware of what clients are using, the frequency of their use, and if they are using more than one substance:

- A client who is using in high-risk situations, such as using more than one substance at once, may need to be referred to a higher level of care.
- A client who wants to stop using substances that are known to have dangerous withdrawal effects may need to be referred to a higher level of care.

The development of new or worsening mental health concerns can be common. Such concerns can include anxiety and depressive symptoms. If clients share that they are struggling with depressive symptoms, the ADC must assess for suicidal ideation and intent. Other factors to be mindful of include loss of hope, isolation behaviors, and a sudden improvement in symptoms.

QUICK REVIEW QUESTIONS

11. How can the counselor use a crisis to facilitate the recovery process?

12. What should the counselor consider if a client is using more than one substance at once?

Conflict in the Therapeutic Relationship

Conflict in the therapeutic relationship can generate insight and provide beneficial therapeutic moments. **Transference** describes a situation in which clients redirect feelings about someone else in their life onto the counselor. These feelings and subsequent interactions can be positive or negative, but either way, they are unhealthy:

- A positive example of transference might be treating the counselor as a friend.
- A negative example might be directing anger at the counselor when the client is angry with his spouse.

In either case, the counselor's skill at bringing awareness to the interaction and processing it with the client can be a constructive therapeutic moment. For example, if the client behaves toward the counselor in anger, the counselor can direct the client's attention to the emotion of anger. The counselor could ask the client to describe what she is feeling in the moment and determine the cause and object of that anger. The counselor might also invite the client to engage in a dialogue in which she imagines the counselor is the object of her anger, which allows her to process the emotion through role-play.

When discussing transference, it is also appropriate to bring attention to **countertransference**, which is the counselor's transference toward the client's transference. For example, a client treats the counselor as if she were a friend, perhaps telling her that she reminds him of his friend, and then discloses a painful experience. The counselor reacts to the client's transference by sharing a similar painful experience instead of simply listening to the client. That disclosure is countertransference and can happen without the counselor realizing it, which is another reason counselor self-awareness and self-reflection are important:

- Countertransference can shift the focus from the client's therapeutic needs and toward the counselor.
- It also compromises the counselor's objectivity because the professional boundary has been blurred by the disclosure of personal information.

Defense mechanisms are another source of conflict within a therapeutic relationship. These are techniques clients use to protect themselves from feelings of anxiety or hurt. There are a number of defense mechanisms that people use. Some of the more common ones appear in Table 7.3.

TABLE 7.3. Defense Mechanisms

MECHANISM	DEFINITION	EXAMPLE
denial	ignoring reality	A parent denies that his child is misusing substances despite obvious signs.
repression	deciding to avoid thinking about something distressing	A client pushes away memories of an ex-partner who treated her badly.
regression	engaging in childlike behavior or emotions	A client speaks in baby talk when someone gets angry with him.

intellectualizing	focusing on rationalizing an issue rather than the emotions	A client's loved one dies, and the client only talks about the person's illness, the course of treatment, and the inevitability of death without acknowledging the sad emotions.
compartmentalizing	keeping a part of one's life separate from the others to reduce distress	A client has a very dangerous job but keeps it completely separate from her home life.

Constructive confrontation is a helpful therapeutic tool counselors use to call attention to the client's behaviors and feelings in the present moment, especially when there is incongruity. This method is useful to confront transference and defense mechanisms.

For example, if a client is talking about something distressing but is smiling or laughing, the counselor might stop the client and share observations about this behavior. By confronting the client about the difference between the painful experience being discussed and the client's outward emotional expression, the counselor can guide the client to increased self-awareness and, possibly, some insight.

Risk assessments for **crisis** situations should be part of every assessment counselors conduct with clients. It is also necessary to ask clients how they define a crisis and what a crisis might look like for them. Everyone's interpretation of a crisis is different; counselors cannot rely solely on their own judgment. Potential crisis situations can include

- suicide risk;
- self-harm;
- danger to self;
- danger to others;
- interpersonal violence;
- situational violence;
- a health emergency for self or loved ones;
- sudden changes in education, employment, or housing;
- natural disasters;
- accidents;
- a sudden change in relationship status;
- psychotic episodes;
- substance use lapse; and
- sudden strong mood changes, such as mania or depression.

Safety planning is a client-led process whereby the counselor and the client discuss

- what determines a crisis,

HELPFUL HINT

Risk assessment should occur at intake and periodically throughout the counseling relationship.

- what the client will do in a crisis,
- whom the client will reach out to in a crisis, and
- under what conditions outside help will be sought.

Depending on the client's situation, a safety plan will be put in writing so that the client and counselor can each keep a copy and the client can share it with others who will be involved in the plan. As clients progress through treatment, their needs will change, so safety plans should be revisited and revised over the course of treatment. Safety plans include the following information:

- how to tell if the client is in crisis
- whom to call when the client is in crisis
- whom not to call when the client is in crisis
- what supporters should do
- what supporters should not do
- under what circumstances to call for outside help
- which outside help to call
- how to tell when the client is no longer in crisis

Counselors need to keep boundaries with clients and ensure that they understand when it is appropriate to contact the counselor if in crisis and when to call others. Most counties in the United States have a crisis hotline; some provide hotlines specific to issues like sexual assault and domestic violence. If a counselor works for an organization or agency, there will likely be emergency and crisis policies in place for clients.

DID YOU KNOW?

Counselors must establish boundaries in crisis planning: some clients use crisis situations to seek attention from counselors.

QUICK REVIEW QUESTIONS

13. Which term describes when clients redirect feelings for someone else onto the counselor?

14. In which defense mechanism does the client ignore reality?

Conflict Resolution Strategies

Conflict resolution is important in both the counseling relationship and the group counseling context. Some strategies to resolve conflict include conflict avoidance, giving in, standing one's ground, compromising, and collaborating:

- **Conflict avoidance** involves not acknowledging the conflict.
- **Giving in** means acquiescing to the other party, thereby giving the other person what she wants or letting her have her way.
- **Standing one's ground** is a way of competing with the opposing party in the hopes that he does not win the battle.
- **Compromising** involves seeking common ground as a stepping stone to negotiating and resolving the conflict.

- **Collaborating** consists of actively listening to the opposing party's perspective, discussing areas of like-mindedness and common objectives, and confirming that both parties understand each other's viewpoints. This strategy is sometimes difficult, but it can be rewarding when it is effective.

QUICK REVIEW QUESTIONS

15. What term describes not acknowledging the conflict?

16. What strategy are parties using when they seek common ground to approach negotiation and resolution of the conflict?

Engaging Families and Concerned Others

Social Interactions and Support Systems

Social support systems are an integral part of a healthy functioning life and include the people an individual can turn to with emotional, physical, or spiritual needs. Social support systems may include

- friends,
- family members,
- practitioners,
- religious congregations,
- clergy,
- mentors,
- teachers,
- neighbors, and
- other community members.

Family of origin and close friends make up the majority of most people's social support networks. Church congregations, clergy, mentors, teachers, neighbors, and other community leaders may also be part of the wider network of a person's support system.

Strong support systems are ideally rich in depth and breadth, with a variety of people who can offer different levels of support. People with a robust social support network can more easily deal with life challenges, such as financial difficulties, health issues, or relationship problems.

Some clients have very poorly developed support systems. This is especially common among adults who experienced abuse as children, since their family ties may be tenuous. Individuals with weak support systems are at high risk for feelings of loneliness and depression. **Loneliness** and depression can lead a person to retreat even further from society despite craving social interaction. Counselors should encourage clients struggling with loneliness to work on the following:

- strengthening existing support systems
- expanding new support systems
  - taking on new hobbies
  - joining communities with like-minded individuals

The counselor may discover unhealthy **interactional patterns** in a client. For example, a client who habitually breaks up with romantic partners after two to three months might be avoiding intimacy and vulnerability. Some approaches to use with this client may include

- learning to identify intimacy fears; and
- developing coping strategies to self-soothe when faced with anxiety over intimacy.

QUICK REVIEW QUESTIONS

17. Most people's support networks are composed of what?

18. What are the features that indicate a strong social support system?

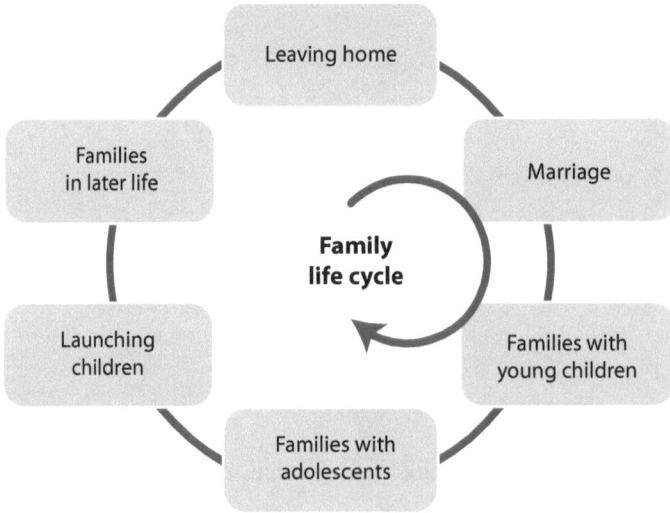

Figure 7.1. Family Life Cycle Stages

The Family Life Cycle

The **family life cycle** is typically divided into six stages, each with its own **stage-critical tasks**:

1. **leaving home**: developing self-identity, differentiating from family
2. **marriage**: adjusting to and developing a satisfying married life, adapting to a new kin network, navigating family planning
3. **families with young children**: adjusting to the high needs of infants and toddlers, creating a satisfying family life for all members

4. **families with adolescents**: encouraging academic success and planning for their future, balancing freedom with responsibility
5. **launching children**: supporting young adults as they navigate careers, college, and relationships
6. **families in later life**: coping with loss, living alone, adjusting to retirement

A counselor should know which stage in the family life cycle the client is in; this way, the counselor can determine which key areas the client is likely to be struggling with and which areas the client needs to succeed in to feel accomplished and ready for the next stage.

Extended families can offer a wealth of resources and joy; they can also contribute to family friction. Couples or individuals who diverge from the rest of the family's values can disrupt family norms and cause friction. Clients who are struggling with extended family relations may benefit from identifying boundaries to keep within their family and how to honor those boundaries in a way in which they are comfortable.

QUICK REVIEW QUESTIONS

19. How many stages are in the family life cycle?
20. In which stage of the family life cycle do individuals develop self-identity and differentiate from family?

Interacting with the Family and Concerned Others

Social support is an important aspect of substance use recovery. **Concerned others** like family, friends, and other close contacts can play a positive role.

However, the counselor must be aware that concerned others—even if well-meaning—can have a negative impact. For example, an adversarial relationship can cause a client to exhibit resistance or ambivalence to treatment engagement.

Ultimately, the counselor's ethical and professional obligation is to the client; the counselor must maintain boundaries with concerned others. The therapeutic relationship is with the client; therefore, the client directs the involvement of concerned others, including giving permission for them to be involved in the client's recovery.

Ultimately, the importance of the relationship with concerned others is not up to the counselor but to the client. The information provided by a concerned other during the assessment may or may not be true; the counselor and the client must process that information.

There are multiple ways a counselor can approach clients' relationships with concerned others:

- Invite clients to help the counselor understand the role of the concerned other in their lives and in their substance use.

 HELPFUL HINT

One way to build trust with clients is to ask them their thoughts about what the concerned other said during the session.

- Ask clients to evaluate their relationships with concerned others in terms of positive and negative resources.
- Involve the concerned other in the client's safety planning and recovery journey.
- Use the perceptions of the concerned others to help clients see themselves from another perspective.
- Help clients recognize how their actions impact those around them.
- Identify enabling behaviors or the codependency of concerned others.
- Work toward repairing relationships, with possible recommendations for couples or family therapy.

Substance use disorders affect society and the family of the person using. The National Institute on Drug Abuse (NIDA) estimates that approximately $600 billion is spent annually on public addiction concerns in the United States. This estimate includes the cost of health care, law enforcement, lost wages, treatment, and substance-related crimes. In addition to the financial burden carried by society, there are other impacts:

- dangers associated with impairment (e.g., driving while impaired)
- impact of loss of employment on a family unit
- disbursement of responsibilities in the work environment when individuals are unable to complete their duties
- problematic behavior to support addiction (e.g., theft, unsafe sexual behaviors)

DID YOU KNOW?

The American Society of Addiction Medicine (ASAM) reports that approximately 40–60 percent of domestic violence incidents involve an individual with a substance use disorder.

Children who grow up in a home where an adult is struggling with a substance use disorder are at a higher risk for various mental health concerns, including

- anxiety,
- depression,
- their own substance use disorders, and
- aggressive disorders.

Families with a member who is struggling with substance use can be significantly impacted by, among other things, loss of trust and new financial concerns. Family members of individuals with SUD can experience their own mental health concerns. The emotional toll of watching a loved one struggle with addiction can be difficult. Family members often suffer when their loved ones are in denial and unable to see the consequences of their use.

Family members may fall into unhealthy relationship patterns, such as enabling and codependency. Enabling can be present in a codependent relationship; however, this is not a causation relationship.

Enabling behaviors occur when family members make it possible for their loved ones to continue engaging in their addictive behaviors. This can happen when families try to support their loved ones. Examples of this include paying a loved one's bills or making excuses for a person's behaviors.

Some relationships may take on a specific pattern known as codependency. **Codependency** is a type of relationship dynamic in which a person enables another person's destructive habits, such as addiction, immaturity, or irresponsibility. The enabling person may take on a role of self-sacrifice and feelings of responsibility for others' actions and behaviors, and thus may experience boundary issues and enmeshment. People who are codependent tend to have

- high rates of anxiety or depression,
- compulsions,
- hypervigilance,
- experiences of recurrent physical or sexual abuse, and/or
- possible addiction issues.

Codependency patterns are typically rooted in childhood issues, often among children who were parentified or whose feelings were ignored or punished. When these children grow up, they might ignore their own feelings and deny themselves, feeling that they do not deserve to be treated well. People who are codependent may even have been expected to care for their parents due to addiction or mental health issues.

Counselors working with clients who are codependent may begin treatment by exploring childhood patterns and working to identify how those impact the client's current life. From there, issues such as developing healthy boundaries, sharing one's feelings, and building self-esteem can be introduced to allow the client to work toward better relationships.

> **HELPFUL HINT**
>
> Individuals who are codependent may help the other person in the relationship maintain unhealthy behaviors by enabling that person, despite insisting that they want the behavior to end. Typically, this is motivated by a desire to be needed by the other person.

QUICK REVIEW QUESTIONS

21. Who directs the involvement of concerned others in the treatment process?

22. Can the counselor rely on information provided by concerned others?

Abuse and Violence

Abuse can occur in any family and lead to lifelong emotional challenges for individuals who experience it:

- **Physical abuse** involves the use of physical force against a person. In addition to hitting or beating, this type of abuse includes shaking a person, holding someone underwater, or throwing things at a person.
- **Sexual abuse** includes coercive sex or sexual acts, taking pictures of a person without permission, exposing minors to pornography, or behaving sexually with minors. It can be done through the use of force or violence, threats, drugging, or emotional manipulation.
- **Emotional abuse** involves belittling language, name-calling, bullying, withholding love and affection, or telling the person that he is worthless or will never amount to anything.

Family abuse can happen between adults in a family, between older and younger siblings, or between parent and child. Some common warning signs of abuse include

- bruises or injuries that are not well explained;
- burns, especially patterned burns that cannot be explained;
- patterned injury marks as from a belt or other object;
- unattended medical issues;
- children expressing fear or dislike of their parents;
- high fight-or-flight response to being touched;
- bruising, bleeding, or pain around genitals;
- pregnancy or STDs;
- acting out sexually at a young age;
- speech problems, emotional development delays;
- depression, low self-esteem;
- poor academic performance;
- unexplained physical pain, such as headaches or stomachaches;
- poor hygiene;
- missing a lot of school;
- being underweight; and
- hoarding.

Domestic violence is not reportable unless the child has witnessed the abuse. Regardless of reporting, the counselor can—and should—continue to stay involved with the family and assist with safety planning, building parenting skills and emotion regulation, and assisting with any next steps that may need to be taken if an investigation is opened.

 HELPFUL HINT

Counselors have a legal and ethical obligation to report any suspected child abuse or cases in which children witness domestic violence. It is not the counselor's duty to investigate to confirm child abuse—only to report it to the appropriate authorities.

QUICK REVIEW QUESTIONS

23. Using belittling language, name-calling, bullying, and withholding affection indicate what kind of abuse?

24. Abuse can occur in which types of families?

Developing Life Skills

Conditions for Learning

Adult learners have several distinct traits that counselors should consider while developing client education plans:

- Adult learners are **independent** and **self-directed**. Counselors should actively engage them in the learning process and encourage them to help develop their treatment plans.

- Adult learners are **results-oriented** and **practical**. Counselors should give them information that they can apply immediately.
- Adult learners may be **resistant to change** and require justification for new behaviors.
- Adult learners may **learn more slowly** than younger learners; however, they may be more skilled at integrating new knowledge with previous experience.

Educational psychologist Benjamin Bloom described three domains of learning:

1. The **cognitive domain** includes collecting, synthesizing, and applying knowledge.
2. The **affective domain** involves emotions and attitudes, including the ability to be aware of emotions and respond to them.
3. The **psychomotor domain** relates to motor skills, including the ability to perform complex skills and create new movement patterns.

When educating clients, counselors should address all three learning domains. For example, a client who is learning about smoking cessation may need to be taught about the negative health impacts of smoking (cognitive domain), how to manage negative emotions related to quitting (affective domain), and how to correctly apply a nicotine patch (psychomotor domain).

Adult clients' **readiness to learn** can be shaped by many factors, including openness to new information, emotional response to illness (e.g., denial, anxiety), religious and cultural beliefs, and social support systems. However, just because a client learns the information does not mean the behaviors will change.

The counselor must assess the **functional status** of a client before developing an education plan. Doing so ensures that the plan aligns with the client's abilities and capacity to learn. Functional status is evaluated during assessment with the mental status exam.

Mental health literacy is the degree to which an individual can obtain, process, and understand basic information needed to make personal decisions. Mental health literacy gives clients ownership over their recovery and empowers them to learn the skills necessary to care for themselves. People do not stay in therapy forever, so the more mental health literacy clients have, the better able they are to care for themselves after therapy ends.

Mental health literacy also helps clients communicate their needs to others who are supportive. For example, someone who improves his mental health literacy about his panic disorder can explain to a loved one how to help him if that person is present during a panic attack. Interventions for clients with low mental health literacy include

- asking clients questions to assess their current knowledge;
- using plain language and short sentences;
- applying the knowledge to the client's situation;
- limiting important points to three or fewer;

 DID YOU KNOW?

Client mental health literacy improves as clients become more involved in their own care.

- using visual materials, such as videos or models, where possible;
- discussing issues in terms of short periods (less than ten years); and
- simplifying procedures and regimens as much as possible.

QUICK REVIEW QUESTIONS

25. Which domain includes collecting, synthesizing, and applying knowledge?

26. How can the counselor determine a client's functional status?

Life Skills

People in recovery from SUD should learn life skills that can help them maintain their recovery and succeed. These skills can be applied to all areas of their life. Examples of common **life skills** discussed in addiction treatment include the following:

- **managing stress**
    - This is a common trigger for individuals who struggle with addiction.
    - Drugs and alcohol are unhealthy coping mechanisms that can temporarily numb emotional discomfort but worsen distress in the long run.
    - Examples of **stress management skills** include using healthy coping skills to manage distress and using mindfulness strategies to increase emotional self-awareness.
- **relaxation skills**
    - These can be used to help individuals cope with the emotional distress they experience.
    - Adding relaxation practices to people's daily routines can improve their emotion regulation skills.
    - Relaxation practices include mindfulness and meditation exercises.
- **communication skills**
    - These help people advocate for themselves in recovery and help them feel as though they can effectively communicate their thoughts and concerns.
    - Role-playing can be an effective tool for clients to practice new communication skills.
- **assertiveness skills**
    - These improve client self-advocacy and help clients establish and maintain the physical and emotional boundaries that support their recovery.
    - Similar to communication skills, assertiveness skills can be practiced in role-playing exercises to work through situations that would challenge clients.

- **refusal skills**
  - These involve learning to say "no."
  - Like assertiveness skills, refusal skills help individuals maintain boundaries that support their recovery and mental health wellness.
  - Refusal skills can be helpful in other areas of a person's life, including interpersonal relationships.

QUICK REVIEW QUESTIONS

27. What tool is effective for practicing new communication skills?

28. Which stress management and relaxation skills increase emotional self-awareness?

Client Education

Counselors should provide educational resources on relevant topics (e.g., stress management, assertiveness training, divorce adjustment). This type of education in the context of mental health is often referred to as **psychoeducation**, or education focused on sharing evidence-based information about a mental health issue and how to cope with it.

Psychoeducation is valuable because it helps clients understand the what, how, and why of what they are experiencing. Strategies for teaching include the following:

- **Lectures** (groups or one-on-one) are effective for conveying cognitive knowledge, particularly to auditory learners. Counselors use this strategy to convey information on a specific subject to clients individually or to a group.
- **Group discussions** in which clients can ask questions and share information are effective for social learners and can help with affective learning (e.g., changing attitudes) and practicing skills in a safe environment.
- **Role-playing** is a good way to teach affective skills (e.g., responding to peer pressure) and to practice relational and communication skills in a safe environment.
- **Instructional materials**, like films or pamphlets, may be used as part of a larger education plan; however, they may be ineffective if clients are disengaged or the materials do not match the client's needs and learning abilities.
  - Counselors may provide instructional materials to clients within the context of treatment to support additional learning. For example, during a session, the client learns about healthy coping skills and discusses coping skills to try during the next week.
  - A counselor might give the client a pamphlet that defines healthy coping skills and provides a list of healthy coping skills to try,

including ones that were discussed in the session. This serves as a reminder for the client and reinforces what happened in the session.

Some specific strategies to engage clients in the learning process include the following:

- Link new information to current behavior; new learning is better received when it focuses on what the client already knows.
- Be clear, explicit, and specific.
- Suggest alternatives or adaptations that apply directly to clients and their situations.
- Be transparent about the goals of the learning process and why these are important.
- Involve other health providers (like dietitians) to engage clients and reinforce learning.
- Invite people from the client's social support network to participate in the learning process.

Finally, technology can engage clients and connect them to providers and support communities. **Webinars** or **live events** are often available in the community and are geared toward specific client populations (e.g., parents). When recommending these resources, counselors should verify the credentials of presenters as well as the validity and quality of the information presented.

QUICK REVIEW QUESTIONS

29. What type of psychoeducation is effective for conveying cognitive knowledge?

30. What type of psychoeducation is effective for social learners and practicing skills?

Answer Key

1. The therapeutic alliance is based on trust, boundaries, and mutual respect.

2. The term *empathetic responding* describes that the counselor has an understanding of what clients are feeling and why they feel that way.

3. A strengths-based assessment investigates strengths and supports that can help clients in their recovery.

4. Person-centered recovery planning (PCRP) refers to a partnership between the client and the counselor and is a process that takes a holistic approach to the client's treatment plan.

5. Intrinsic motivation is driven by enjoyment and personal satisfaction.

6. Clients with an internal locus of control attribute their success or failure to themselves.

7. Clients are more likely to be impacted by the current use of substances and/or withdrawal symptoms in the early stage of treatment.
8. Clients are in the maintenance stage of change during the late stage of treatment.
9. Motivational interviewing can help clients find internal motivation and strengthen existing motivation.
10. Counselors should know the level of treatment and stage of change their client is in.
11. The counselor can tie the crisis to the client's values or explore how the crisis impacts the individual's personal goals.
12. The counselor should consider whether the client may need to be referred to a higher level of care.
13. The term *transference* describes when clients redirect feelings for someone else onto the counselor.
14. In the denial defense mechanism, the client ignores reality.
15. The term *conflict avoidance* describes not acknowledging the conflict.
16. The strategy of compromising involves parties seeking common ground to negotiate and resolve conflict.
17. Family of origin and close friends make up most people's support networks.
18. Strong social support systems include a variety of people who can offer different levels of support.
19. The family life cycle is typically divided into six stages.
20. During stage 1—leaving home—people develop self-identity and differentiate from family.
21. The client directs the involvement of concerned others in the treatment process, including giving permission for their involvement in the client's recovery.
22. The information provided by a concerned other during the assessment may or may not be true; it is up to the counselor and the client to process that information.
23. Using belittling language, name-calling, bullying, and withholding affection describe emotional abuse.
24. Abuse can occur in any family.
25. The cognitive domain includes collecting, synthesizing, and applying knowledge.
26. Functional status is evaluated during assessment with the mental status exam.
27. Role-playing can be an effective tool for clients to practice new communication skills.
28. Mindfulness strategies can increase emotional self-awareness.

29. Lectures are effective for conveying cognitive knowledge.
30. Group discussions are effective for social learners and practicing skills in a safe environment.

8 Group Counseling

Working with a Group

Group counseling is significantly different from individual counseling because the client is considered the entire group—not just one person. Therefore, the focus of intervention is on the interactions among group members. This shift requires a purposeful approach from the group counselor when determining the type, size, and duration of the group.

Group type, size, and duration depend on the goal of the group. Some groups focus on a specific purpose and benefit from interaction among members; others offer support for members with minimal interaction among them. The following section discusses the different types of groups and their characteristics.

Types of Groups

Open groups, or **open-ended groups**, have no set beginning or ending—members can come and go as they please. Open-ended groups might teach members a set of coping skills for substance use or follow a psychoeducational curriculum that starts again once one cycle of the program ends:

- Some open-ended groups follow a **manualized program**, which provides a curriculum for the group counselor and includes instruction techniques and exercises to use for practice.
- Manualized programs can run in cycles, allowing members to start at any time and finish when the cycle is complete.
- Examples of manualized programs include anger management and court-ordered driver education and counseling (for clients with DUIs).
- Other open-ended groups function as support groups, such as mutual aid groups, where members receive support from each other.
- Examples of support groups include open groups for people dealing with depression or grief.

- The level of interaction among group members is superficial.
- The size of the group depends on factors such as
  - the number of group counselors,
  - room size,
  - program capabilities, and
  - state rules regarding group sizes.

DID YOU KNOW?

Some states regulate the ratio of group leaders to members (for example, ten to fifteen members for each facilitator). This way, the group size will depend on the number of facilitators available.

Open-ended groups can last as long as necessary. Some run continually; others have a start and end date. **Closed groups** are the opposite of open groups:

- New members are not allowed to join once the group begins.
- Closed groups tend to have specific purposes as well as start and end dates.

Closed groups are effective for especially delicate matters. For example, closed groups for people who have experienced sexual assault are appropriate due to the level of trust required among group members and the weight of the topics addressed. The success of the group often depends on the trust established and the interaction among members:

- Closed groups may feature a curriculum or schedule of topics.
- Closed groups typically set criteria for membership, such as age, gender, or experience with the topic.

Psychoeducational groups, or **curriculum groups**, focus on specific topics and typically have start and end dates. Psychoeducational groups are usually open, with the stated purpose of teaching a skill or providing information. Topics include

- anger management,
- parenting skills, and
- life skills.

These groups follow an evidence-based program whereby the facilitator presents information to the group. Group interaction focuses on the topic.

Process groups focus on the interaction among group members. In process groups, counselors help members process their thoughts, feelings, and behaviors on a deep level. The purpose is to address challenges that members face in the present. Process groups treat issues such as

- depression,
- anxiety,
- PTSD,
- substance use,
- relationship issues, and
- other mental illnesses.

Interactions among group members allow them to increase self-awareness and gain insight from other members by sharing experiences and perspectives. Additionally, process groups allow members to practice various skills, such as

- assertiveness,
- creating boundaries, and
- working through conflict.

Since process groups require a deeper level of trust among their members, they are often closed or semi-closed.

A **homogenous group** facilitates bonding among members based on what they have in common, which provides a focus for the group's purpose. Members of a homogenous group are chosen because they have characteristics or traits in common, such as

- gender;
- age (for example, members who are under eighteen); and/or
- mental health issues (for example, members with a certain diagnosis).

Members of **heterogeneous groups** are chosen for the diversity of their characteristics or traits. Many open groups are heterogeneous—anyone of any age with any issue may participate. The diversity of experiences, backgrounds, traits, and issues that each person brings to the group can help other members.

QUICK REVIEW QUESTIONS

1. Which type of group counseling has a start and end date and does not allow new members to join once it starts?
2. Which type of group counseling allows interactions among group members in order to address challenges that members face?

Group Activities and Psychoeducation

Structured activities provide overall structure and routine to an open group. A counselor can use structured activities during a session in a variety of ways.

For example, in an open group, members might use the structured activity format to each say their name and provide a brief update on their progress. Then, there might be a presentation of a relevant topic followed by group reactions and commentary on the topic for a set amount of time. Finally, the group might close with a structured activity, such as each member summing up the session.

This structured method gives group members a sense of stability and trust in the group process, helps them feel comfortable with the routine, and keeps sessions predictable. Structured activities may also be used for

- building trust among group members by helping them get to know each other;
- lessons to keep the progress of the group moving toward its end goal;
- sample situations that members may encounter, which allow them to role-play in group;
- moving a group out of stagnation or resolving a conflict;

- teaching skills; and
- engaging new group members.

There are many ways to use **psychoeducation** as part of the group process. In some groups, the focus is on the presentation of educational materials. Psychoeducation can also be used to normalize and validate a group member's experience. For example, if a member of a substance use group talks about having cravings that feel out of control, the counselor can use psychoeducation to explain the effects that drugs have on the brain and what the brain goes through during the processes of healing and recovery.

QUICK REVIEW QUESTION

3. Why are structured activities beneficial in a group?

Interactions in Groups

There are many ways counselors can manage **leader-member dynamics**. The title of "group leader" can be misleading because group counselors act more as facilitators than leaders. The purpose of a group leader is to facilitate interactions among group members, and while a counselor may present material or topics for the group to address, the real work takes place when members inspire insight in each other.

Many interactions between leaders and members are positive, but an effective group leader will remember the group's function and resist trying to control all aspects of it. The following are some ways to keep leader-member dynamics from becoming disruptive to the group:

- Have the members establish group rules and reiterate them at each meeting. When the group creates the rules, the leader is no longer in an authoritative position.
- Defer to the group. For example, if a member challenges the leader's qualifications or reasons for being there, the leader can reflect that question back to the group and ask if anyone else feels that way, why they feel that way, and what impact that has on the group. This takes the focus of discussion off of the leader and back to the members.
- Remind members that the group is not about the leader. This is another skill whereby the group leader reflects the interaction between a member and the leader back to the group.
- Invite the group to decide. If a member's behavior toward the leader becomes too disruptive, it may be appropriate to ask the group to determine if the member's behavior violates group rules and, if so, to act. Deferral to the group puts the power of the member's fate in the hands of the members and not the leader, thus giving group members authority over each other.

Managing leader-member dynamics is similar to the relationship between basketball players and the referee. The action of the game is the ball between the players, but sometimes the ball bounces to the referee. The referee's job is not to take the ball and join the game but to direct the ball back to the players to continue the game. Most groups require a **leader** or **facilitator**:

- For some groups, the counselor acts as the group leader or facilitator.
- Some group types require the presence of the counselor, but the counselor may defer group leadership to a member.
- Other groups may not need a counselor as a leader, especially if they are support groups and not therapy groups.
    - Examples include mutual aid groups like Alcoholics Anonymous (AA) or peer support groups, which have facilitators or chairpersons.
    - In such groups, it is wise to have someone act as a leader if only to get the group started and ended on time.
    - Chairpersons, coordinators, or facilitators manage logistics and ensure adherence to the group format and rules.

By having a coordinator or facilitator, the groups can remain open to all potential participants, and members and potential participants will know what to expect when they attend. Effective group leaders understand the group's purpose and function, which then determines the level of facilitation the group will require:

- In psychoeducational groups, the leader might be responsible for presenting the material and coordinating discussion afterward.
- In process groups, the leader might be responsible for noticing interaction among members, calling attention to something happening in the group for deeper processing, or addressing issues related to members who are either too quiet or too overpowering.
- An effective group leader can facilitate resolutions for therapeutic purposes when conflict arises.

TABLE 8.1. Characteristics and Skills of Effective Leaders

CHARACTERISTIC/SKILL	DEFINITION
Detachment	the ability to keep the focus of the group on the members and not on the leader
Observation	the ability to notice therapeutic events when they happen in a group and point them out
Empathy and encouragement	the ability to draw out group members who are not participating and include them
Reflection and summarization	the ability to rephrase what group members are saying to make a connection with what other members are experiencing
Confrontation and mediation	the ability to recognize conflict or the potential for conflict and guide group members through fixing it themselves

Teaching and clarifying	the ability to share educational information (that applies to what is going on in the group) during group discussions and to find ways members can use what they learn outside of the group
Management	the ability to keep members on task or focused and help them enforce group rules when necessary

Co-leaders can be very effective in groups since one person cannot always notice or address everything that happens. A co-leader can be

- another licensed counselor;
- a counseling intern; or
- a peer.

Co-leaders can take on various roles: training new counselors as group counselors, presenting specialized material, or acting as additional observers. Peers, or people further along their recovery journey than other members, can also be very helpful in engaging group members.

Before the group session begins, the co-leaders should discuss each of their roles. For example, one co-leader may take the role of lead facilitator while the other observes and interjects, or each co-leader may divide up responsibilities equally.

Although **leader-member interactions** are not usually the focus of group counseling, it is helpful when group members trust the leader. The counselor can promote and encourage interactions between the leader and members through

- introductions;
- self-disclosure;
- asking clarifying questions; and
- other counseling skills (for example, reflection, summarization, and attending).

The counselor's role in facilitating the group is to promote and encourage interactions among members. There are several ways to do this:

- Using **direct questioning**, the counselor might ask one group member how he reacted to what another member said.
- To **establish commonality** among members, when one member shares something about a family member who died, for example, the counselor might ask if anyone else has experienced the loss of a family member.
- **Linking** is a technique group counselors use to connect what one member says or experiences to another member to establish a connection, empathy, or understanding.

- **Feedback** in group therapy can be used by the counselor or members to share reactions to another group member—what that person said, did, or shared.
    - In addition to sharing reactions, feedback can include providing encouragement or recommendations.
    - An effective group counselor will facilitate feedback among members but may also use feedback as an instructive tool for the rest of the group.
- **Self-disclosure** is the process of sharing one's perspectives or experiences and generally refers to the counselor's sharing of personal experiences for a therapeutic purpose.
    - Self-disclosure can be useful for establishing a trusting relationship with the group members or for instructive purposes, but it should be used with care.
- Finally, the counselor can bring up **previous information** shared by a member in group to apply to a current situation.
    - For example, if a member shared a coping skill in a previous session that could help someone in the current session, the counselor might ask the first member about what she did and request that she explain it again.

Confidentiality in group therapy is held by the counselor, not necessarily the group. This means that the counselor has a legal and ethical obligation to keep what happens in group and the names of group members confidential. The agency hosting the group may have rules regarding group confidentiality that all members will be expected to uphold.

Group members are not legally or ethically obligated to uphold the same standards as the counselor; however, confidentiality is essential for groups to be successful, which is why members need to establish rules of confidentiality. This is one of the first items of business in a new group:

- Counselors should facilitate the creation of confidentiality rules to include how group members recognize each other outside of group and on social media.
- The group should determine the consequences of breaking confidentiality and how such a situation will be handled if it happens.

Another key role of the group counselor is to identify therapeutic moments that occur and point them out to members. The counselor can do this purposefully by asking questions of members and inviting feedback.

For example, if someone shares an experience, the counselor might ask the group if anyone else has experienced something similar or if they have any feedback for that member. The counselor can also do this indirectly by allowing the group to interact and then interjecting on occasion to share an observation of a theme or pattern. The counselor can also use summarization at the end of group sessions to identify patterns and themes that emerged in that session.

 HELPFUL HINT

A word of caution when bringing up previously shared information: it is a breach of confidentiality to bring up information that the client shares with the counselor outside the group.

QUICK REVIEW QUESTIONS

4. What term describes a group leader in a mutual aid group?

5. A counselor connects what one member says or experiences to the experience of another member to encourage empathy. What term describes this?

6. A counselor shares personal experiences for a therapeutic purpose. What is this technique called?

Group Stages

There are several defined **stages in the group process**:

- forming
- storming
- norming
- performing
- mourning

The **forming** stage of the group process is the start of the group when members join, introduce themselves, and determine their positions in the group. This part of the group process involves establishing the group rules, getting used to the format, and gaining an understanding of what the group will accomplish.

The **storming** stage involves conflict among group members. This can include testing boundaries, ascertaining whether other members really belong in the group, challenging the authority of the counselor, or resisting the way the group has decided to operate. Not every group goes through this stage, but the group's success depends on a healthy resolution; otherwise, members will be stuck in this stage and not get to the group's actual work.

The **norming** stage involves healing and repairing following the storming stage. If there is no conflict within the group, it occurs immediately after the forming stage. This is the stage when group members become comfortable with each other, understand what is expected of them, and settle into the routine of the work.

The **performing** stage describes the phase of real group work being done. The leader's function is reduced because members take on the roles of encouraging interaction with each other. It is in this stage that much of the therapeutic work is accomplished.

The **mourning** stage occurs at the end of the group and begins the process of group termination. During group therapy, members can become close and the end of group can be a sad event. Therefore, to ensure a successful termination of the group, the leader might facilitate an event or ritual to commemorate the successes of the members and to celebrate their accomplishments. Honoring this stage of the group process helps members transition out of the group.

Counselors need to be aware of which stage the group is in to make sure members are ready for a particular intervention. If a proposed intervention is not appropriate for the stage, then it will not be effective. For example, a role-play intervention to teach assertiveness might not be effective during the storming stage because of the level of group conflict; however, adjusting that intervention to teach healthy conflict resolution skills would be appropriate. A counselor should therefore always think about whether members are ready for a particular intervention and if it will help them move toward the stated goals.

QUICK REVIEW QUESTIONS

7. Which stage in the group process describes when members begin introducing themselves?

8. In what stage of the group process is most therapeutic work accomplished?

Attributes in a Group Counseling Context

Group Therapeutic Factors

A counselor demonstrates all of the core counseling attributes in a group context. Important core counseling attributes include

- self-awareness,
- genuineness,
- congruence,
- nonjudgment,
- positive regard,
- active listening,
- attending,
- reflecting, and
- empathy.

The following attributes are also important for group counseling:

- facilitation of group topics and group membership
- management of time, rules, and tasks
- observation of group members
- redirection of topics back to the group
- modeling appropriate behavior and healthy relationship skills
- identification of therapeutic moments
- enforcement of group rules
- fairness of treatment of and among group members
- conflict resolution skills
- calling out inappropriate behavior
- facilitating behavioral corrections
- teaching skills and therapy concepts

There are multiple therapeutic events and factors that occur in group therapy that a counselor watches for and facilitates. Group counselors foster the emergence of **group therapeutic factors** by knowing what they are and how to recognize them in a group context. Once a counselor recognizes when these factors occur, it may be appropriate to call attention to them in the group.

Self-disclosure is the sharing of personal information and experiences; it usually refers to the counselor. The purpose of self-disclosure is to further the therapeutic process. Often this is done with the intent to establish trust with the client, to move the client out of stagnation, or to inspire insight.

Self-disclosure can also include the counselor sharing feelings in the present to bring something into awareness. For example, a counselor may disclose feelings of tension within the group to initiate a conversation about conflicts among members.

Self-disclosure among group members is a key component of group therapy and requires that members share their thoughts, feelings, and experiences. The counselor may need to navigate self-disclosures by inviting reticent members to share and limiting the sharing of those who tend to dominate discussions.

Interaction in group therapy refers to the interpersonal engagement among group members. The interaction should not be between members and the counselor but among the members themselves so that they can learn from each other rather than from the counselor. A counselor who notices how members interact may draw attention to more quiet members to encourage their participation.

In group therapy, **acceptance and group cohesiveness** refers to members feeling like they belong in the group, that other members accept them for who they are, and that the member relationships are important to them. Group members feel safe and not judged, which results in a healthy environment for therapeutic progress.

When group members come to an understanding of their issues, or if they gain a new perspective or awareness of what they experience, this is referred to as **insight**. The new understanding or perspective helps members see their experience a little differently and even provides what they need to move beyond their issues.

Catharsis refers to an internal experience of change or a sudden realization that leads to a strong emotional reaction. The sudden realization may be associated with something that happened in a person's past or the identification of a triggering event.

Guidance occurs when either the group counselor or other group members provide educational information or advice.

Altruism is an aspect of group therapy whereby group members help each other, thus shifting the focus from themselves to other people. Helping other members provides a sense of value and gratitude among all members, which can improve how members think about themselves. A counselor may point out situations in which one group member helped another in order to draw attention to it and thus magnify the therapeutic effect.

Vicarious learning is learning from the experiences of other people. The self-disclosure of group members allows the other members to hear the good—and the bad—in the hopes that the listener makes different choices based on the experiences of someone else.

Hope is a strong motivator, and it can fuel a person's desire for change. Without hope, people feel helpless to change their situation. Within a group situation, the **instillation of hope** can come from members who share a common experience and who can show other members that healing is possible. Hearing the stories of someone who has been in the same situation can provide members with inspiration and a model of how healing is possible.

Existential factors involve recognizing what gives life meaning and the shared experience of being human. This may include discussions about big questions surrounding life and death, universal truths, and spirituality. Existential discussion in group therapy can help members come to terms with what they are dealing with by giving it some meaning or purpose outside of themselves.

QUICK REVIEW QUESTIONS

9. What term describes the interpersonal engagement among group members?

10. What term describes learning from the experiences of other people?

Conflict in Groups

The counselor can use many strategies to facilitate the resolution of **interpersonal conflict in the group setting**. First, the counselor needs to approach all conflicts as if they are a therapeutic opportunity from which group members can learn. Conflict has a way of bringing issues to the surface and inspiring insight; therefore, the counselor should approach conflict with an attitude of curiosity and exploration.

It is essential to focus on the present when doing this in the group. Often, conflict among two or more group members is representative of something else, but that something else cannot be discovered without exploring what is happening in the moment. Counselors should follow certain steps to make the most of conflict:

1. The counselor should first call attention to the conflict and bring it into the present.

2. The counselor should then encourage each party to consider their individual experiences of the conflict.

3. Group members should be asked to offer their observations and feedback about the conflict.

4. The counselor should guide the parties while they work through the conflict, after which the group processes how it went and what they learned from it.

Group counselors should not let conflict go to waste. Each conflict presents a learning opportunity for group members to not only gain insight into their behaviors but also to learn how to work through conflict in a healthy way.

Counselors must recognize and address harmful group behaviors and intervene if members do not. Often, that intervention includes pointing out the person's behavior and exploring it. This intervention shows everyone that the counselor values the cohesiveness of the group by enforcing group rules and protecting members. If the behaviors violate group rules, then the group must decide whether to enforce the rules and determine the consequences. One method of intervention is blocking. In **blocking**, the group counselor immediately stops a member's behavior if it is

- inappropriate,
- counterproductive, and/or
- harmful to others.

After stopping the behavior, the counselor references the group rules and the reason for blocking the member's behavior. If the member violates the group's rules, the counselor may defer to the group to determine what to do about the member.

For example, if the group decides that name calling is not allowed and a member calls another member an inappropriate name, the counselor should immediately stop the group and block the offending member from continuing.

Unfortunately, a counselor has no power to regulate the behaviors and interactions of members outside of the group; however, part of establishing group rules would include every member agreeing to confidentiality and the way in which people interact outside of the group. If a member violates the agreed-upon rules, then it would be appropriate to address that in the group and let the group decide whether that person is allowed to continue as a member. Additionally, the counselor may speak to members one-on-one, but the most effective interventions occur within the group.

QUICK REVIEW QUESTIONS

11. A group member begins shouting at another member, so the counselor intervenes to stop the behavior. What method is the counselor using?

12. What is a benefit of conflict in the group?

Answer Key

1. A closed group has a start and end date and does not permit new members to join once the group starts.

2. Process groups help members address challenges by focusing on the interaction among group members.

3. Structured activities are beneficial in a group because they promote stability and trust in the group process and keep sessions predictable.

4. The terms *facilitators* or *chairpersons* describe mutual aid group leaders.

5. The term *linking* describes when counselors connect what one member says or experiences to the experiences of another member to establish a connection, empathy, or understanding.

6. In self-disclosure, a counselor shares personal experiences for a therapeutic purpose.

7. The forming stage of the group process is the start of the group and the time during which members begin introducing themselves.

8. Most of the therapeutic work is accomplished in the performing stage of the group process.

9. The term *interaction* describes the interpersonal engagement among group members.

10. The term *vicarious* learning describes learning from the experiences of other people.

11. The counselor is using blocking, wherein the group counselor stops a member's behavior if it is inappropriate, counterproductive, or harmful.

12. Conflict offers a learning opportunity for group members.

9 Professional Practice

Multicultural Counseling

Cultural Sensitivity

Culture refers to the collective behaviors and beliefs characteristic of a particular group, be they ethnic, social, or religious. Culture includes the shared values, language, and religion of the people living in a location or region. It also includes how people feed, clothe, and shelter themselves. Shared traits include

- norms of behavior (greetings and interactions on a day-to-day level);
- values (the moral beliefs and codes that guide a culture's textual and subtextual behavior); and
- language (cultural communication, including through formal language, slang, and colloquialisms).

Some cultures view the rest of the world through the lens of **ethnocentrism**, the belief that one's culture is superior to others, and those other cultures are judged by the former's values and assumptions. **Cultural bias** is a phenomenon whereby a people's worldview is informed by their own culture, and they therefore perceive the rest of the world through that lens.

Cultural bias impacts interpersonal relationships, including therapeutic relationships, especially when it comes to practicing nonjudgment and empathy. Competent counselors will practice self-awareness regarding their cultural biases and take steps to reduce these so they do not interfere with the therapeutic relationships they have with clients.

Additionally, cultural bias can influence a counselor's diagnosis of a client. Cultural bias provides a lens through which the counselor views a client's behavior, thereby preventing the counselor from seeing the client's concerns through the client's unique experiences.

Multicultural issues play a significant role in mental health and can affect

- the way people think about mental health issues,
- the causes for mental health issues,

 HELPFUL HINT

Cultural bias is evident in research: most psychological research has been conducted using White, middle-class participants. Therefore, the results do not reflect or apply to the experiences of people of other populations.

- seeking treatment,
- appropriate diagnosis and treatment,
- recovery, and
- a client's preferences for and expectations of a counselor.

Culture can also impact internal and external stigmas related to mental health. Cultural issues also influence family relationships, friendships, and social support networks, and define what constitutes socially acceptable behavior. Counselors must educate themselves about the potential multicultural issues they may encounter with clients. A culturally competent counselor asks clients about their own cultural perspectives and understands how important cultural perspectives are to them.

> **HELPFUL HINT**
>
> In some cases, counselors must be prepared to acknowledge that a client would be better served by working with another counselor who is more able to meet the client's cultural needs.

QUICK REVIEW QUESTIONS

1. What term describes the collective behaviors and beliefs that are characteristic of a particular group?

2. What term describes the belief that one's culture is superior to others?

What Is Multicultural Counseling?

In **multicultural counseling**, issues of culture and identity are openly addressed as concerns how they impact a client's functioning. When clients present for therapy, they often focus on the symptoms they experience in an effort to fix them; however, in multicultural counseling, a counselor will redirect to further explore issues such as

- race,
- ethnicity,
- family,
- religion,
- socioeconomic status,
- environment, and
- identity.

Multicultural counseling explores how those factors contribute to a client's symptoms. It also considers how those cultural factors function as risk or protective factors. Multicultural counselors might also discuss with clients how they view therapy and what their expectations are for the therapeutic process.

Culture impacts the way people experience mental health issues. It is therefore also appropriate to ask clients who say they are depressed how they experience depression and how the cultural factors that impact them most play a role in what they experience.

For example, a client might report experiencing depression as sadness, fatigue, loss of appetite, and a desire to socially isolate. Perhaps the client feels a family expectation to not feel depressed because the family comes from a culture that does not believe depression is a mental health issue or that it requires treatment. The family's invalidation of the client's depressive symptoms may be a contributing factor to the client's treatment plan in addition to addressing the symptoms of depression.

Multicultural competence is demonstrated by counselors who

- regularly practice self-awareness regarding their own cultural bias,
- pursue knowledge of other cultures, and
- can interact effectively and respectfully with people from different cultural backgrounds.

Counselors must continually pursue multicultural competence. For example, a non-Native counselor might live in a state with a significant Native American client population. That counselor should network with counselors in the Native American community to learn about available resources and how to integrate appropriate Native American concepts or ideas in treatment.

Multicultural competence also requires a degree of cultural humility, especially when the counselor is not immersed in the client's culture. Using the Native American population as an example, a White counselor might ask a Native American client about his tribal affiliations and how important that connection is to him. The counselor might also ask the client how he feels about discussing his personal issues with a non-Native counselor. A multicultural counselor will be able to have that conversation respectfully and honestly while inviting the client to discuss cultural issues of importance to him.

The **emic perspective** is a way of learning about and perceiving culture by becoming a part of that culture. Taking this perspective can lead to a more in-depth understanding of the values and beliefs inherent to a culture in a way that an outsider cannot perceive.

The **etic perspective** is a way of learning about and perceiving culture from the outside of that culture. This perspective enables a person to acquire knowledge and to answer questions about a culture but often does not go deeper than a superficial understanding.

The **transcultural perspective** is an approach to counseling that references five dimensions:

1. cultural knowledge
2. understanding power, privilege, and oppression
3. positionality and self-reflexivity
4. partnership
5. cultural competence

A culturally competent counselor understands that a client may already experience hardship due to cultural issues and seeks to understand the client's cultural perspectives on issues related to counseling.

Counselors using a transcultural perspective will explore culture on the client's terms and discuss what it means for the counseling process. Counselors understand that clients are the experts on their own lives, experiences, and struggles.

The **Association for Multicultural Counseling and Development (AMCD)** is a professional counseling organization dedicated to providing professional development for counselors to improve cultural competence. The AMCD also advocates for human rights and policies to enhance cultural diversity within the counseling profession.

QUICK REVIEW QUESTIONS

3. What perspective refers to learning about and perceiving culture by becoming a part of that culture?

4. What perspective refers to learning about and perceiving culture from the outside of that culture?

Considerations in Multicultural Counseling

A multicultural counselor practices the basic skills and core attributes of counseling (genuineness, congruence, nonjudgmental stance, positive regard) and keeps sessions focused on clients and their needs. Additionally, counselors pursue knowledge of cultural issues by learning about the populations within their community that they may encounter in a therapeutic setting. This means that they learn about the general values, beliefs, and behavioral norms of each group. Acquisition of knowledge leads to awareness of

- the counselor's own cultural biases,
- the counselor's attitudes toward people of different cultural groups, and
- the attitudes of various cultural groups toward each other.

Acquiring knowledge enables the counselor to put knowledge and awareness into practice with clients by

- asking about cultural issues during the assessment process, and
- creating a safe environment for the client to discuss cultural issues.

The counselor can further demonstrate knowledge about cultural differences by drawing attention to the differences between the counselor and the client and seeking understanding about how culture influences a client's mental health.

Psychologist Charles Gilbert-Wrenn drew attention to the culturally encapsulated counselor. **Culturally encapsulated counselors** are counselors who

- look at the world and other people only through their own cultural lens,
- do not venture outside that lens,
- ignore anything contrary to that lens,
- treat clients as if they can all be treated the same way, and
- view themselves as free of bias and are therefore not open to learning.

To avoid becoming culturally encapsulated, the counselor must practice and demonstrate respect for and acceptance of diversity. The first way to do this is to recognize the various aspects of diversity that affect people.

The **RESPECTFUL counseling** acronym provides a useful framework for counselors to approach multicultural issues. Each of the letters represents areas of diversity within people. This model can serve as a template for discussing issues during assessment or throughout the counseling process:

- **R**eligious/spiritual issues
    - Does the client hold religious or spiritual beliefs? Why or why not?
    - How do those beliefs or lack thereof influence the client? Are they important to the client?
- **E**conomic class issues
    - What is the client's experience with socioeconomic class?
    - How has this socioeconomic experience affected the client's life, worldview, and choices?
- **S**exual identity issues
    - How does the client identify sexually? Is this important to the client?
    - How has this identity affected the client's life, relationships, and family?
- **P**sychological developmental issues
    - Did the client have any developmental or psychological issues during childhood that had a positive or negative impact?
    - Did the client get treatment for any of these issues?
    - How did the experience impact the client?
- **E**thnic/racial identity issues
    - How does the client identify ethnically/racially?
    - How has this identification shaped the client's values and beliefs?
    - Has the client encountered discrimination? How has that impacted the client's life?
- **C**hronological issues
    - How old is the client? What is the client's developmental stage?
    - How were previous developmental stages resolved?
    - What impact does age have on the client's life now?
- **T**rauma/threats to well-being
    - Does the client have a history of trauma?
    - What does the client experience in terms of the effects of trauma?
    - How does that trauma influence the client's perception of herself and others?
    - How does it impact the client's relationships?
- **F**amily issues
    - How does the client define family?
    - How does the client describe his family of origin?
    - How are those relationships now?
    - How does family influence the client's choices and identity?

- **U**nique physical issues
  - Does the client have different or limited physical abilities?
  - Are those differences something the client was born with or acquired?
  - How do the client's unique physical issues impact her life, functioning, and relationships?
- **L**anguage/location of residence issues
  - Is the client a native of the location in which he lives, or did he immigrate there from another city, state, or country?
  - Does the client have a non-Native immigration status?
  - Does the client speak a second language?
  - Is English the client's first or second language?
  - How do these issues and experiences impact the client?

QUICK REVIEW QUESTIONS

5. What term describes counselors who see the world and other people only through their own cultural lens and are not open to learning?

6. How can a counselor avoid becoming culturally encapsulated?

Specific Cultural Groups

Every client who presents for therapy is a unique individual, and each session with that client will be unique. Counselors should check their assumptions about clients—whether based on cultural bias or any other preconceived ideas—at the counseling office door. By maintaining a client-focused approach to therapy and adopting the core attributes of a counselor, one can approach each session with each client with an open, nonjudgmental mind.

Counselor self-examination is a practice of consistent self-reflection whereby counselors examine their own cultural diversity, attitudes, beliefs, and values, and how those influence how they interact with clients. Several concepts aid in self-examination and working with clients from different cultural backgrounds:

- **White privilege** refers to the unearned social status and advantages held by White people.
  - For example, White characters and figures generally have more widespread positive representation in the media than do people of other races. Perhaps a White child sees more characters or toys that look like him than would a Black, Latino, or Asian child.
  - This disparity can be harmful to individuals who are not White, as they will not grow up and live with similar experiences.
- **Racial microaggressions** are small behaviors and messages that occur in everyday situations and are characterized by bias toward a marginalized group.

- They include questions, comments, and actions.
- They can be both intentional and unintentional.
- One example would be to presume that an individual is dangerous because of her race, ethnicity, or gender; for instance, a pedestrian crosses the street to avoid a person of a different race.

- The term *model minority* describes myths that are commonly associated with Americans of Asian descent.
  - This can include the idea that children of Asian descent are smarter than other children, more musically inclined than others, and pushed harder by their parents than are other children.
  - These seemingly positive stereotypes might be downplayed or considered less offensive or harmful than negative stereotypes about education or ability.
  - Stereotypes associated with positive attributes can be just as harmful to the individual as negative stereotypes.

- **Unconscious bias** refers to the attitudes and stereotypes people do not consciously realize they have about others.
  - Unconscious bias results in behaviors that can be interpreted as offensive.
  - Education and self-reflection can help bring unconscious bias into the conscious mind so the counselor can reduce it.

Counselors should also be aware of **historical hostility** and **minority racial identity development (MRID)**. According to MRID, trauma is passed from one generation to the next. The following are all vehicles for historical trauma:

- how a group of people feels about themselves
- how a group views others
- how the group perceives systems
- how the group interacts with other people and systems

These attitudes, values, beliefs, and behaviors can be passed through generations. Groups of people who have been subjected to hostility, oppression, and discrimination throughout history carry the trauma of those experiences throughout the subsequent generations within their families.

The MRID model is a framework that explains the various stages groups go through to develop their cultural identities. It includes four stages that range from devaluing their identities to developing confident identities as members of historically marginalized communities.

Cultural groups often contain more **within-group differences** than **between-group differences**. For example, there are distinct differences between collectivist and individualist cultures; however, within the collectivist culture, there will be even more differences.

Within-group differences are even visible within families. Therefore, even if a counselor knows someone from a particular cultural group, that does not mean the next person she meets from that group will hold the same values, beliefs, and behaviors.

QUICK REVIEW QUESTIONS

7. What term describes small, everyday behaviors and messages that are characterized by bias toward a marginalized group?

8. What model argues that trauma passes from one generation to the next?

Gender Issues

Culturally competent counselors also recognize diversity regarding gender. They must demonstrate knowledge of and sensitivity to gender orientation and issues pertaining to gender. Congruence, unconditional positive regard, and empathy are important during sessions with lesbian, gay, bisexual, transgender, queer, intersex, agender, and questioning (LGBTQIA+) clients:

Gender refers to a person's subjective experience of gender, which may or may not be congruent with the gender assigned to that person at birth. Gender characteristics may fall within a range of masculinity and femininity. A person's identified gender will impact that person's gender roles and gender identity:

Gender issues can refer to a variety of experiences, including

- gender orientation;
- gender identity;
- gender dysphoria;
- how to talk to family about gender;
- discrimination at school or work; and
- navigating intimate/romantic relationships.

Gender socialization is the process individuals undergo when learning and conditioning themselves to the societal expectations and attitudes of their gender. Gender socialization is a lifelong process that can impact a person's beliefs, thoughts, feelings, and behaviors. Early socialization is most often shaped by parents, caregivers, and others within the family of origin. As a child grows up, socialization is further shaped by friends, school, the media, and the community.

Gender role conflict occurs when people are in a rigid or restrictive environment that leads them to devalue themselves or restrict how they express themselves. These individuals are unable to live as their true selves in their environment, which is harmful and distressing.

QUICK REVIEW QUESTIONS

9. What term describes the process individuals undergo when learning and conditioning themselves to the societal expectations and attitudes of their gender?

10. What conflict can occur when people are in a rigid or restrictive environment that leads them to devalue themselves or restrict how they express themselves?

Professional Development

Continuing Education

There are multiple education and training opportunities for personal and professional growth for SUD professionals. Useful organizations and their examples are outlined in the Table 9.1.

TABLE 9.1. Organizations Offering Education, Training, and Professional Development

TYPE OF ORGANIZATION	EXAMPLES	FUNCTIONS
Government agencies	• Substance Abuse and Mental Health Services Administration (SAMHSA) • National Institute on Drug Abuse (NIDA)	• monitors nationwide needs and trends • provides resources for education and training (publications, webinars, and reading materials)
National organizations	• Recovery Institute • American Addiction Centers • Addiction Technology Transfer Center (ATTC) Network	• focuses on substance use, mental health treatment, and efficacy of treatment • offers training, continuing education, updates on current trends, and resources for information sharing
Professional organizations	• NAADAC, the Association for Addiction Professionals	• offers resources for professional literature • coordinates the newest research • helps professionals access information sources for current trends in the SUD field • offers conferences and online meetings to keep updated on SUD counseling news and skills

Substance use disorder counselors are licensed by state. Each state determines the number of **continuing education** hours (including hours specific to ethics or cultural competency) required to maintain a license, which helps professionals set training and professional development goals.

States maintain a list of continuing education providers approved by that state. Some of these continuing education providers are private or nonprofit entities that offer education and training online and in person.

Personal training and professional development go beyond attending and accruing continuing education. Even after counselors are licensed, working with

DID YOU KNOW?

The ATTC Network also has regional centers that tailor resources for a specific region of the country based on the needs of that region and provides networking among SUD professionals.

a **supervisor** can help them examine their skills and determine areas that need improvement. Typical personal areas of improvement might include

- cultural humility,
- reducing bias,
- building advocacy skills, and
- addressing compassion fatigue and burnout.

Supervision and consultation with peers can also reveal areas in which a counselor would like to receive training, such as intervention skills or learning how to facilitate a new type of group. **Client feedback** can also provide insight. Some agencies distribute client feedback forms or evaluations at certain times of the year and encourage clients to discuss the positive—and negative—aspects of their treatment. Counselors may also invite clients to give feedback during a termination session.

Evaluating **client trends** within the agency or community may also inspire a counselor to pursue further training. For example, the agency might have experienced an increase in the number of clients who are going through medication-assisted treatment with buprenorphine. In this case, counselors may seek additional training so they can modify their approach to clients and the intervention methods used. This applies to new populations as well. For example, the community may have experienced a growth in the number of immigrants in the community. A counselor may seek education to learn more about that immigrant group and the kinds of issues the people in that group face to proactively become culturally competent.

Learning **evidence-based practice methods** and applying them to client treatment plans is a vital part of ethical substance use treatment. Another aspect of providing ethical services is to ensure that a counselor is competently delivering those evidence-based practices. Counselors who wish to use interventions such as Acceptance and Commitment Therapy (ACT) or specialized cognitive behavioral therapy (CBT) techniques should pursue education and training to ensure they are delivering evidence-based practices proficiently.

Counselors should always seek to improve their skills, and a professional development plan that includes both personal and professional goals can help. The plan may include topics to pursue for continuing education credits, skills to develop based on feedback from clients or supervisors, and personal goals that keep the counselor motivated to continue working in the substance use treatment profession.

QUICK REVIEW QUESTIONS

11. Who determines how many continuing education hours a counselor must obtain to remain licensed?

12. Who can help counselors examine their skills and determine areas that need improvement?

Self-Assessment

Counselors must continually assess their **competency** to work with a specific client through a process of self-awareness and objective evaluation. Choosing to work with a client when not qualified to do so violates professional ethics and could potentially harm the client:

- Counselors must be honest about the education and training they have received.
- Counselors should pursue continuing education and additional training to keep up with best practices.
- When meeting a client for the first time, counselors must objectively evaluate whether they are qualified to work with the client based on the client's presenting problem.

Being forthcoming about training and education usually applies to certain interventions with clients. For example, counselors who have not received training and certification to perform eye movement desensitization and reprocessing (EMDR) must disclose this to clients who request EMDR and offer another method of therapy or refer the client to someone who is trained in this intervention.

Self-evaluation about competency to work with clients is more complicated. For example, if a client presents with a severe eating disorder and the counselor is not trained in working with eating disorders, this must be disclosed, and the client should be referred to someone who is qualified. Consultation with a supervisor can help counselors evaluate their effectiveness and competencies, including creating plans for professional development.

QUICK REVIEW QUESTION

13. A client recovering from alcohol use disorder wants to learn about DBT skills with a SUD counselor who is not trained in that intervention. What should the counselor do?

Clinical Supervision and Consultation

A prominent adage among counselors is, "When in doubt, consult." Counselors who work in community mental health clinics or organizations have access to an on-site supervisor, clinic director, or someone who acts as the senior counseling professional. **Supervision and consultation** are not just for inexperienced counselors; they provide support at all levels of the counseling profession. A counselor should seek supervision or consultation in specific situations:

- difficulties with client assessment, diagnosis, and treatment planning
- when a client's progress appears to stagnate
- when a client is in crisis
- when presented with an ethical situation
- when faced with a court order or other legal issue

Documented evidence that additional help was requested with an incident is a significant benefit of seeking supervision and consulting with a colleague when dealing with ethical or client issues. In legal situations, this documentation can act as a level of protection and ensure that proper procedures are followed.

When consulting with a supervisor or colleague within the organization that employs a counselor, client confidentiality should be honored, but those consultations tend to fall under the confidentiality exception that clients agree to via informed consent. Counselors in private practice who establish a consultation relationship with another colleague should also disclose to clients the potential for consultation and explain how the counselor will keep the client's information confidential.

Consultation and supervision should be limited to issues pertaining to the counseling process, not gossip or disclosure of client information that is not relevant to treatment.

QUICK REVIEW QUESTION

14. Does the director of a clinic ever need to consult with others when dealing with clients?

Self-Care

Being a counselor can be a challenging, stressful job. Counselors often work with clients who are dealing with illness, death, or financial hardship. The emotional toll of managing these clients can be immense.

At the same time, counselors may also have to navigate complex systems like hospitals, insurance companies, and government agencies. The impact of these stressful situations cannot be underestimated.

Because of these strains, counselors should not overlook their own **self-care**. The first step in practicing self-care is practicing **self-awareness**. Understanding one's limits and the signs of strain can let the counselor know when it's appropriate to engage in self-care.

Counselors who work with clients who have experienced traumatic events are subject to **secondary trauma**, a condition that mimics the symptoms of PTSD. Although less severe than PTSD, secondary trauma interferes with the counselor's ability to function. Furthermore, when stress is left unattended for too long, counselors can suffer from burnout. **Burnout** is one of the primary reasons counselors leave the profession. Signs of exhaustion, stress, and burnout can include

- increased anxiety,
- worrying about clients after hours,
- taking work home,
- difficulty concentrating,
- sleep disturbances,
- emotional lability,

 **DID YOU KNOW?**

Counselors cannot serve clients well if they are not taking good care of themselves. In fact, counselors who do not practice self-care become more at risk of harming their clients either through ignorance or negligence.

- social isolation, and
- increased irritability.

Counselors should develop proactive practices for self-care and self-awareness. This may include regularly scheduled activities to promote health and happiness. There are many ways a counselor can fulfill the goal of being healthy and happy:

- routine exercise
- eating a well-balanced diet
- getting adequate sleep
- enjoying hobbies
- relaxing
- spending time with friends and family
- refraining from overuse of alcohol and/or other substances

The counselor should also set physical and emotional boundaries with clients and be willing to ask for assistance when confronted with unmanageable tasks. A crucial boundary for counselors is the one between work and personal life. While counselors should check in with themselves, it is also recommended that counselors in an agency setting check in with each other. Counselors should also talk with spouses, partners, or family members about signs of stress and let them know how to point out those signs when they notice them. Sometimes others will notice the signs of stress before the counselor does.

QUICK REVIEW QUESTIONS

15. Counselors who work with clients who have experienced trauma are at risk of what condition that mimics PTSD?

16. When counselors do not manage their stress, they are at risk for what?

Answer Key

1. The term *culture* refers to the collective behaviors and beliefs that are characteristic of a particular group.

2. The term *ethnocentrism* describes the belief that one's culture is superior to others.

3. The emic perspective is a way of learning about and perceiving culture by becoming a part of that culture.

4. The etic perspective is a way of learning about and perceiving culture from the outside of that culture.

5. The term *culturally encapsulated counselors* describes counselors who see the world and other people only through their own cultural lens and are not open to learning.

6. To avoid becoming culturally encapsulated, the counselor must practice and demonstrate respect for and acceptance of diversity.

7. The term *racial microaggressions* describes small behaviors and messages that occur in everyday situations and are characterized by bias toward a marginalized group.

8. According to the minority racial identity development (MRID) model, trauma is passed from one generation to the next.

9. The term *gender socialization* describes the process individuals undergo when learning and conditioning themselves to the societal expectations and attitudes of their gender.

10. Gender role conflict can occur when people are in a rigid or restrictive environment that leads them to devalue themselves or restrict how they express themselves.

11. Each state determines the number of continuing education hours required to maintain a license.

12. Clients (through feedback) and supervisors can help counselors examine their skills and determine areas that need improvement.

13. The counselor should explain that she is not trained in dialectical behavior therapy (DBT) and refer the client to a colleague who is trained in that intervention.

14. Yes. Clinical supervision and consultation apply to all levels of the counseling profession.

15. Secondary trauma is a condition that mimics the symptoms of post-traumatic stress disorder (PTSD). Secondary trauma can affect counselors who work with clients who have experienced trauma.

16. Counselors risk burnout when stress is left unattended for too long.

10 Ethics and Documentation

Documentation

Counselors must create and maintain documentation appropriate for each aspect of the counseling process in compliance with state law, for insurance reimbursement, and to document client progress.

Creating and Maintaining Documentation

The counselor is responsible for maintaining accurate, objective documentation of the client's care. Accurate documentation has obvious benefits for the client's care, but it is also important for the counselor. Counselors can use accurate, timely documentation to prove they have complied with standards of care and practice, which is important for professional advancement and a possible legal defense. Counselors should

- only document facts—opinions do not belong in the official documentation;
- record details of the client visit as soon as possible after the visit;
- always record if the client agrees or refuses case management, interventions, or other types of care;
- record all communication with people or organizations involved in the client's care, including the client's family, medical providers, employer, and insurance companies;
- document the care plan, including assessments, interventions, evaluations, and the outcomes of each;
- document all instances of consultation about the client with supervisors and colleagues, including what was discussed and with whom, and recommendations;
- document modifications of the care plan, the rationale for the changes, and whether the client agreed;

- include all legal documents, including advance directives and informed consent forms; and
- document discharge plans and client education.

Many organizations require documentation and regular review by the clinic director to ensure compliance with state law. There are two types of notes taken by the counselor that are added to the client's documentation: progress notes and process notes.

Progress notes are the official record of a session and tend to follow a **SOAP note** format:

- <u>s</u>ubjective information about the client and what the client is experiencing
- <u>o</u>bjective findings from assessments or observation
- <u>a</u>ssessments that include findings of the client's diagnosis or evaluations of how the client is progressing in the treatment plan
- <u>p</u>lans that include next steps (therapeutic and otherwise)

Progress notes may be shared with others:

- Insurance companies receive progress notes when determining reimbursement.
- Progress notes may be included in requests from other providers for client records.
- Progress notes are subject to inspection by agency quality control personnel and government regulators.

When clients request a copy of their records, these are the notes that are included. When the courts request records, these are the notes that are subject to a subpoena.

HELPFUL HINT

When writing progress notes, keep them clinical and focused on the client's treatment plan.

The second type of notes, **process notes**, are considered a counselor's private notes. Process notes are not required to be part of the client's official record. Process notes generally include

- hypotheses,
- theories,
- the counselor's thoughts regarding client treatment, and
- questions to address during supervision.

Process notes are considered privileged and are not generally accessible to the client or other parties except in certain circumstances:

- If a client is involved in a legal action, it is possible that the counselor's records, notes, and documentation will be shared with the court.
- When a counselor leaves an agency, the documentation stays with the agency; the counselor's notes will influence how future providers interact with that client.

Not all counselors use process notes. Still, counselors should consider the impact of every piece of documentation concerning the client. There are certain times when the counselor should **review client records**:

- When starting with a new client, reviewing records can provide relevant historical information about the client's issues. These can be requested as part of the intake process or by asking the client to bring the records to the first session.

- When taking a referral from another counselor, the client's records can be helpful for understanding which therapeutic interventions worked and which did not. These can be requested as part of the referral process.

- During a quarterly review process—often required by state law or for funding purposes—client records are subject to review. For example, many agencies that provide substance abuse treatment services must conduct client reviews every thirty or sixty days to determine the client's progress in treatment. It is also considered best practice to review client records quarterly to determine if the present course of treatment is appropriate, to evaluate client engagement, and to ensure that documentation is compliant with state law.

- Before discharging a client, the records must be reviewed to create a discharge summary.

QUICK REVIEW QUESTIONS

1. Which type of notes are considered the official record of a session?

2. What term describes a counselor's private notes?

Payment, Fees, and Insurance Benefits

Counselors should be aware of payment, fee, and insurance benefit issues. Agencies and clinics generally have staff or departments to address these issues. It is best practice to allow the administrative staff to handle billing and insurance so that any challenges do not infringe on the therapeutic relationship.

However, to be able to answer questions and navigate the treatment process, counselors must be aware of the policies governing care:

- Insurance providers decide how many sessions are appropriate for a particular diagnosis.

- Payments, fees, and insurance benefits also determine session length, frequency, and mode of delivery.

- Insurance companies do not reimburse counselors for the time it takes to complete documentation.

- Some insurance companies will not provide reimbursement for therapies that are not evidence based; some even list which therapeutic interventions are acceptable.

DID YOU KNOW?

If counselors provide therapy they are not trained to do, the insurance company can refuse to provide reimbursement.

- The insurance company may also dictate the mode of service delivery that is acceptable for reimbursement.

QUICK REVIEW QUESTIONS

3. Who decides how many sessions are appropriate for a particular diagnosis?

4. Are counselors reimbursed for time spent on documentation?

Health Care Laws and Legislation

Counselors should be familiar with the important elements of several pieces of health care legislation.

The **Affordable Care Act (ACA)**, popularly known as "Obamacare," changed behavioral health care coverage. Key elements of the ACA include the following:

- Insurance companies cannot deny coverage due to a preexisting condition or charge more because of the condition or based on gender.
- Adults who cannot obtain health insurance through a job may remain on their parents' policies until the age of twenty-six.
- Essential health benefits must be covered, including those for mental health and substance use disorders.

Congress passed the **Health Insurance Portability and Accountability Act (HIPAA)** in 1996. HIPAA allows workers to continue or transfer health coverage when they change or lose a job. HIPAA also focuses on how health care information is handled.

The HIPAA Privacy Rule and the HIPAA Security Rule, developed by the Department of Health and Human Services, both protect the privacy and security of certain health care information. This **protected health information (PHI)** includes

- demographic information, such as name, address, phone numbers, SSN;
- information included in the medical record; and
- payment history.

The counselor must follow HIPAA privacy and security policies. PHI must be safeguarded, released, and disposed of in the manner described by HIPAA. Only personnel who require clients' PHI should have access to that information for treatment or administrative purposes, such as billing and scheduling.

When medical records are no longer needed (a period usually specified by state regulations), they must be destroyed so that the information cannot be retrieved.

PHI can only be released under specific circumstances:

- A **Privacy Rule Authorization form**, which allows the provider to release information to the parties included in the form, must be signed by the client.

HELPFUL HINT

HIPAA's Security Rule establishes rules pertaining to the transfer of electronic records. The Privacy Rule sets national standards for the protection of health care information.

- Clients may also authorize the provider to release their PHI to others, usually family members.
- PHI can be shared within the health care team only when it is considered relevant to treatment; it should never be shared with anyone who is not directly involved in the client's care.

Counselors may also need to share PHI with outside government agencies:

- State law specifies that the practitioner must warn authorities if harm (e.g., exploitation or abuse) to the client is suspected.
- If counselors are aware of HIPAA violations and do not report them, they and the organization at fault can be held liable.

Annual HIPAA training is a component of most mental health providers. This ensures that faxing, internet communications, and phone delivery of clients' health care records, including personal notes and billing, are properly handled.

The **Mental Health Parity and Addiction Equity Act (MHPAEA)** was enacted in 2008 to fill in the gaps in the Mental Health Parity Act of 1996 (MHPA). The MHPAEA outlines the following requirements:

- Insurance plans that offer mental health care benefits must manage them as they manage medical/surgical benefits.
  - The insurance company cannot place limits on mental health benefits that it does not place on medical/surgical benefits.
  - These rules also apply to substance use disorders.
- The MHPAEA specifies limitations on how insurance companies can cover mental health and substance use disorder benefits.

Agencies or counselors who provide services to clients with substance abuse issues must also abide by **42 CFR Part 2**, a federal law that offers strict confidentiality rules for clients with substance use disorders. It was originally written for agencies that receive federal funding to provide substance abuse treatment only, and those organizations and providers are not allowed to acknowledge that a person is a client at the organization.

In agencies and organizations that provide both mental health and substance abuse treatment, it is best practice to include the privacy provisions of 42 CFR Part 2 as part of the confidentiality policies.

 DID YOU KNOW?

Not every health insurance plan is required to offer mental health benefits under the MHPAEA; however, the ACA greatly extended insurance plan coverage and lists mental health care as an essential health benefit.

QUICK REVIEW QUESTIONS

5. Are substance use disorders covered by health insurance?

6. What law protects the privacy and security of certain health care information?

7. Is a client's payment history considered PHI?

Electronic Health Records

The **Health Information Technology for Economic and Clinical Health (HITECH) Act** was written to encourage the use of electronic health records (EHRs) and related technology. The Centers for Medicare and Medicaid Services (CMS) have several objectives for using EHRs:

- Electronic exchanges of summary of care: An **exchange of summary of care** (also referred to as a discharge summary) refers to the movement of a client from one setting to another. For example, the exchange of summary of care is used when a client is discharged from an inpatient to an outpatient facility.
- There is greater ease of sharing records with supervisors and other members of a client's care team.
- Documentation compliance is improved.
- Clients can access an online portal to check on appointments and reminders.

QUICK REVIEW QUESTION

8. What document is used when a client is discharged from an inpatient to an outpatient facility?

Ethics

Terms, Definitions, and Principles

Ethics are moral principles, values, and duties. Whereas laws are enforceable regulations set forth by the government, ethics are moral guidelines established and enforced formally or informally by peers, the community, and professional organizations. Ethics include norms and duties.

Norm is short for *normal*, a term used for a behavior or conduct that is valued and usually expected. Norms are also often described as aspirational ethical principles because they are not enforceable by law, but counselors aspire to the highest ethical standards to maintain trust between the public and their profession.

Duties are commitments or obligations to act in an ethical and moral manner. These fall under the minimum ethical standards and are usually part of the state regulations. Counselors can be held legally accountable for violating ethical standards.

Core ethical principles include autonomy, beneficence, nonmaleficence, justice, veracity, and fidelity:

- **Autonomy** is acknowledging that a client is a unique individual with the right to personal opinions, values, beliefs, and perspectives.
- **Beneficence** describes acting with the intent of doing the right thing or the most good. The counselor has an obligation to act in the best interest of the client, regardless of other competing interests.

- **Nonmaleficence** describes the intent to do no harm. This principle addresses the counselor's responsibility to keep the client from being harmed in the care setting.
- **Justice** can be considered fairness. The counselor should be fair to clients in counseling matters and regarding administrative issues.
- **Veracity** is the practice of complete truthfulness with clients and families.
- **Fidelity** concerns honoring promises or commitments made to a client.

QUICK REVIEW QUESTIONS

9. Moral principles, values, and duties refer to what?

10. Acting with the intent of doing the right thing or the most good is called what?

Nonmaleficence

Nonmaleficence is the principle of not doing harm. It requires counselors to consider the impact of their actions (and inaction). The potential for nonmaleficence in counseling includes referrals. (See Chapter 5 for more on referrals.) A counselor should refer a client to another provider if

- the client's treatment progress seems stagnant, and/or
- the counselor does not have the expertise to treat the client's particular condition.

While a counselor might have good intentions in wanting to continue working with a client, not referring a client when necessary can be harmful—another counselor might be able to help the client progress through issues more quickly.

Another example of nonmaleficence application in clinical practice is hospitalization, especially **mandatory psychiatric treatment**. Some states have a provision that stipulates people can be committed to psychiatric facilities against their will for a minimum period—often seventy-two hours—if they present a danger to themselves or others. While this may sound like a positive action to save someone's life, it must be considered whether that forced commitment will prove to be more harmful than helpful to the client.

For clients who show signs of being suicidal, proactive measures, such as developing a crisis plan, can be instrumental in providing them with the help they need without resorting to a potentially traumatic experience.

In any type of ethical dilemma, a counselor needs to balance state laws and agency policies with the principles of beneficence and nonmaleficence. Consultation and documentation are vital in these situations for the reasons previously noted.

QUICK REVIEW QUESTION

11. What is the principle of not doing harm?

Dual Relationships

The clinical therapeutic relationship requires the counselor to refrain from any type of **dual relationship** with clients. A dual relationship is when the counselor has both a counseling relationship with the client and a relationship outside the clinical setting.

Avoiding dual relationships reduces the chance of a counselor exploiting a client or conveying the perception of power and authority. For example, if a counselor has any type of personal relationship with a client outside of the treatment setting, it is unethical for the counselor to provide services to that client. In general, counselors should avoid

- any sexual or romantic relationship with former or current clients; and
- a counseling relationship with someone with whom the counselor had a previous sexual or romantic relationship.

Any counselor who becomes aware of another counselor engaged in dual relationships or of sexual harassment or exploitation is obligated to follow procedures for reporting the legal and ethical violation.

A dual relationship can also apply to business relationships. In some states, business relationships are permissible with clients; however, these relationships are still unethical. For example, if a client is a carpenter and the counselor needs work done on her home, it is unethical to hire that client as a carpenter. Business relationships such as these have the potential for exploitation and the expectation of favors.

QUICK REVIEW QUESTIONS

12. What term describes a counselor who has both a counseling relationship with the client and a relationship outside the clinical setting?

13. A counselor's ex-boyfriend wants to join a group that the counselor is facilitating. Is this considered a dual relationship?

Privacy

In the age of social media, privacy is of particular concern for counselors and clients. Clients may share personal information in a public forum, but it is unethical for a counselor to use social media, technology, or other resources to find information about clients without their written permission.

Social media privacy is also appropriate to address in group therapy. Group members may have access to information about other members. Group rules should stress the importance of both confidentiality and privacy.

Counselors consulting with supervisors or other care team members about the client should consider the client's privacy and only provide information relevant to the client's treatment plan.

Counselors should also avoid accepting gifts from clients except in cases of cultural or therapeutic significance. Gift exchanges can create confusion about the nature of the therapeutic relationship, and the counselor needs to consider that as well as the impact that nonacceptance could have on the client's well-being.

QUICK REVIEW QUESTION

14. Can a counselor use social media to find out information about a client?

Consent

Client **consent** is required for treatment. A client must provide **informed consent** in order for counselors to perform a treatment or procedure or if the client is going to take part in a research study. For informed consent to be valid, the counselor must cover key elements:

- description of procedures
- risks
- benefits
- alternatives

The counselor must also assess **client competency** to provide informed consent. A competent client understands

- the procedure or practice;
- the risk and benefits involved; and
- the possible consequences.

Finally, the client must acknowledge having provided consent. Most states have regulations for practices that include having a signed informed consent form for each client.

State regulations vary regarding the age of consent. The age of consent to sign informed consent forms ranges from fourteen to sixteen. Regardless of the legal age of consent, a good way to establish trust with adolescent clients or with clients unable to provide legal consent for themselves is to gain the client's assent for treatment. Obtaining **assent** means

- going through the entire informed consent process with the client;
- explaining the role of the counselor;
- making sure the client understands the therapeutic process; and
- ensuring that the client agrees to participate freely.

Obtaining assent helps establish trust with clients and engages them in the therapeutic process. This can be especially powerful for clients who may feel they are being coerced into treatment.

HELPFUL HINT

If the counselor decides it is appropriate to accept a gift, the reasoning should be documented.

DID YOU KNOW?

To remain valid, informed consent forms may need to be updated once per year.

HELPFUL HINT

To obtain assent, many counselors use a form similar to the informed consent form.

QUICK REVIEW QUESTIONS

15. What elements must the counselor cover for informed consent to be valid?

16. How can a counselor build trust with clients who are unable to provide informed consent?

Confidentiality

Confidentiality means that the counselor will keep the client's personal information confidential according to state and federal laws. The counselor must also explain to the client when and under what circumstances confidentiality may be broken. In general, confidentiality requires that counselors must not disclose client information to anyone not authorized by the client.

Confidentiality is a vital aspect of the counseling relationship and is protected not only by professional ethics but also by law. There are several **limits to confidentiality** that are usually explained in writing in the informed consent process:

- Client information will be shared with clinic personnel for record-keeping and billing purposes.
- Client information may be shared with a clinical supervisor or colleague for the purposes of consultation for the benefit of the client.
- Client records may need to be included in state or federal auditing procedures.
- Client information may be shared if the client expresses a desire to hurt themselves or someone else.
- Client records may be shared in the case of a medical emergency.
- Records may be shared if the client discloses having experienced (or perpetrated) abuse that falls under the requirements of mandated reporting.
- If the client brings someone else to the session and grants the counselor permission to waive confidentiality, client information may be shared.
- A court order may require a counselor to break confidentiality.

Counselors should abide by the principle of sharing the least amount of information needed to get the job done. Furthermore, it is best practice that any breaches of confidentiality be shared with the client either before or immediately after the breach, including what information was shared. Also, the counselor should document the incident, along with the personal information disclosed, in the client's records.

Social media and electronic communication should be considered risks for confidentiality breaches. Information posted on social media is not private, as the platform owners can access a person's data at any time. Therefore, counselors should be careful what they post about themselves on social media.

Some counselors use social media as a professional referral opportunity that includes a business page with how to contact them. However, connecting with clients as friends on social media is unethical. Also, communication with clients via social media is not recommended due to the confidentiality risks.

It is not ethical for counselors to look up clients on social media to learn more about them. Electronic communication may be used for setting appointments, but it is recommended to only use electronic communications for therapeutic purposes if that is part of an agency's protocols for conducting telehealth or distance counseling.

Communicating with clients on social media outside of the counseling relationship would ethically be considered a dual relationship unless it is conducted outside of the legal time allotted. States set the rules about this period; in some cases, a counselor may have to wait two to five years before engaging in a dual relationship with a client, and that includes social media friendships.

QUICK REVIEW QUESTIONS

17. A counselor alerts CPS when a client admits to offering his child drugs. Is this a breach of confidentiality?

18. A counselor tells her family the name of the celebrity whom she is treating for SUD. Is this a breach of confidentiality?

Legal Aspects of Counseling

Counselors are vulnerable to legal action. There are multiple situations that may result in legal system involvement, including

- disability evaluations;
- workers' compensation evaluations;
- workplace accommodations;
- school accommodations for children;
- custody disputes;
- divorce disputes;
- abuse and neglect cases of children, adults, people with disabilities, or older adults;
- use of therapeutic interventions that are not evidence-based or are unlawful;
- criminal cases involving mental illness or substance misuse (or abuse); and
- duty to warn cases.

Counselors must be aware of and understand

- state laws,
- regulations,
- standards of care,

- agency policies,
- the differences between subpoenas and court orders in their state, and
- the procedure for responding to subpoenas and court orders.

Consistent supervision and consultation on client cases, and thorough documentation of these, help protect the counselor by showing that policies and regulations were followed. Counselors should seek advice from a supervisor or legal representative in such cases. Agencies usually have policies for handling these situations, but legal requirements will determine how a counselor must respond to requests for information by attorneys.

Not every state requires a counselor to provide records to a subpoena. Furthermore, when presented with a request for client records by someone within the legal system, it is important to discuss this with the client and document what and how the information was shared. Therefore, two rules of best practice apply to protect counselors in legal situations:

1. If it is not documented, it never happened.
2. Consult, consult, consult.

Many clients are referred for treatment by courts or systems affiliated with the courts. For example, child protective services may require that families or individuals engage in services. Also, mental health courts and drug court programs are becoming more widespread as incarceration diversion efforts. In these cases, there are special considerations for documentation requirements and sharing information with the courts and the rest of the client's care team.

Counselors should take extra care during the informed consent process to not only meet the needs of the referring system but also protect the privacy and confidentiality of the client to preserve the therapeutic relationship.

 DID YOU KNOW?

Complaints against a counselor, including HIPAA violations, can be made against both the agency and the individual counselor; therefore, counselors should carry professional liability insurance to protect their interests and not rely on their employer to do so.

QUICK REVIEW QUESTIONS

19. How can counselors demonstrate adherence to policy and legal requirements?

20. What programs are an alternative to incarceration?

Answer Key

1. Progress notes are considered the official record of a session.
2. The term *process notes* describes a counselor's private notes.
3. Insurance providers decide how many sessions are appropriate for a particular diagnosis.
4. No, counselors are not reimbursed for time spent on documentation.
5. Yes. Under the Affordable Care Act (ACA), substance use disorder treatment is considered an essential health benefit and must be covered.

6. The Health Insurance Portability and Accountability Act (HIPAA) protects the privacy and security of certain health care information.

7. Yes. A client's payment history is considered protected health information (PHI).

8. An exchange of summary of care (or a discharge summary) is used when a client moves from one health care setting to another.

9. Moral principles, values, and duties refer to ethics.

10. Beneficence is acting with the intent of doing the right thing or the most good.

11. Nonmaleficence is the principle of not doing harm.

12. The term *dual relationship* describes when the counselor has both a counseling relationship with the client and a relationship outside the clinical setting.

13. Yes. Dual relationships include a counseling relationship with someone with whom the counselor had a previous sexual or romantic relationship.

14. It is unethical for a counselor to use social media to find information about clients without their written permission.

15. The counselor must describe the procedure and cover risks, benefits, and alternatives.

16. Gaining the client's assent can help build trust.

17. No. Client information may be shared if clients express a desire to hurt themselves or others, or if they disclose having experienced—or perpetrated—abuse that falls under the requirements of mandated reporting.

18. Yes. A counselor's family members are not entitled to information about clients, and protected health information (PHI) includes identifying information, such as names.

19. Consistent supervision and consultation on client cases and thorough documentation help protect counselors by showing that they followed policy and regulations.

20. Mental health courts and drug court programs exist as incarceration diversion efforts in many states.

11. Practice Test

1. Studies reveal that alcoholism has negative effects on interactions with a person's family, friends, and society. What is a counselor's primary responsibility when working with clients with a history of alcoholism?
   A) finding the point of origin of the drinking problem, formulating a diagnosis, and creating a viable treatment plan
   B) providing clients with addiction psychoeducation to help them understand how their addiction affects their loved ones
   C) encouraging clients to consider a family therapy program so every family member can receive help
   D) helping clients get their family, friends, and other associates to be supportive of their recovery efforts

2. Terry is about to complete his sixty-day inpatient treatment program for opioid abuse disorder. His clinical team recommends that he continue engaging in addiction treatment since this was his second time at the inpatient rehab. He is being referred to a higher level of care that depends on having a safe and sober home environment. He will attend treatment for six to eight hours each day. Terry lives with his wife, who doesn't use any substances, and their three children who range from six to nine years old. Terry has a great network of sober friends, including individuals with whom he attends Narcotics Anonymous. Which level of care would be an ideal fit for Terry?
   A) outpatient treatment
   B) detoxification
   C) partial hospitalization program
   D) aftercare programming

3. Which example of a peer support group would you recommend to a client who struggles with social support?
   A) volunteering at a local community center
   B) attending a Narcotics Anonymous meeting
   C) joining a support group for family members
   D) going to an educational session about addiction

4. Which of the following behaviors helps an ethical counselor stay informed of best practices?
   A) group supervision
   B) additional certifications
   C) case conferences
   D) continuing education courses

5. A new client reports struggling with "oxy." In the past two months, the client has tried twice to stop using but has been unsuccessful, experiencing severe muscle pain, anxiety, depression, nausea, and intense cravings. Which diagnosis would the counselor likely investigate?
   A) stimulant use disorder
   B) cannabis use disorder
   C) opioid use disorder
   D) sedative, hypnotic, or anxiolytic use disorder

165

6. You are working in an addiction treatment program and met with Nathan, who shared that he came to his appointment after his parents gave him an ultimatum. To continue supporting him financially, they want him to be in therapy and stop drinking. Nathan feels his drinking is sometimes a problem, but he does not think he needs to make any changes. He shared that he is only there to appease his parents. Which of the five stages of change is Nathan in?

   A) precontemplation
   B) contemplation
   C) preparation
   D) action

7. During your session with Nathan, you noticed that his motivation for treatment is external and coming from his parents. Although external motivation can be impactful, you know that internal motivation can be even more significant. Which therapeutic approach could you use to find sources of internal motivation?

   A) cognitive behavioral therapy
   B) behavioral therapy
   C) motivational interviewing
   D) solution-focused brief therapy

8. After eight weeks of working with you on his alcohol use, Nathan realizes that his drinking behaviors are hurting his work performance. This includes decreased focus, concentration, and feeling sick at work. Nathan has recently been open to talking about changes he can make to his behavior that would promote sobriety. Which of the five stages of change is Nathan in?

   A) contemplation
   B) preparation
   C) action
   D) maintenance

9. What is a behavioral change associated with drinking alcohol?

   A) motor impairment
   B) nausea and vomiting
   C) visual hallucinations
   D) auditory hallucinations

10. You are working in an addiction treatment program with Martha, who has been diagnosed with alcohol use disorder and binge eating disorder. You have had no exposure to eating disorder treatment since earning your degree three years ago. Which of the following should you do?

    A) talk to your supervisor about your competency with this client
    B) work with the client individually and focus on her addiction
    C) work with the client and research eating disorder treatment
    D) refer her to a colleague with more experience in eating disorder counseling

11. You work at an addiction treatment center providing group and individual counseling sessions and encourage your clients to consider attending a support group for people in recovery, by people in recovery. What group would you recommend to Jane, a twenty-nine-year-old female recovering from alcohol addiction?

    A) Narcotics Anonymous
    B) Alcoholics Anonymous
    C) your aftercare group
    D) a colleague's group session

12. A counselor is working with a client who has similar problems as several other clients. Which action is MOST appropriate for the counselor to take?

    A) let the client know she has problems that many others have
    B) try to learn if this client's problems have any significant differences
    C) talk about this situation with a coworker
    D) handle it like any other case

13. While conducting a case consultation, which of the following pieces of information can be omitted to protect the client's privacy?

    A) client's substance use history
    B) client's mental health concern
    C) client's age
    D) client's name

14. Which substance has the highest rate of abuse among adults in the United States?

    A) marijuana
    B) alcohol

C) opioids
D) cocaine

15. You are working in an outpatient addiction treatment center and believe there is a gap in your treatment program. Several clients at the center are military veterans. Some began using substances after their military service to cope with PTSD; others began to use heavily during active duty. What would be an effective method to address this treatment gap?
    A) develop psychoeducation groups
    B) refer to the VA for treatment
    C) increase individual sessions
    D) create a special-interest group for veterans

16. During an educational session with high school students on the dangers of drinking, the counselor asks them to wear modified goggles and then walk in a straight line. What is the purpose of this exercise?
    A) to show how alcohol affects decision-making skills
    B) to show how alcohol affects perceived vision
    C) to show how alcohol affects thought processes
    D) to show how alcohol affects judgment skills

17. Which of the following accurately describes quantitative research?
    A) It relies on data that can be measured.
    B) It is not intended to be applied to practice.
    C) It uses a small number of participants.
    D) It investigates how and why things happen.

18. You are meeting with a client who recently received a DWI. According to his paperwork, his charge is related to a zero tolerance law. What does this tell you about your client?
    A) He was caught drinking alcohol.
    B) He is under the legal age for drinking.
    C) He drove with a BAC over 0.00.
    D) He drove with a BAC over the legal limit.

19. You are working as a youth counselor in an after-school program. Your supervisor has provided you with a guide to your group sessions that includes a variety of topics, such as emotion regulation, healthy boundaries, and effective communication. After the group began, you learned that a close friend of several members recently died from an overdose. How would you proceed with the group?
    A) run a processing group that talks about grief
    B) briefly address the loss and continue as planned
    C) encourage those group members to talk privately
    D) have a psychoeducational group about drug use

20. You are meeting with a new client who is a teacher at your child's school. She has not taught your student, and your child is past the grade she teaches. What is an appropriate concern to discuss during her intake session?
    A) how to handle seeing each other in public
    B) concerns for your child's current teacher
    C) the school's attendance policy for students
    D) where the teacher can park for therapy

21. A counselor is meeting with a new client for the first time. Nader shares that he has never been in treatment and appears uncomfortable: he cannot sit still, is bouncing his leg, and says he is having trouble concentrating. The counselor takes a few moments to explain what Nader can expect from his session and how it can help guide the counselor's work with him. Which intervention is this?
    A) normalizing the client's experience
    B) validating the client's experience
    C) psychoeducation
    D) therapy road map

22. You are meeting with a new client for an intake interview at an outpatient addiction treatment program. While conducting the assessment, it becomes clear that the client is struggling with alcohol use and depressive symptoms. What is the BEST therapeutic strategy for this client?
    A) treat the client's addiction concerns and then address the depressive symptoms
    B) treat the client's depressive symptoms first, followed by addiction treatment
    C) treat the presenting addiction, then reassess for depressive symptoms

D) treat the addiction concerns and the mental health concerns at the same time

23. In all US states except Utah, what is the legal BAC limit for driving a motor vehicle?

    A) 0.02
    B) 0.04
    C) 0.06
    D) 0.08

24. What is the BEST way for an interviewer to secure reliable data and reduce the possibility of misunderstanding?

    A) use casual, undirected conversation, enabling interviewees to talk about themselves
    B) ask direct questions
    C) obtain the desired information from interviewees by putting them on the defensive
    D) explain to interviewees the information desired and the reasons for needing it

25. You are conducting an intake session with a new client at an IOP addiction counseling center. Clients are asked not to wear clothing referencing alcohol, such as a Bud Light T-shirt. How can you apprise the client of this policy?

    A) briefly touch on the policy during the intake session
    B) give her a printout instead of discussing the policy
    C) discuss the policy and ask if she has questions about it
    D) address it if the client comes to group wearing something restricted

26. Salma is a twenty-two-year-old female who began binge drinking during her second year of college. Her drinking then progressed into an alcohol use disorder. She left school for a year to attend an inpatient rehab program and focus on her recovery. As her outpatient addiction counselor, you have been working with her to develop an effective and realistic relapse prevention plan for when she returns to school. Which of the following should Salma include in her relapse prevention plan?

    A) only attend parties with a sober friend
    B) volunteer to be a designated driver for friends
    C) attend AA meetings regularly
    D) go to online courses to avoid campus

27. You have been working with a transgender woman, Tasha, throughout her transition. Tasha originally came to you with SUD, and throughout your time together she has been responsive to new coping skills and begun going to AA. She currently reports six months of sobriety and feeling "much better." Tasha has limited social support and has been working hard to make healthy connections with individuals in the LGBTQIA+ community. What treatment recommendations could you suggest to her?

    A) biweekly individual sessions with you
    B) medication-assisted therapy
    C) an LGBTQIA+ support group
    D) volunteering at a local youth center

28. In your work as a counselor, you gravitate toward a client-centered approach. This is evidenced by the fact that you do not judge clients for what they say during sessions and continue to support them despite your personal beliefs and opinions. Which of the following concepts are you using?

    A) congruence
    B) unconditional positive regard
    C) transference
    D) unbiased mindset

29. A counselor is leading an educational session for at-risk individuals. When discussing how substances affect behavior, an attendee asks how alcohol use would impact someone with depression. What is the MOST appropriate response?

    A) Alcohol can help people cope with depressive symptoms.
    B) Depressive symptoms worsen the effects of alcohol.
    C) Drinking alcohol can worsen depressive symptoms.
    D) Alcohol is not known to impact depressive symptoms.

30. You are meeting with a new client. Which topic should you be familiar with?
    A) payment, fee, and insurance benefit issues
    B) the client's availability
    C) your upcoming overtime schedules
    D) alternative office locations

31. You are running a group therapy session that focuses on relapse prevention skills for individuals in early recovery. Some group members have just completed an inpatient rehab program; others have recently relapsed. Some individuals will be in this group longer than others, and new members will be joining. Which therapeutic approach would work BEST for your group?
    A) motivational interviewing
    B) cognitive behavioral therapy
    C) solution-focused brief therapy
    D) behavioral therapy

32. One of your current clients sent you a friend request on social media. How should you proceed?
    A) block the request
    B) ignore the request
    C) wait until your next session
    D) consult with your supervisor

33. Which of the following can occur with polysubstance abuse?
    A) respiratory failure
    B) increased focus
    C) motor coordination
    D) gallbladder damage

34. You have been working with Sara, a seventeen-year-old female, for four months after she was referred to treatment by her school counselor. Sara's teachers had noticed she was acting strange, and when she met with her school counselor, she shared that she had been drinking before and during school with friends. Sara has been actively engaged in therapy, has attended all group and individual sessions, and has not consumed alcohol in two and a half months. You meet individually with Sara weekly and are scheduled to see her tomorrow. Sara's mother has requested a family session to talk about her. How would you approach this?
    A) schedule the family session without telling Sara
    B) talk to Sara in her next session and schedule the session together
    C) kindly tell her mother that the request needs to come from Sara
    D) refer her mother to the school counselor

35. A counselor is discussing the damage social media use can cause clients, including body dysmorphia, anxiety, and depressive symptoms. When it comes to mental health, what is a positive use of social media?
    A) creating a mental health educational account
    B) limiting exposure to germs and viral infections
    C) creating new employment opportunities
    D) helping avoid boredom

36. The counselor is reviewing her treatment plan for Michael, a twenty-eight-year-old male who was diagnosed with opioid use disorder. Which of the following is an effective method to track his progress?
    A) administering the Beck depression Inventory
    B) reports from his family
    C) Michael's self-report of use
    D) random urinalysis screenings

37. An intake coordinator in an outpatient addiction treatment program is meeting with an individual who is concerned about ambulatory detoxification and presents with nausea, vomiting, muscle pain, restlessness, and anxiety. Which substance is this person likely to be withdrawing from?
    A) alcohol
    B) caffeine
    C) opioids
    D) cocaine

38. You have been working with Lou, a twenty-four-year-old male with a history of opioid use disorder. He shared with you that he relapsed and feels that he cannot stop using. You recommend inpatient treatment. He is

resistant at first, but after you use motivational interviewing strategies, he is willing to try it. Which of the following is an MI skill that could have been used in this situation?

- A) core mindfulness
- B) rolling with resistance
- C) the miracle question
- D) exception questions

39. A client is expected to complete an inpatient rehab program in two weeks and wants to continue with outpatient treatment when she returns home. Which of the following options can you discuss with her?

- A) local detoxification treatment program
- B) local residential treatment program
- C) local intensive outpatient program
- D) local medication-assisted treatment

40. A counselor is telling new clients how she can be contacted and gives them a phone number and email address. What should clients know about exchanging emails?

- A) Counselors are available 24/7 via email communication.
- B) Emails will be received by an automated service.
- C) Clients should not email personal or confidential information.
- D) Emails are not documented in a client's chart.

41. You are conducting an initial assessment with a client who identifies with a different ethnicity and religion than you do. How would you proceed?

- A) refer the client to a colleague who shares his ethnicity
- B) cancel the appointment
- C) conduct the initial assessment
- D) speak with your supervisor for guidance

42. Your supervisor wants you to include a disclaimer at the end of your email signature. Which information is MOST appropriate to include?

- A) a reminder that email is not a secure form of communication
- B) your phone number
- C) your office's location
- D) your hours of work

43. You are providing an educational session for college freshmen on the dangers of alcohol and drug use and create a hypothetical situation in which a group of friends are at a party. One of the friends drinks more than the others, cannot walk, and falls asleep. Her friends cannot wake her up. How should the friends deal with this situation?

- A) let her sleep it off
- B) position her on her side
- C) contact emergency services
- D) put her in a cold shower

44. You offer a family therapy program in your addiction treatment program. As part of this, you provide psychoeducation about the disease concept of addiction, recovery, communication, and healthy boundaries. A common boundary concern is when a person takes on a caretaker role with a loved one who is struggling with an addiction. This role may involve some enabling. How would you describe this relationship pattern?

- A) codependency
- B) gaslighting
- C) controlling
- D) dependence

45. Your outpatient client shares that his family members are trying to support him, but they do not understand addiction and the recovery process. What would be an appropriate recommendation for your client's family members?

- A) Al-Anon meetings
- B) Alcoholics Anonymous meetings
- C) family therapy sessions
- D) group therapy for family members

46. A counselor facilitates a relapse prevention group in an outpatient addiction treatment facility. He refers a client to the group because she drank over the weekend. What should the counselor tell the client to expect from the group?

- A) She can actively participate in the group sessions.

B) She can just listen in the group.

C) She can talk first because the counselor referred her.

D) She does not need to do random urine screens with other group members.

47. Which of the following mental health concerns commonly uses spirituality in treatment approaches?

    A) bipolar disorder
    B) substance use disorder
    C) post-traumatic stress disorder
    D) depressive disorder

48. You have been working individually with Scott in an outpatient addiction treatment program. He has been in treatment for ten months and has twelve months of sobriety. Scott was in an inpatient treatment program for eight weeks before outpatient treatment. Which of the following factors BEST supports the decision to complete his treatment?

    A) He has maintained sobriety in his toxic home environment.
    B) He has made changes to his routine and friendships and uses healthy coping skills.
    C) He has not missed an individual session since he started treatment.
    D) He has paid off the remaining balance of his copays.

49. A new client is interested in ambulatory detox. After learning about the client's substance use, the counselor realizes that he is ineligible for ambulatory detox due to the risk of seizures and death during the withdrawal process. Which substance has this client likely been using?

    A) opioids
    B) cocaine
    C) alcohol
    D) tobacco

50. You have been seeing Lucia, a thirty-six-year-old woman, individually for nine weeks. Lucia has been learning to cope with the distress over her relationship with her husband. She began dating her husband in college, where they would binge drink together frequently. Lucia feels like she "grew out of it," while her husband drinks more than she would like. She shared that he drinks most days after work, is irritable, and is reluctant to help her with the children's bedtime routine. She has tried talking to him about her concerns, but he brushes them off, saying that he does not have a problem and she is overreacting. What would be a helpful recommendation for Lucia?

    A) referral to local inpatient addiction treatment centers
    B) referral to local outpatient addiction treatment centers
    C) list of local Al-Anon meetings she can attend
    D) list of local Alcoholics Anonymous meetings he can attend

51. You are working in an outpatient addiction treatment program and are meeting with a new client, Sam, who recently completed a local inpatient addiction rehab program. You learn that Sam does not have sober support: his close family and friends struggle with their own addiction issues. Sam would like to find other options for support. What is an appropriate recommendation?

    A) social media connections
    B) group therapy
    C) Alcoholics Anonymous
    D) a dating app

52. A counselor facilitates a family therapy program at an outpatient addiction treatment program. The beginning portion of the program focuses on psychoeducation. Which of the following topics would be the MOST appropriate for that client population?

    A) overview of common mental health concerns
    B) the disease concept of addiction
    C) therapeutic interventions like EMDR
    D) the effectiveness of medication-assisted treatment

53. Which of the following is an example of a trigger that clients in an inpatient rehab program can actively avoid or remove from their day-to-day lives?

    A) anger
    B) sadness
    C) financial responsibilities
    D) impaired people

54. Which of the following is necessary for a client to give informed consent?
    A) must be physically present for the practice or study
    B) must understand the associated risks of participating
    C) must receive financial compensation for participating
    D) must give verbal consent, not written

55. During an education session on substances, a student mentions a friend who is usually shy and reserved becoming outgoing and social when he goes out to bars. How can you explain this change to the student?
    A) Alcohol impairs judgment and can change behaviors.
    B) Alcohol is an effective tool to cope with social anxiety.
    C) Alcohol can be used to calm nerves in small amounts.
    D) Alcohol makes everyone comfortable in social situations.

56. Marla is a forty-two-year-old woman who began working with you individually after struggling to support her daughter who is living with opioid addiction. After a few weeks, you recognize that Marla struggles with codependent behaviors. She has been so focused on her daughter's needs that she has been neglecting her own. This has led Marla to feel overwhelmed, irritable, and exhausted. How would you proceed with Marla regarding her codependency behaviors?
    A) introduce DBT skills
    B) introduce goal setting
    C) improve boundaries
    D) introduce mindfulness

57. When working with a client who is under the age of consent in your state, what should you get from her in addition to her legal guardian's signed informed consent?
    A) the client's assent
    B) verbal participation
    C) written participation
    D) approval of study content

58. You are running an intensive outpatient program group. A group member shares that she received Narcan last night after relapsing and overdosing on heroin. She denied seeking medical attention. Your clinic has a medical staff member present when it is open. What is the BEST action to take?
    A) process her relapse and continue with the group
    B) consult with your supervisor after the group session concludes
    C) focus on relapse prevention skills
    D) escort her to meet with the medical staff for assessment

59. Which of the following can reverse an opioid overdose?
    A) naltrexone
    B) naloxone
    C) methadone
    D) buprenorphine

60. Ayana is a counselor at an addiction treatment center providing medical-assisted therapy (MAT). A client asks to borrow fifteen dollars during an interview. How should Ayana respond?
    A) inform the client that policy prohibits her from lending money to clients
    B) give the client the money on the condition he pays it back at the next session
    C) ask him to check with some of the other staff members
    D) tell the client to ask a relative or friend

61. You have been working as an initial assessment counselor in an outpatient addiction treatment program. Your new client arrives for her session, and you notice the smell of alcohol in the room. She reports driving herself to the appointment. She consents to taking a breathalyzer; her BAC comes up as 0.10. You inform her that you cannot complete the intake with her under the influence, and the client is agreeable to rescheduling. What is the appropriate next step?
    A) refer her to AA
    B) arrange for her to be picked up
    C) call the police
    D) reschedule the assessment

62. After developing a treatment plan that you feel is realistic and feasible, your client expresses concerns about the goals identified in the plan: the client's motivation does not align with the plan. How would you proceed?
    A) work with the client to make changes that you both are comfortable with
    B) leave the treatment plan as you originally wrote it
    C) allow your client to create a new treatment plan
    D) explore the disconnect with your understanding of the client's motivation

63. Alana is a client in an outpatient addiction treatment program. She began treatment three weeks ago to get sober from opiates and has been attending individual and group counseling and twelve-step meetings. In an individual session, Alana shared that she is only attending treatment because she wants to avoid criminal court for a possession charge. She lives with her partner, who actively uses opioids, and she works in a pub where her coworkers use drugs during their shifts. Which type of challenge has she been experiencing?
    A) consequences of addiction
    B) barriers to sobriety
    C) failure to comply with treatment
    D) lack of motivation

64. You are concerned that a member in your IOP group is not sober and cannot engage in a group session. Which of the following is a sign of being under the influence of a benzodiazepine?
    A) slurred speech
    B) restlessness
    C) increased hunger
    D) restricted pupils

65. You have been working with Rachel, a nineteen-year-old female with trauma symptoms and a history of childhood abuse and neglect. Rachel said that you remind her of her childhood neighbor who would give her juice boxes and invite her for lunch. She shared that she was fond of this neighbor because she seemed to care when her parents did not. She said that she feels the same about you and that no one else in her life has taken the time to listen to her thoughts and feelings. Based on the information, what is Rachel exhibiting?
    A) codependency
    B) transference
    C) countertransference
    D) building rapport

66. A client shares that she has moodiness, cravings, and fatigue, and cannot focus at work. Knowing that she recently detoxed from alcohol, you suspect that she is experiencing post-acute withdrawal symptoms. How can you BEST assist with her symptoms?
    A) explore ways to increase her social support
    B) focus on her treatment plan goals
    C) return to the topic from your last session
    D) schedule a family therapy session

67. A counselor is reviewing the limitations of confidentiality with new clients. What is a limit clients should be aware of?
    A) Their spouse can have limited access to their records.
    B) Their emergency contact can have limited access to their records.
    C) Their records may be viewed during a state or federal audit.
    D) Their records are not protected by confidentiality in death.

68. What is a de-escalation skill that you can use when a client becomes defensive in an individual session?
    A) end the session
    B) raise your voice to match the client's
    C) deep breathing exercises
    D) label the client's feelings

69. Your new client reports agitation, restlessness, depression, hunger, and nightmares. She denies experiencing physical signs of withdrawal, such as nausea, vomiting, or aches and pains. Which substance do you suspect she is withdrawing from?
    A) alcohol
    B) opioids
    C) benzodiazepines
    D) cocaine

70. During an interview, a client relates his family situation, saying, "Two of my kids are in school, but my oldest, who is now nineteen..." He pauses and does not continue. What should the counselor do?

    A) ask if the oldest child works
    B) ask if the oldest child left school
    C) quickly ask about the last child
    D) patiently wait for the client to continue

71. How can counselors stay active and up to date on professional concerns?

    A) watching the news
    B) taking continuing education courses
    C) joining professional organizations
    D) talking to colleagues

72. You and several colleagues have discussed a get-together outside of the office. Knowing that one of your colleagues is in recovery, which of the following could you recommend?

    A) going out for drinks after work
    B) having snacks and drinks at the office
    C) going for hot chocolate and ice-skating
    D) attending a bottomless mimosa brunch

73. You have been working with Veronica for four months and noticed that she has a hard time developing relationships with women. When you brought this up in a session, Veronica agreed. After further exploration, she traced this back to her mother, whose involvement in her life has been inconsistent. How could a counselor build rapport with Veronica?

    A) schedule her sessions on varying days
    B) show unconditional positive regard
    C) normalize inconsistent relationships
    D) share about your own relationships with women

74. You have been working with Adrien at an inpatient addiction treatment program for two and a half months. He has successfully met his treatment goals and is expected to complete this program in two weeks. After speaking with Adrien about his goals after treatment, you have both agreed that he would benefit from continuing in treatment. Adrien states that his days have little structure since he is unemployed, and he is worried about being bored at home. He reports having a healthy home environment that is sober and supportive of his recovery. Which treatment option would provide him with a structured environment that will allow him to focus on his recovery?

    A) outpatient treatment program
    B) intensive outpatient treatment program
    C) aftercare programming
    D) partial hospitalization programming

75. One common assessment is a simple four-question screener that can often be completed without papers if the counselor can remember the questions. Scoring for this assessment is standard; clients who answer "yes" to two or more of the questions may have a substance use disorder. Which assessment fits this description?

    A) AUDIT
    B) CAGE
    C) DAST
    D) TAPS

76. You are running a group therapy session in an outpatient treatment program and notice that group members are hesitant to be vulnerable in their sessions. Which exercise would help create trust within the group?

    A) develop group rules together
    B) use icebreaker exercises
    C) call on group members to share
    D) avoid processing group exercises

77. A counselor is working with a young man who has bipolar disorder and an opioid use disorder. His treatment is mandated by his probation officer. Who should the counselor coordinate with in treating this client?

    A) client's psychiatrist
    B) client's parents
    C) client's employer
    D) client's lawyer

78. You are meeting with a new client who has been admitted to your inpatient program. This client has shared that she is uncomfortable with group therapy and does not believe that attending group sessions will be helpful. She later explained that her ambivalence came from how

group therapy has been portrayed in movies and television, not her own experience. How could you provide education about group therapy to her?

- A) The group facilitator will provide feedback when needed but otherwise is relatively quiet.
- B) The group is led by peers, which can help her learn to speak up for herself.
- C) One group member will talk for most of the session; she would likely have little opportunity to do so.
- D) Group therapy allows her to feel validation in terms of emotions and experiences.

79. Which of the following is a symptom associated with burnout?
- A) anxiety at home about work
- B) regular self-care practices
- C) regular supervision
- D) having work-life balance

80. During an interview, a curious client asks several questions about the counselor's private life. How should the counselor respond?
- A) refuse to answer such questions
- B) answer the questions fully
- C) explain that your primary concern is with her problems and that discussion of your personal affairs will not help meet her needs
- D) explain that it is the responsibility of the interviewer to ask questions and not to answer them

81. A counselor meets a new client for an intake assessment and administers the DAST-10. The client scores a 4, showing a moderate level of problems. What would be an appropriate response?
- A) no response at this time
- B) monitoring and reassessment in thirty days
- C) further investigation
- D) intensive assessment

82. Why is it inappropriate for a counselor to have a personal relationship with a client?
- A) The client may benefit from favoritism.
- B) The client may receive special treatment.
- C) The client may falsely accuse the counselor of wrongdoing.
- D) The relationship could interfere with the counselor's objectivity.

83. You have just completed an intake assessment with a sixty-eight-year-old female at an inpatient addiction treatment program. Laura has been binge drinking on and off since she was in her twenties. She says that she has been able to stop drinking when she wanted to, so she has never thought her drinking was a concern. She has been drinking about five days a week for the past few months and confirms feeling "shaky" in the mornings after she drinks. She denies that her job, family, or other responsibilities are impacted by her drinking. Laura was referred to treatment by her doctor following a fatty liver diagnosis. What would you recommend to Laura?
- A) partial hospitalization program
- B) detoxification
- C) intensive outpatient program
- D) inpatient rehab program

84. You are running a family therapy program for family members with a loved one attending an inpatient rehab program. Which of the following is an appropriate psychoeducation topic for this group?
- A) different methods of substance use
- B) financial cost of addiction
- C) the disease concept of addiction
- D) common mental health concerns

85. Which of the following does NOT describe client autonomy?
- A) focusing on defending individuals who cannot represent themselves
- B) referring to clients having control over their own health care decisions
- C) describing a client's freedom to make choices
- D) fostering client independence

86. You have been working with Jonah, who has been in a domestic partnership for nine years. Jonah has discussed several times that his partner has been physically abusive, leaving him with bruises. After this occurs, his partner buys an expensive gift as an apology and promises to get help. Everything seems fine for a week or

two, but then his partner becomes aggressive and eventually abusive again. To the best of Jonah's knowledge, his partner has not gotten help for his anger issues. Which of the following would be an appropriate psychoeducation topic?

A) emotion regulation skills
B) the cycle of violence
C) antisocial personality education
D) self-defense skills

87. Your client agrees that an IOP would be the best fit for her needs and schedule. How would you proceed?

A) encourage your client to search for local IOP providers
B) provide your client with a list of local IOP providers
C) provide your client with the contact information for one IOP provider
D) assist the client in scheduling an intake assessment with a local IOP provider

88. Your client is a twenty-four-year-old female who has tried to stop using opioids but has been unable to remain sober. She often uses more than she intends and is preoccupied with her use, which takes her attention away from her work. How would you specify the severity of her opioid use disorder?

A) low
B) mild
C) moderate
D) severe

89. Which of the following does NOT describe beneficence in client care?

A) an obligation to do good for the client
B) providing informed consent
C) the act of telling the truth
D) removing the client from harm's way

90. You are about to conduct an initial assessment with a new client. Your supervisor encouraged you to summarize more during these appointments to make sure you fully understand the client. How often would you summarize during the appointment?

A) twice; halfway and at the end
B) at the end of each section
C) at the end only
D) dismiss your supervisor's suggestion

91. A counselor administers the Alcohol Use Disorders Identification Test (AUDIT) to a client who reports concerning drinking behaviors. Which of the following is important to discuss with the client before administering the test?

A) Answers should reflect standard drink sizes.
B) This test impacts the test taker's mental health diagnosis.
C) An emergency contact will not be alerted.
D) There is no need to explain anything before administering the test.

92. Anthony, a nineteen-year-old male with SUD, struggles with procrastination. Even talking about setting goals is overwhelming. The counselor discusses the components that go into making healthy goals and describes the acronym *SMART* for goal setting. What does this acronym stand for?

A) sensitive, measurable, attainable, realistic, tailor-made
B) specific, measurable, attainable, realistic, time-restricted
C) sensitive, meaningful, attainable, realistic, time-restricted
D) specific, meaningful, attainable, realistic, tailor-made

93. You are meeting with a client who presents as anxious with rapid speech and are having a hard time following what he is sharing with you because he jumps between topics. What would be an appropriate skill to use?

A) summarizing
B) redirecting
C) taking notes in session
D) breathing exercises

94. You are concerned that your client may need detoxification services and are unsure whether outpatient treatment is appropriate. Which of the following should you discuss with your supervisor to reach your treatment recommendation?

A) client's age, employment status, and treatment goals

B) client's employment status, motivation source, and treatment goals

C) client's treatment goals, substances used, and current withdrawal symptoms

D) client's motivation source, treatment goals, and mode of transportation

95. A counselor is discussing goal setting with a client—specifically, the difference between intrinsic and extrinsic motivation. Which of the following is an example of intrinsic motivation that the counselor could share?

    A) receiving a bonus after a year of work at a new clinic
    B) working out because it is fun and feels good afterward
    C) making the honors list after working hard at school
    D) buying a nice house in a desirable neighborhood

96. You are working in an outpatient addiction treatment program. During your initial assessment with a new client, she appeared resistant to treatment, so you tried to validate her experiences and provide support. In return, the client asked what business you have helping someone with an addiction, because it is obvious you do not have one. You have been in recovery for five years and feel that self-disclosure may help the client be more open with you. What is an appropriate way to share your experience?

    A) be dishonest about your experience to avoid embarrassment
    B) provide all the details of how you hit rock bottom
    C) share that you are in recovery with minimal details
    D) encourage the client to come to an AA meeting with you

97. Lauren has been in your outpatient addiction program for about three months, receiving treatment for her alcohol addiction. She recently lost her job due to downsizing and will also lose her insurance, which means she cannot continue with counseling. Understanding her financial concerns, what would you suggest Lauren do next?

    A) apply for unemployment
    B) attend Alcoholics Anonymous
    C) find cheaper counseling services
    D) return when she has insurance

98. You are meeting with a new client who was referred to treatment by his primary care physician. The referral paperwork includes the following:
    - an inability to stop using
    - development of a tolerance
    - taking his pain medication for a longer period than was prescribed
    - loss of employment from being sick at work
    - interpersonal concerns with family and friends
    - presence of withdrawal symptoms

    Based on the information provided, which diagnosis would you investigate?

    A) opioid use disorder, mild
    B) opioid use disorder, moderate
    C) opioid use disorder, severe
    D) unspecified opioid use disorder

99. Which of the following accurately describes qualitative research?

    A) It relies on data that can be measured.
    B) It is not intended to be applied in practice.
    C) It uses many participants.
    D) It investigates how and why things happen.

100. While walking in a common area of your office you overheard a colleague share with his client that he was tired because his baby was up all night and he was struggling before their session began. What is an appropriate action for you to take?

    A) confront your colleague before his session
    B) confront your colleague after his session
    C) reach out to his client personally
    D) voice your concern to your supervisor

101. In a common space of your office, you overhear two colleagues discussing private information that is unique to a client. How would you proceed?

    A) confront them immediately
    B) share your concern with your supervisor
    C) ignore the event and let it go
    D) inform the client of the encounter

102. A fifty-seven-year-old man has been meeting with a counselor to address his alcohol dependence and has cut down on his drinking over the past few weeks. He arrives at his appointment sweating, says that he has been vomiting, and has a noticeable tremor in his hands. What should the counselor do?

   A) call 911, even if the client refuses to consent, as he is likely detoxing and may experience seizures or possibly death
   B) explain the possible dangers of alcohol withdrawal and collaborate with the client to decide whether to seek medical help
   C) encourage the client to withstand the uncomfortable symptoms for a few days, as they will likely pass after the painful detox process
   D) encourage the client to decrease his alcohol intake more slowly, as he will be less likely to experience such serious withdrawal symptoms

103. At the end of a one-hour interview with a client, she begins to discuss another issue that will take additional time to consider. You have another client scheduled shortly after this interview. What is the BEST way to proceed?

   A) finish the initial interview and schedule a second appointment with that client to discuss the new issue
   B) skip the next client's appointment and allow the current client to continue, using all the time she needs to explain the new issue
   C) ask the client to give a clear rationale for why she feels the need to talk about the new issue near the end of the interview
   D) let the client know that her scheduled hour has expired, and you have someone else to meet

104. A counselor working at an inpatient addiction rehab program plans to give a psychoeducational lecture to the program participants. What would be an appropriate topic for this lecture?

   A) vocational opportunities
   B) coping with trauma
   C) nutrition
   D) relapse prevention

105. Peter is a twenty-eight-year-old male who has been drinking heavily since he began binge drinking in college at the age of nineteen. He recently noticed that his cravings have intensified, and he uses alcohol to cope with grief since the unexpected loss of his father. Peter does not feel that his drinking is a concern and has never experienced withdrawal or physical dependency symptoms. In which stage of addiction would you place Peter?

   A) stage 1: experimentation
   B) stage 2: regular use
   C) stage 3: high-risk use
   D) stage 4: addiction

106. You are meeting with a client who you feel could benefit from attending Alcoholics Anonymous meetings. When you explore her reasons for not going, she explains that she is not religious and is not interested in going to meetings to hear about God. How could you explain spirituality?

   A) feeling connected to other aspects of organized religion
   B) identifying with other religious materials
   C) a deep connection to something that makes you feel whole
   D) a deep connection to others that makes you feel whole

107. Your client recently saw his addiction physician, who ordered testing. The client shares that he is confused about the tests and their purpose. Assuming you have the consent of release, how would you proceed?

   A) encourage the client to call his doctor and report back to you
   B) ask the client if he would like to call the doctor together
   C) send the doctor an email explaining the client's confusion
   D) wait for the doctor to send you the test results

108. Lucas chose to attend addiction treatment rather than serve a jail sentence for a recent drug-related arrest. As a condition of his deal, he must provide an update from the treatment provider to the court once every eight weeks. Lucas does not like these updates and believes his treatment should be kept private. How

can the counselor comply with his deal while maintaining a therapeutic rapport?

A) omit from the report the challenges Lucas has faced in the past eight weeks

B) exaggerate the details of his progress in the past eight weeks

C) be truthful, and review the report with Lucas before sending it

D) allow Lucas to fill out his own progress forms for the court

109. You are running an intensive outpatient program in an outpatient addiction facility. You have established a one-time five-minute window for when group members are allowed to come to group late. Today Karl was late for the second time this week. What should you do next?

A) allow him to participate in the group and say nothing to him about breaking the rules

B) allow him to participate in the group and ask him to talk to you after the group ends

C) ask him to come into the hall and tell him that he is late for the second time and cannot join the group

D) tell him he cannot join the group and assume he understands why

110. You are discussing screening, brief intervention, and referral to treatment (SBIRT) in your addiction counseling class. Which of the following would be an appropriate explanation for prescreening?

A) to make completion of the rest of the approach easier

B) to figure out aspects to focus on in the session

C) to identify individuals who are at risk of developing an addiction

D) to evaluate the effectiveness of outreach and prevention efforts

111. Your client Sheila is a single mother of three children. She shared that she has not been able to feed her children well lately because she has no money. She has been asking her children to play at their friends' houses so they can eat full meals. You are concerned about her children's safety despite their mother's efforts. What should you do next?

A) give her some money and ask her to buy her children more food

B) empathize and try to change the topic of conversation

C) explain your legal responsibilities and call CPS

D) empathize, change the topic, then call CPS

112. You are working with Sarah, a thirty-one-year-old female with alcohol use disorder. Which statement about her use indicates that she is in the fourth stage of addiction?

A) She drinks in the morning to avoid experiencing withdrawal.

B) She continues to drink despite knowing that it hurts her partner.

C) She continues to drink despite having pending charges for a DWI.

D) She consumes two to three drinks per occasion three days each week.

113. Regarding goal setting, what is the counselor's role when working with clients?

A) let them know what has worked for the counselor personally

B) allow them to identify their own goals

C) explain what would be appropriate

D) provide an objective perspective

114. A counselor is working on value clarification with a client who has alcohol dependence. He is also assisting her in recognizing the consequences and the impact her behaviors have on others. The counselor uses a readiness ruler to help assess the client's readiness to change. These methods are most likely to be effective when the client is in which stage of the transtheoretical model?

A) action

B) maintenance

C) preparation

D) pre-contemplation

115. You do not fully agree with a colleague's recommendation for a client but are uncomfortable sharing your thoughts with the colleague. How would you proceed?

A) take the colleague's recommendation despite your concerns

B) disregard the recommendation and develop your own plan without further input

C) seek feedback on the case and your concern about voicing your thoughts with your colleague

D) seek feedback for the case only

116. The focus of interviews is always on clients and their situations. Accordingly, which statement is MOST correct regarding interview focus?

    A) Counselors should get clients to focus on factual information.
    B) Counselors are responsible for assisting clients to focus on anything related to their problems.
    C) Counselors must help clients focus on their feelings, which are often behind many of the problems they face.
    D) Counselors should not direct interviews; rather, they should allow clients to speak as they wish.

117. Using SBIRT allows for screening assessments that are available to the general population, as well as some that have been validated for specific populations. Which of the following are the specific populations that have validated full screening assessments?

    A) adolescents, adults, older adults, pregnant persons
    B) men, women, and members of the LGBTQIA+ community
    C) veterans, first responders, professionals, students
    D) college students, tradespeople, professionals, and housewives

118. You have been providing individual therapy in an outpatient addiction treatment program. One of your clients who struggles with anorexia nervosa shared that she is five months pregnant. When you assess her disordered eating patterns, she told you that she has been struggling more recently because of the changes to her body due to pregnancy. She denied sharing this with her ob-gyn and explained that she is worried about being judged because she understands the importance of having a healthy diet while pregnant. How would you proceed?

    A) have her call her ob-gyn in your presence
    B) refer her to an inpatient hospitalization program
    C) refer her to a nutritionist
    D) increase the frequency of her sessions

119. When should clients be informed of the office's policies for case consultation regarding their confidentiality?

    A) during their initial intake assessment
    B) before you engage in a case consultation
    C) after you engage in a case consultation
    D) during admission when receiving paperwork

120. You are running a relapse prevention group in an outpatient addiction treatment program. One of the group rules is that members do not come to group impaired. When the group begins, you observe that a member appears impaired. You ask her to step outside, then have another staff member take her to the doctor on staff for assessment. Which behavior are you demonstrating?

    A) blocking
    B) linking
    C) facilitating
    D) creating safety

121. Which of the following scenarios would MOST require a counselor to consult with a supervisor?

    A) client is ten minutes late to an individual session
    B) client's safety may be in jeopardy
    C) client has concerns about making a payment
    D) client wants to end counseling

122. Franco is a twenty-four-year-old male in outpatient treatment for SUD. He recently decided to tell his family that he is gay, and he did not get the positive and supportive reactions he was hoping for. Franco explained that he comes from a large, loud, extended family where everyone is active in each other's lives. This includes weekly Sunday dinners, which he has been asked not to attend for the past two weeks. This has led to him feeling sad, let down, and angry. How can you best support him?

    A) encourage him to distance himself from his family
    B) invite him to your family dinners

C) provide him with unconditional positive regard

D) encourage him to go to dinner this weekend

123. Which of the following assessments is the FIRST one a counselor should conduct with a new client?

A) IQ test

B) personality assessment

C) clinical interview

D) neuropsychological assessment

124. You and your group co-leader are running the first process group of the day in an addiction treatment rehab. A client named Jeanine began complaining about the care she has received. Agitated, she made negative comments and judgments about other group members. What is the BEST course of action?

A) redirect the group to change topics

B) ask her to step out with your co-leader while you process the experience with the group

C) have the group engage in a box breathing exercise followed by processing the experience

D) wait to see what other group members' reactions and responses are before acting

125. A group counselor working in an outpatient addiction treatment program is leading a relapse prevention group. The group discussed goal setting. Which of the following was MOST likely a long-term goal that a group member had?

A) going to a job interview in two and a half weeks

B) attending ninety twelve-step meetings in ninety days

C) remaining sober at a wedding in two weeks

D) finding a sponsor in the next six weeks

126. You are a counselor in an inpatient rehab setting and have just completed an intake assessment for a twenty-two-year-old female who has been struggling with heroin addiction for about a year and a half. During your assessment, you learned that she has a history of trauma and binge eating. Which treatment approach would you recommend?

A) focusing on her opioid addiction

B) focusing on her trauma history

C) focusing on her disordered eating behaviors

D) a holistic approach addressing all concerns

127. Which of the following is the correct order of the stages of change?

A) precontemplation, contemplation, action, relapse, maintenance

B) contemplation, preparation, action, relapse, maintenance

C) precontemplation, contemplation, preparation, action, maintenance

D) action, precontemplation, preparation, contemplation, maintenance

128. Which of the following is an example of high validity?

A) a math exam to determine how well the students know the material

B) an oven that can consistently change temperatures but does not display the correct temperature

C) using GPA to determine athletic ability

D) a scale that is five pounds off but always reads the same weight

129. Diego, a client in your outpatient addiction treatment program, shares that he struggles with a lack of social support. What should you recommend?

A) connect with old friends, even if he used with them

B) connect with family he lost touch with during his addiction

C) join a local Alcoholics Anonymous group

D) join a church

130. Which of the following is an element of a mental status exam?

A) client's level of insight

B) case notes from prior counselors

C) an IQ assessment

D) client's past drug use

131. Which of the following therapeutic groups encourages interactions among its members OUTSIDE of the group setting?

A) process groups

B) support groups

C) psychoeducational groups

D) mindfulness groups

132. You have been working with Robert for five months. You review his treatment plan with him, as it has been four weeks since you last did so. He asks why you do this every month. What is the BEST response?

A) You are mandated to do so monthly.

B) It decreases your professional liability.

C) It lets you track his progress from last month.

D) It helps guide a conversation about changes he needs to make.

133. You are working in an outpatient addiction treatment program and recently received a referral for a new client who just completed an inpatient rehab program. Sam was diagnosed with alcohol use disorder while at his inpatient rehab program. During your session, you learn that Sam has limited social support because his family and friends do not know how to respond to him identifying as homosexual. How can you help him regarding his friends?

A) discuss coping skills for his distress

B) provide psychoeducation about sexuality

C) improve his communication skills

D) focus on his addiction treatment

134. What are some signs that a client in an outpatient addiction treatment program may be at risk of relapsing?

A) The client expresses being happy in day-to-day life.

B) The client recently received recognition for progress at work.

C) The client shares that depressive symptoms have returned.

D) The client's self-care routine has changed.

135. Shawn is a thirty-four-year-old male who has an intake session at the addiction clinic where you work. Shawn began abusing prescription opioids after being prescribed oxycodone for an injury. Before the injury, Shawn worked full-time as a real estate agent. Since his injury, he has been slipping at work by not getting back to clients promptly and has not made a sale in three months. Shawn began purchasing oxycodone illegally and is now unable to pay his bills. He is now using heroin because it is more affordable. Shawn knows he needs to stop using and still has his medical insurance. What would you recommend?

A) career counseling

B) addiction counseling

C) meet with a financial advisor

D) ask his family for financial help

136. During your group session, you notice that Eddie has been quiet and shared very little. He does appear engaged while others are talking by making eye contact and nodding. You do not know Eddie and his case well, but you would like to encourage group participation. Which of the following would you consider?

A) put him on the spot in group

B) talk to him individually after group

C) facilitate a group activity

D) give him a week to get comfortable

137. The counselor is seeing a fourteen-year-old client for the first time. She was referred for missing school and poor family relationships. Her mother suspects she has been using marijuana with friends. Which of the following would be the BEST tool to screen for drug usage?

A) TAPS

B) CRAFFT

C) COWS

D) SBIRT

138. Your office is in a building with an elevator, which has a pass code to deter people from using it excessively. You have an initial intake with an individual who is unable to walk long distances due to medical concerns. How would you proceed?

A) refer the client to a different practice

B) have the meeting on the first floor

C) provide the code to the client before the session

D) see if he can use the stairs before providing the code

139. A heterosexual counselor has been asked to start a therapy group that specializes in working with members of the LGBTQIA+ community. How can the counselor build rapport with the group?

A) allow group members to lead the group

B) allow the group to identify their group norms and rules

C) have a group session focused on the counselor's personal and educational experiences

D) allow heterosexual individuals into the group

140. Which of the following is the FIRST thing to determine in assessing for suicidality?

A) if the client has access to weapons

B) if the client has any suicidal thoughts

C) if the client has a specific plan for killing himself

D) if the client has planned a time and place where she would kill herself

141. You have been working with Dan, a twenty-seven-year-old male with opioid use disorder who entered treatment to appease his family. Dan has been struggling to stay clean because he cannot see the benefits of being sober. Which strategy could you use to help Dan recognize the benefits of sobriety?

A) motivational interviewing

B) recovery education

C) cognitive behavioral therapy

D) group therapy

142. A counselor is working at a clinic that specializes in alcoholism and is interviewing a client who is obviously intoxicated. What is the MOST appropriate action the counselor can take?

A) end the interview session and inform the client that she cannot continue when he is intoxicated

B) focus the entire interview on the negative consequences of alcoholism

C) firmly let the client know that his case will be closed

D) suggest that he seek medical assistance since counseling is not beneficial to him

143. A counselor is nearing the end of a session with a client. What is the BEST thing to do before ending the session?

A) talk about the client's plans for the week

B) ask what the client got out of the session

C) begin talking about a new source of distress

D) let the client continue sharing until the time is up

144. Which of the following behaviors is MOST likely to encourage your group members to talk to you?

A) be available before or after the group session

B) provide them with your email and phone number

C) consistently arrive on time for group

D) have a snack during the group

145. An outpatient client who reported relapsing on heroin has been unable to stop using. She wants to pursue recovery, but she has been struggling to cope with withdrawal symptoms. When she begins to experience extreme nausea and muscle pains, she uses to stop the symptoms. What would you recommend?

A) that she taper her use to decrease the severity of withdrawal symptoms

B) that she enroll in a detoxification program for medication-assisted treatment

C) that she increases the number of NA meetings she attends during the withdrawal

D) that she goes through the withdrawal process at a family member's home for support

146. You are running a relapse prevention group in an outpatient addiction treatment program. The group members have either recently completed an inpatient rehab program or have had a recent relapse after a period of sobriety. Based on the population of your group, which of the following would be the MOST appropriate topic for psychoeducation?

A) coping skills for depressive symptoms

B) emergency mental health services

C) the disease concept of addiction

D) the benefits of Narcotics Anonymous

147. Which of the following BEST describes comorbidity?

A) Joe was diagnosed with PTSD after ending his military career and was diagnosed with alcohol use disorder five years later.

- B) Rob was diagnosed with social anxiety disorder when he was sixteen and with bipolar I at eighteen.
- C) Nicole was diagnosed with selective mutism and a specific phobia when she was seven.
- D) Jaime was diagnosed with erectile disorder, and a year later with prostatic hypertrophy.

148. The federal law HIPAA was enacted in 1996 to create national standards to protect client health information, such as mental health care records. What does HIPAA stand for?
- A) Health Information Privacy and Advocacy Act
- B) Health Insurance Portability and Accountability Act
- C) Health Institution Privacy and Advocacy Act
- D) Health Insurance Privacy and Accountability Act

149. You have noticed throughout your group session that members' concerns tend to have a similar theme: they feel that they are not being heard by their loved ones. Since this theme has come up for several members, you want to provide some psychoeducation related to their concerns. Which of the following would be the BEST choice for you to introduce?
- A) communication skills
- B) self-regulation skills
- C) codependency patterns
- D) mental health resources

150. You are working as a counselor in an inpatient addiction rehab program. When should you begin planning to discharge your clients?
- A) during their intake
- B) halfway through treatment
- C) one month before discharge
- D) two weeks before discharge

Answer Key

1. **A**
   The counselor's primary responsibility is to provide a full range of assistance, including creating a treatment plan with a diagnosis and goals.

2. **C**
   Partial hospitalization programs are appropriate for individuals who need more support after completing an inpatient rehab program. These programs have a similar structure to a typical day at inpatient rehab, the key difference being that the individual can return home at the end of the day. People at this level of treatment are in the early stages of their recovery and require a healthy and supportive home environment. Being active in Narcotics Anonymous, Terry is more likely to succeed in a partial hospitalization program, where he can work to build healthy relationships. Terry should not necessarily expect his family to forget about his past transgressions, but he should feel like he can be open about his struggles and successes at home. Family therapy can be used to help strengthen the support that can be found at home.

3. **B**
   Narcotics Anonymous (NA) is an example of a worldwide peer-led support group; other options include Alcoholics Anonymous (AA) and Smart Recovery.

4. **D**
   Continuing education (CE) courses are required for counselors to maintain an active license in most states. These courses offer new training certifications and provide an opportunity to learn about new practices while refreshing the counselor's knowledge on existing practices.

5. **C**
   "Oxy" refers to oxycodone or oxymorphone, both opioids. The symptoms resemble those associated with opioid withdrawal.

6. **B**
   Contemplation is the stage during which individuals begin to see that a behavior is a concern, but they are not ready to change that behavior.

7. **C**
   Motivational interviewing skills, such as rolling with resistance, open-ended questions, and summarizing, can be useful when working with clients who are struggling to find motivation regarding their substance use disorder. Having any motivation at the beginning of recovery—including external motivation—is enough to get the individual through your door. From there, you can use evidence-based approaches to find sources of internal motivation that will help the client recognize potential benefits of sobriety.

8. **B**
   Nathan has recognized that his behavior is a concern and is beginning to see the benefits of changing his behaviors, which has added internal motivation. At this point, he is talking about changes rather than acting to make changes. When he begins making the changes, then he will be in the action stage.

9. **A**
   Motor impairment is a known consequence of drinking alcohol. Nausea and vomiting are not behavioral changes. Hallucinations may occur in severe withdrawal but do not generally manifest in acute use.

10. **A**
    You should discuss with your supervisor your ability to ethically provide treatment. Individuals with co-occurring disorders have more success if they receive treatment for both concerns at the same time. If you cannot provide a particular treatment, you should refer the client to the appropriate professional.

11. **B**
Bill Wilson (Bill W.) founded Alcoholics Anonymous (AA) in 1935. Since then, the fellowship has expanded and meetings can be found across the world. These meetings are run by alcoholics in recovery, so they differ from a therapeutic support group. There are two types of meetings: those that are open to the public, and those that are open only to those in recovery. Alcoholics Anonymous encourages participants to work through a twelve-step model to strengthen their recovery.

12. **B**
Although problems among clients may be similar, every situation is unique and may require a different solution. Counselors must learn as much as possible about each client before working on a solution.

13. **D**
During a case consultation, the client's name can be omitted to protect the client's privacy. Relevant information includes the client's age, use history, mental health concerns, physical health concerns, treatment history, and treatment goals. The counselor may disclose the client's name if the consultation is with another professional who has had clinical interactions with that client (e.g., group therapy or crisis interventions).

14. **B**
The 2019 National Survey on Drug Use and Health (NSDUH), produced by the Substance Abuse and Mental Health Services Administration (SAMHSA), identifies alcohol as the most abused substance in the United States. According to SAMHSA, 14.5 million Americans have an alcohol use disorder.

15. **D**
Establishing a specialized group helps clients who share a unique background. A specialized group, like a veterans' group, fosters an environment where individuals feel comfortable being vulnerable and discussing difficult topics.

16. **B**
Modified goggles can be used as a tool to demonstrate the impact alcohol can have on vision and, subsequently, coordination. It can be an effective tool in prevention efforts.

17. **A**
Quantitative research uses standardized assessments and measurable data to investigate behaviors. Important components of this research include the methods that are used, limitations of the study, and whether other research supports its findings.

18. **B**
Zero tolerance laws are in place for individuals who are underage and driving while under the influence. The most common blood alcohol concentration limit for underage individuals is 0.02, with the exception of the following states: Alaska, Arizona, the District of Columbia, Illinois, Maine, Minnesota, North Carolina, Texas, and Wisconsin.

19. **A**
It would be best to give the group a safe space to talk about their thoughts and emotions related to the loss. Other members should also get the chance to talk about how grief has impacted them. Then you can talk about the five stages of grief and provide healthy suggestions for coping with their emotions.

20. **A**
Since you may see the client in public settings, it is appropriate to establish boundaries so you both understand how to act toward each other.

21. **C**
The counselor is providing Nader with psychoeducation about his intake assessment. It makes sense that he would be apprehensive if he has never been in treatment before and is unsure what to expect. All clients will come to sessions with an expectation of what they will experience; unfortunately, this expectation is not always accurate or helpful. Taking time to explain the process can also help build rapport with Nader.

22. **D**
Research has shown that the best approach is to treat both addiction and mental health concerns at the same time. Individuals struggling with dual diagnosis often have intertwined symptoms. For example, the client's depressive symptoms could lead to cravings and triggers, which would challenge her sobriety. By providing mental health treatment in conjunction with addiction treatment, the

client will learn to manage her mental health symptoms in a healthier manner.

23. **D**
Throughout the United States, the legal limit for blood alcohol concentration (BAC) is 0.08 when operating a motor vehicle. The exception is Utah, where the BAC limit is 0.05.

24. **D**
The best way to obtain reliable information and lessen the chance of misunderstandings in an interview is to make sure the client understands both the reasons for the questions and how truthful, accurate answers will help solve problems. Option A may result in misunderstandings, option B in prevarication, and option C in resentment.

25. **C**
The best option is to discuss the policy up front and answer any of the client's questions. Printing the policy is an additional option, but the client may not read it.

26. **C**
Regular engagement in Alcoholics Anonymous (AA) meetings can provide Salma with sober support while she readjusts to school. Finding sober support and activities to keep her busy can strengthen her recovery.

27. **C**
Now that Tasha has several months of sobriety, she would likely benefit from engaging in an LGBTQIA+ support group, where she would be with individuals who can relate to her and validate her thoughts and experiences.

28. **B**
Unconditional positive regard is a mindset used by client-centered counselors. This concept helps build therapeutic alliances because it creates an environment where clients feel safe talking about things they may not have previously felt comfortable talking about. Being mindful of your body language and facial expressions plays a role in unconditional positive regard.

29. **C**
Alcohol is a depressant that can worsen a person's depressive symptoms. While alcohol may temporarily ease depressive feelings, the effect does not last.

30. **A**
Counselors should be aware of payment, fee, and insurance benefit concerns. For example, if a client's insurance requires prior authorization, you may need to provide the relevant clinical information. Counselors with an administrative staff may not need to know all the details about these concerns, but they should have a working understanding so they can inform potential clients.

31. **C**
Solution-focused brief therapy (SFBT) applies in this situation because it is effective in three to ten sessions. In a relapse prevention group, members can identify their goals and determine which solutions have helped them before. This approach can also help members identify plans to address any barriers they face in working toward their goals.

32. **D**
Unless you are using a social media account as a psychoeducational platform, being friends with clients online can change your relationship's dynamics and harm your therapeutic alliance.

33. **A**
Polysubstance abuse—abusing more than one substance—can cause respiratory failure, coma, heart problems, stomach bleeding, liver damage, slowed breathing, and brain damage.

34. **B**
Because of Sara's age, it is appropriate for her parents to want to be involved in and informed of her treatment. To maintain a rapport with Sara, it would be effective to speak with her about her mother's request. This allows Sara to talk about her concerns and identify anything she would like to discuss during the session.

35. **A**
Social media can be used to provide psychoeducation about mental health concerns and healthy coping skills, thereby increasing awareness and decreasing the stigma associated with mental health concerns.

36. **D**
Random urinalysis screenings are an effective strategy for monitoring opioid use. There is no mention of Michael struggling with depressive symptoms. Family and self-reports are useful,

but they are subjective and not as reliable as other assessment options.

37. C
The symptoms described indicate opioid withdrawal. Other possible symptoms include stomach cramping, dilated pupils, rapid heart rate, and high blood pressure.

38. B
Rolling with resistance is the only strategy that is part of motivational interviewing (MI). Core mindfulness is a skill used in dialectical behavior therapy. The miracle question and exception questions are used with solution-focused brief therapy.

39. C
Intensive outpatient programs (IOPs) are a common recommendation for individuals who have completed an inpatient treatment program. These programs vary in length and the number of hours involved. For example, clients might be expected to participate in nine to twelve hours of group therapy weekly in addition to an hour of individual counseling. Medication-assisted treatment (MAT) may be a component of a client's aftercare program; however, MAT providers often require behavioral therapy.

40. C
Clients should not share personal information in emails because confidentiality cannot be ensured. Most counselors are not available 24/7. Any emails sent or received should be documented in the client's chart as a form of communication.

41. C
Canceling appointments based on a client's demographics is unethical. The best option is to proceed with the scheduled appointment. If you have concerns about working with clients with different backgrounds from yourself, you should process this with a supervisor.

42. A
Your signature should always include your phone and fax numbers and office location. Option A is an appropriate disclaimer: content of emails is confidential and intended only for the person addressed in the email.

43. C
If an intoxicated individual is unresponsive, emergency services should be contacted. Alcohol is a depressant: it slows down bodily functioning, including heart rate and breathing.

44. A
Codependency is a common unhealthy relationship behavior found among individuals who are struggling with an addiction. The co-dependent person tends to focus on the individual who is struggling, which leads to the codependent person putting her needs on the back burner. This behavior can also enable the individual in active addiction.

45. A
Al-Anon offers meetings for loved ones of people with substance use disorder (SUD). In Al-Anon, family and friends receive support from others in similar situations, learn about unhealthy relationships, and find ways to establish healthy boundaries.

46. A
The client should not be treated differently than the other group members. If members are expected to participate in discussions, the new client should behave accordingly.

47. B
Addiction treatment can take a holistic approach and address a person's mind, body, and spirit. Spirituality is a topic that can arise in self-help groups, such as Alcoholics Anonymous and Narcotics Anonymous. Spirituality does not necessarily have to tie into religion.

48. B
Treatment is completed when the client has shown growth and achieved identified treatment goals. Since Scott is in treatment for an addiction, he should be able to effectively manage stressors and triggers, have healthy sober support, and not struggle with other mental health concerns.

49. C
Seizures, delirium, and death are possible side effects of alcohol withdrawal. Detoxification from alcohol should always be monitored by a medical professional.

50. C
Lucia would likely benefit from psychoeducation regarding denial, the disease concept of addiction, and the importance of internal motivation. She can find support at local Al-Anon meetings, which are specifically

for individuals who have a loved one who is struggling with an addiction. This could help validate her thoughts and feelings as well as provide additional support.

51. **C**

    Support groups, such as Alcoholics Anonymous and Narcotics Anonymous, help individuals in recovery make connections with other people in recovery. Individuals who are active in these groups are encouraged to work closely with a sponsor who can provide guidance and support in their recovery. Group counselors often advise against building relationships with other group members because it can change the dynamic of the group. A support group in a clinical setting would be an exception to this.

52. **B**

    For a family therapy program in an addiction setting, the most appropriate topic is the disease concept of addiction. There are many misconceptions about both addiction and recovery. Providing family members with a solid understanding of how addiction changes the way our bodies work and effective treatments can help families navigate their future together. Sessions on medication-assisted treatment (MAT) could be helpful for some clients, but not every client will have a family member using MAT.

53. **D**

    While options A, B, and C are triggers a client might face at home, they are unavoidable realities of life. The counselor can recommend that clients avoid people, places, and things associated with substance use: people who use substances, places where substances are present, and things that remind clients of their use or items that can be tools used to abuse drugs.

54. **B**

    To provide informed consent, the client must understand the risks associated with participating, the potential benefits, the procedure, and the possible consequences. Most states require that an informed consent be signed and dated rather than offered verbally.

55. **A**

    Alcohol impairs judgment. When drinking, people may do things they would not otherwise do. Poor judgment is also a sign that someone is becoming impaired and should be removed from a situation where alcohol is available.

56. **C**

    Codependency occurs in relationships with poor or no boundaries. Providing Marla with an understanding of codependency can help lead to a discussion about how she can shift her boundaries in her relationship with her daughter.

57. **A**

    Obtaining assent from a client who is under the age of consent in your state can help build rapport before the study or procedure, which in turn could reduce potential limitations on your study.

58. **D**

    All of the options are appropriate in this situation; however, the first priority should be the client's well-being and safety. Since there is a medical professional in the office, the client should be evaluated to see if further medical attention is necessary.

59. **B**

    Naloxone (Narcan) can temporarily reverse the effects of an opioid overdose. The individual will require medical attention to avoid a subsequent overdose. Naloxone will not help individuals who are overdosing on other substances and may be ineffective for a fentanyl overdose.

60. **A**

    It is a violation of the counselor-client relationship to lend money to clients. Doing so risks crossing boundaries into a dual relationship and could be a form of enabling addictive behavior, which can include not having the necessary funds to support the habit. It is important to explain the situation in a compassionate and understanding manner. Counselors can help clients develop a plan to develop financial security.

61. **B**

    While it may be appropriate to discuss Alcoholics Anonymous (AA) and reschedule the appointment, your focus should be on the client's safety. Since her blood alcohol concentration (BAC) is 0.10, she should not drive herself home. You can work with her to find a safe alternative, like a ride share, bus, friend, or family member.

62. **A**
Treatment plans should be developed by both the counselor and the client. The counselor provides knowledge and suggestions about recovery and effective treatment goals, and the client discusses motivations, personal goals, and concerns about recovery. Treatment plans should be a realistic tool to guide the client's treatment and should be modified continuously to reflect both progress and setbacks.

63. **B**
Everything Alana has listed is a barrier to sobriety. She does have extrinsic motivation to stay sober (pending legal charges). Even though her motivation is extrinsic, she is still attending sessions and meetings, so she is compliant with treatment. The term *consequences of addiction* usually refers to negative consequences that might push a person to addiction treatment (for example, loss of relationships, financial insecurity, or career and/or health problems).

64. **A**
Signs that someone may be using a benzodiazepine include dilated pupils, slurred speech, dry mouth, drowsiness, sluggish behavior, and being easily confused. If a group member appears to be impaired, he should be assessed by a medical professional. Removing him from the group respectfully decreases the likelihood that his impairment will distress other members.

65. **B**
This is a clear example of transference. Rachel has redirected the feelings she had toward her neighbor onto you. While these are positive feelings, addressing them during a session will benefit your therapeutic alliance in the long run.

66. **A**
Social support can allow clients to talk about what they are experiencing and receive emotional support and validation. This can include meeting with a counselor individually and speaking with a sponsor or another sober individual. Other helpful topics for this client include reviewing healthy sleep hygiene, coping skills for cravings, and grounding skills.

67. **C**
Limits to confidentiality include
- being reviewed during a state or federal audit,
- sharing records for record keeping and billing purposes,
- sharing records with a supervisor or colleagues for consultation that would benefit the client,
- sharing records if the counselor is concerned clients may harm themselves or others,
- sharing records in a medical emergency,
- sharing records if the client discloses abuse that falls into required mandated reporting,
- sharing information if the client brings another person into the session, and
- a court requiring that a counselor disclose client information.

68. **C**
Encouraging your client to engage in deep breathing exercises with you can help him manage his emotions. You can also use this as a learning moment to process the use of breathing as a coping skill that the client can use when he feels distressed.

69. **D**
Individuals can experience intense cravings for an extended period if they have a long history of heavy cocaine use. People in withdrawal from cocaine may also have increased appetite, restlessness, and suicidal thoughts.

70. **D**
Sometimes clients get lost in discussing a topic due to another thought. If they pause, avoid leading or prompting their speech and allow them to work through their thought processes.

71. **C**
Participation in professional organizations keeps counselors apprised of important advocacy concerns and opportunities to take action. The other options are good ways to stay informed but may not offer opportunities for activism.

72. **C**
Finding a sober activity can help foster healthy relationships with colleagues who are in recovery.

73. **B**
Showing Veronica unconditional positive regard means showing her kindness and acceptance despite what she brings to your sessions. For example, if she is talking about passing judgment on others and being inconsistent

herself, you are giving her a safe place to come as she is to work through her needs.

74. **D**

At a partial hospitalization program (PHP), Adrien would attend treatment for six to eight hours a day. For many, this form of treatment can be a bridge from inpatient treatment to returning home. Adrien is a candidate for a PHP program since he has a healthy and supportive home environment. While the other three options are possible, they will not provide Adrien with the structure that he is seeking for his routine at home.

75. **B**

The cut down, annoyed, guilt, and eye-opener (CAGE) questionnaire can be used as a screening tool to help counselors determine the need for further addiction assessments. The CAGE questionnaire does not include diagnostic information, so further exploration would be needed to sufficiently assess for a clinical diagnosis.

76. **A**

Having the group work together to develop rules or norms can help create an environment where members feel safe. They can address their concerns, such as keeping what is said in group sessions private, which can help members feel that they are all on the same page.

77. **A**

Care coordination refers to working with other health care professionals to ensure that clients receive the full spectrum of care they require. While the counselor may also consult with the client's lawyer, attorneys are not health care professionals and therefore are not involved in care coordination.

78. **D**

Group therapy can provide clients with an opportunity to work on social skills that they may be lacking. They will also have the opportunity to feel validated by their peers when they notice similarities in their experiences. Group therapy sessions are led by a professional who will keep the session focused, productive, and healthy.

79. **A**

A variety of factors are associated with burnout, including anxiety about work, frequently working from home, depressive symptoms, and a lack of self-care. Regular supervision can serve as a protective factor and help monitor for mental health concerns.

80. **C**

The best way to handle the situation is to remind the client that the two of you are focusing solely on her problems. A discussion of your personal affairs will not be useful in resolving any of her issues.

81. **C**

According to the Drug Abuse Screening Test (DAST-10) interpreting information, the moderate level warrants further investigation.

82. **D**

Counselors should not enter into any kind of relationship with a client that could interfere with their objectivity.

83. **B**

Knowing that Laura has a history of binge drinking, a fatty liver, and has been drinking recently, she should go to a medical detox center. While Laura has not yet experienced some of the negative consequences typically associated with problematic drinking, long-term misuse of alcohol can have significant impacts on health, including cancer and heart and liver concerns. For many, it can take years to develop health consequences from binge drinking. Laura would likely benefit from psychoeducation about the potential dangers of sudden, unsupervised alcohol withdrawal, such as seizures and death.

84. **C**

Family programming in an addiction setting commonly provides education about the disease concept of addiction. This can help family members better understand how addiction changes the way the brain works and the challenges this can cause. Additionally, this would be an ideal time to discuss how the family could support their loved one's recovery efforts.

85. **A**

Autonomy describes clients' personal freedom to make their own choices in health care decisions.

86. **B**

The cycle of violence would address the several stages that can help Jonah identify the pattern within his partner's behaviors, including being abusive, buying a gift as an apology, a honeymoon phase, and a repeated tension buildup.

87. **D**
The counselor should help the client schedule her first intensive outpatient program (IOP) session whenever possible. Depending on the progression of discharge, counselors may not be able to do this with every client. Scheduling a session with or for clients can help them maintain their sobriety and limit anxiety about reaching out to a new provider.

88. **B**
This client has three symptoms: she cannot stop using, she is using more than intended, and she is having trouble at work. Clients with two to three symptoms from the *DSM-5* all into the "mild" category.

89. **C**
The term *beneficence* relates to the ethical principle of doing what is in the client's best interest; the term *veracity* describes a commitment to being truthful.

90. **B**
Summarizing at the end of each section will likely make it easier for the client to understand the session and will avoid confusing different topics, like family and medical concerns. This will allow your client to add any forgotten details.

91. **A**
Clients should be informed about why assessments are used and how they can impact their treatment. The Alcohol Use Disorders Identification Test (AUDIT) is not a diagnostic tool. For the AUDIT to be valid, clients should answer the questions using standard drink sizes.

92. **B**
The SMART strategy breaks down a large goal into smaller goals that can feel more attainable. Each small goal provides the client with the steps needed to meet the large goal, which can help set the client up for success. After a successful experience, the client can feel the positive emotions that come from accomplishing a goal. This approach also helps the client track progress moving forward.

93. **A**
Summarizing would be appropriate and would give you the clarifying details you need. Additionally, you can check in with your client about how he is feeling and note any changes you observe in his speech.

94. **C**
While all of the options are relevant, the substances being abused and the client's withdrawal symptoms directly impact the treatment recommendation. For example, withdrawal from alcohol or benzodiazepines can be fatal; in such cases, detoxification should be monitored by a medical professional.

95. **B**
Extrinsic motivation comes from sources outside of the self, such as material rewards, validation or acclaim from others, and recognition. Intrinsic motivation is internally powered, making outside recognition irrelevant.

96. **C**
Self-disclosure would likely make the client feel more comfortable by knowing that you also have struggled with an addiction. It is not necessary to share the details of your use, but you could talk about what has helped you in your recovery. It is important to make sure that whatever you do share is to the client's benefit—not yours.

97. **B**
The beginning stages of recovery are challenging, and Lauren would benefit from continued support. The stress of losing her job can easily trigger a relapse, so having a connection to sober support can be beneficial. She may not be able to afford counseling services, so Alcoholics Anonymous (AA) is a good option because it is free. You can also provide her with free hotline support numbers and resources in her area and invite her to return if she does obtain insurance in the future.

98. **C**
The paperwork notes six symptoms associated with an opioid use disorder diagnosis. Regardless of the source of the referral, it is important to investigate the presence of symptoms to understand the client's use and subsequent diagnosis.

99. **D**
Qualitative research aims to investigate how and why things happen. It focuses on a small number of participants, which allows topics to be further explored than other forms of studies.

Results from these studies tend to produce additional topics for research.

100. D
It would be best for your supervisor to handle the situation. You heard only a brief part of the conversation, so there may be more to it than you realize.

101. B
If you are not in a management role, confronting your colleagues may be inappropriate. You should discuss your concerns with a supervisor who can handle the situation in a professional manner.

102. B
Vomiting and tremors do not necessarily indicate a medical emergency, but they do signal withdrawal. The counselor should explain the possible risks of alcohol withdrawal to the client and discuss whether he wants to seek medical treatment. The client should be encouraged to consult with a medical professional if these symptoms occur again.

103. A
Counselors must stick to their appointment schedules. Appointments should stay intact and only be interrupted if an emergency has arisen. When clients have additional issues to discuss, a new appointment should be scheduled to address those concerns.

104. D
Relapse prevention is an appropriate psychoeducational topic for an addiction rehab program. While some of the participants could benefit from the other topics, all participants are engaging in treatment for an addiction concern.

105. C
Peter falls into stage 3: high-risk use. His use has negatively impacted his life, which he is in denial of. He notes that his cravings have intensified, which does not occur during stages 1 or 2. He does not fall into stage 4 because he is not physically dependent on alcohol and has not experienced withdrawal symptoms.

106. C
While the Big Book and other Alcoholics Anonymous (AA) literature do talk about God, one does not have to believe in God to benefit from the program. Spirituality is believing in something bigger than oneself. Research has shown that having a spiritual connection can benefit one's mental health. Other benefits include a sense of love, patience, faith, and hope.

107. B
Offering to call the doctor with the client can help him feel more comfortable asking questions and can also allow the counselor to clarify issues with him. Additionally, it is important to be mindful of clients' physical health, as that can directly impact their mental health and addiction.

108. C
Embellishing or neglecting relevant information is unethical. Reviewing the report with Lucas before sending it can open a dialogue about his concerns. For example, he may feel that he made progress in an area that is not mentioned in the report.

109. C
It is important to be consistent with rules and expectations, especially in a group setting. Karl may be upset about not being able to join the group, so you should take a moment to talk privately rather than calling him out in front of others, which may make him uncomfortable in future group sessions.

110. C
Prescreens identify individuals who are at risk of developing an addiction. These are quick assessments that can be done before a full assessment. Examples of a prescreen are the Alcohol Use Disorders Identification Test (AUDIT-C), Drug Abuse Screening Test (DAST-10), NIAA Single Alcohol Screening Question (SASQ), NIDA Single Question Screening Test for Drug Use, Substance Use Brief Screen (SUBS), and the Older Adult Brief Screen.

111. C
To maintain your therapeutic relationship, you can discuss with Sheila your concern about her children and the need to contact the proper authorities. Having this conversation is a way to be honest with her while fulfilling your legal and ethical responsibilities.

112. A
Option A indicates that Sarah is physically dependent on alcohol and experiences withdrawal if she does not drink. The other

options may occur in earlier stages of addiction, but option A does not.

113. **D**
A counselor should help clients by providing them with an objective perspective. This helps ensure that goals are realistic and attainable, and that they work toward the progress clients would like to see.

114. **D**
All of these strategies are most likely to be effective with clients who are in the pre-contemplative stage, which means that they are not exhibiting an intention to take the actions needed to change their behaviors in the near future (typically defined as within the next six months).

115. **C**
It would be appropriate to receive feedback from another colleague regarding the case. You should also explore what kept you from sharing your thoughts during your initial consultation and how you can manage this if it happens again.

116. **B**
Helping clients focus on the actual situation is the best practice technique because it is the most conducive to resolution.

117. **A**
In addition to the general population screenings, screening, brief intervention, and referral to treatment (SBIRT) has identified specific screenings that can be used for adolescents, adults, older adults, and pregnant persons.

118. **A**
The main concern should be for the health and welfare of your client. If she is apprehensive about telling her doctor about her mental health struggles, having you in the room while she talks to her doctor can help her feel supported. If she does not want to call with you in the room, you can talk to your supervisor about contacting the doctor yourself, provided you have the necessary Health Insurance Portability and Accountability Act (HIPAA) consents.

119. **A**
The process for case consultation and related confidentiality should be discussed during the client's initial assessment. The client can ask questions and know what to expect before a concerning situation arises. Having a conversation about the process normalizes the experience.

120. **A**
Blocking occurs when a counselor stops a behavior that could harm the group. An impaired group member violates the rules and expectations. Having the member assessed by a medical professional is an added measure to ensure her safety.

121. **B**
Counselors concerned for their clients' safety should discuss the situation with their supervisor. Concerns could include breaking confidentiality and the need for a mental health evaluation.

122. **C**
You can best support Franco by providing him with unconditional positive regard while he navigates the changes within his family relationships. You can give him a safe area to process his thoughts and emotions that he may not be getting from others in his life.

123. **C**
A clinical interview, also known as an intake interview, is an informal assessment that makes up the first part of any clinical relationship.

124. **B**
Since you have a co-leader, you can ask him to step out with Jeanine while you stay and process what happened with the group. Other members may have various reactions, including anger, empathy, and confusion. It would be unhealthy for the group if Jeanine continued talking negatively about other members during the session. The colleague who steps out with Jeanine can provide her with one-on-one support and try to understand what contributed to her behavior.

125. **B**
Goals for three or more months out are considered long-term goals. Attending ninety twelve-step meetings in ninety days is a common goal in early recovery. It typically refers to attending a meeting every day for three months. If daily meetings are not possible, clients can occasionally attend more than one meeting in a day during that period. A short-term goal working toward this long-term goal would be to attend seven meetings in one week.

126. D
Research has shown that for co-occurring disorders, the best treatment outcomes are seen among individuals who are treated for all of their mental health concerns. In this case, the individual would likely receive specialized treatment for her trauma and disordered eating while engaging in the addiction treatment program. Her aftercare recommendations should continue to address all mental health concerns that she is struggling with.

127. C
Precontemplation occurs when clients are beginning to see that their substance use is a concern. Clients are in contemplation when they start to see more benefits to stopping their use than continuing. During preparation, clients identify a plan and commit to it. Action refers to the phase when clients follow through with the plan and make the necessary changes. Maintenance describes when the changes in clients' behaviors are now part of their everyday life.

128. A
Generally, performance on math tests shows fairly accurately how well students understand the material, which makes it a valid measure of student knowledge.

129. C
Alcoholics Anonymous, Narcotics Anonymous, and other similar twelve-step groups help individuals in recovery connect with other people in recovery. A client who chooses to work a twelve-step program will also connect with a sponsor, who can be a source of support and guidance in recovery. At some point he may wish to reconnect with family, but building a recovery-oriented community first will help strengthen his recovery. If Diego is religious, joining a church may be a good idea, but a twelve-step program will strengthen his social connections while strengthening his recovery.

130. A
A client's level of insight, or how aware she is of the content of her thoughts, appearance, behavior, and condition, is a key part of a thorough mental status exam.

131. B
Process groups do not encourage group members to interact out of the group setting because doing so can change the group dynamics. Group interactions can be healthy among support group members, as long as members are not excluded.

132. C
Reviewing a treatment plan monthly allows the client to reflect on progress made over the past month and better understand what can be expected in future sessions. It also allows the client to verbalize any changes he would like to be reflected in his treatment plan.

133. C
Discussing sexuality can be difficult if a person's loved ones and friends are not understanding or have a history of making hurtful comments about members of the LGBTQIA+ community. To improve Sam's communication skills, you could try a role-playing exercise to practice verbalizing his thoughts. This would also allow you to discuss coping skills that could help him if the conversations do not go as planned.

134. C
Counselors should be attentive to clients who exhibit low mood, sleep disturbances, lack of appetite, or withdrawal from their sober support—these are signs that could point to relapse. For clients with a dual diagnosis, mental health conditions can affect their substance use disorder and may contribute to relapse. The presence of depressive symptoms does not necessarily mean the client is going to relapse.

135. B
For individuals currently in active addiction, the focus should be on starting their recovery before dealing with their finances. Shawn still has medical insurance, so he would be able to get professional help for his addiction. If he does not take time to focus on his recovery, he will likely end up in similar situations if he continues using.

136. B
Since you do not have a rapport with Eddie, you should talk to him outside of group and explore barriers impacting his participation. Once you have learned more, you can work together to develop a plan to increase his participation.

137. B
The Car, Relax, Alone, Forget, Friends, Trouble (CRAFFT) is the only assessment that is

endorsed for use with adolescents and screens for drug usage.

138. C
If the client has a physical condition that hinders his ability to use stairs, he should receive reasonable accommodations to allow him access. Providing the code before the session will make it easier for the client to get to therapy.

139. B
The counselor does not need to spend an entire group session on herself. Allowing the group to identify their norms and rules can help members develop rapport among themselves as well as with the counselor.

140. B
The first step in assessing for suicidality is to determine if the client has any suicidal thoughts.

141. A
Motivational interviewing (MI) is a strategy that counselors can use with clients who are struggling to find intrinsic motivation for their recovery. Using MI techniques, such as open-ended questions, promotes client engagement in sessions.

142. A
An intoxicated client can be inattentive, defiant, or dangerous. The best approach is to reschedule the meeting when the client is sober.

143. B
Counselors who review their time with clients at the end of a session can better understand what has been helpful for them and what they need to focus on in the next session. Clients can reflect on their participation and which issues to address before the next session.

144. A
All of the options can help you build rapport with group members, but being available to them before and after sessions gives them a consistent opportunity to speak with you individually. This is more effective than communicating via phone and email because you will not miss important body language cues. Being on time for the group can help members feel that you are dependable, but you will not have time to speak with them individually if you arrive right when the group starts. Snacking during group can be a distraction and serve as a barrier to participation.

145. B
Detoxification programs provide clients with medical supervision and support while they go through withdrawal. Due to the changes in dopamine levels, individuals who stop using opioids do experience physical discomfort, including muscle aches and pains, nausea, and vomiting. This client may require medical supervision. Medication-assisted treatment can ease withdrawal symptoms and support sobriety.

146. C
The disease concept of addiction can help group members gain a better understanding of factors that can contribute to a relapse and how to cope with triggers. While the other topics would be beneficial, they may not be as relevant as option C.

147. C
For comorbidity to be diagnosed, both disorders need to be present at the same time. Nicole is the only individual with two conditions at once.

148. B
The acronym *HIPAA* stands for Health Insurance Portability and Accountability Act.

149. A
When several group members verbalize difficulty with a life skill, such as communicating, others can likely relate to the challenge in some way. Other common concerns include self-care, healthy boundaries, and emotion regulation.

150. A
Discharge planning should begin at the time of intake. While a client may expect to be in treatment for a certain length of time, things change. Starting to plan at intake gives you ample opportunity to talk with your clients about their thoughts for discharge. Depending on the setting you work in, discharge planning can include continued mental health treatment at a different level of care.

Online Resources

Trivium includes online resources with the purchase of this study guide to help you fully prepare for your exam.

Practice Test

In addition to the practice test included in this book, we also offer an online exam. Since many exams today are computer based, practicing your test-taking skills on the computer is a great way to prepare.

From Stress to Success

Watch "From Stress to Success," a brief but insightful YouTube video that offers the tips, tricks, and secrets experts use to score higher on the exam.

Reviews

Leave a review, send us helpful feedback, or sign up for Trivium promotions—including free books!

Access these materials at: www.triviumtestprep.com/addiction-counselor-online-resources

To access your SECOND practice test, follow the link below:
www.triviumtestprep.com/addiction-counselor-online-resources

Made in United States
Troutdale, OR
01/27/2025